T0257983

Understanding Machine Learning

Understanding Machine Learning

Margaret Nash

CLANRYE
INTERNATIONAL
www.clanryeinternational.com

Clanrye International,
750 Third Avenue, 9th Floor,
New York, NY 10017, USA

ISBN: 978-1-63240-911-9

Cataloging-in-Publication Data

Understanding machine learning / Margaret Nash.
p. cm.
Includes bibliographical references and index.
ISBN 978-1-63240-911-9
1. Machine learning. 2. Artificial intelligence. 3. Machine theory. I. Nash, Margaret.
Q325.5 .U53 2019
006.31--dc23

For information on all Clanrye International publications
visit our website at www.clanryeinternational.com

Contents

Preface VII

Chapter 1   **Machine Learning** **1**
- a. Supervised Learning   4
- b. Unsupervised Learning   5
- c. Reinforcement Learning   6

Chapter 2   **Machine Learning Theories** **8**
- a. Computational Learning Theory   8
- b. Statistical Learning Theory   9
- c. Adaptive Resonance Theory   12
- d. Hebbian Theory   16

Chapter 3   **Statistical Classification** **20**
- a. Probabilistic Classification   24
- b. Multiclass Classification   38
- c. Linear Classifier   42

Chapter 4   **Unsupervised Learning** **50**
- a. Competitive Learning   54
- b. Vector Quantization   58
- c. Generative Adversarial Network   69
- d. Self-organizing Map   79
- e. Generative Topographic Map   87

Chapter 5   **Supervised Learning** **94**
- a. Semi-supervised Learning   116
- b. Similarity Learning   120
- c. Structured Prediction   123
- d. Support Vector Machine   127

Chapter 6   **Dimensionality Reduction** **141**
- a. Feature Extraction   144
- b. Feature Selection   148
- c. Linear Discriminant Analysis   154
- d. Principal Component Analysis   166
- e. Kernel Principal Component Analysis   182
- f. Non-negative Matrix Factorization   186
- g. Independent Component Analysis   194

Chapter 7   **Reinforcement Learning**..**211**

    a. Q-learning   214

    b. State–Action–Reward–State–Action   221

    c. Temporal Difference Learning   228

Chapter 8   **Ensemble Learning**..**237**

    a. Bootstrap Aggregating   246

    b. Boosting   247

    c. AdaBoost   249

    d. Gradient Boosting   253

Permissions

Index

Preface

Machine learning is a branch of computer science concerned with the application of statistical techniques to improve performance of computer systems in the execution of specific tasks. It is significant where designing and programming algorithms for the effective operation of computing tasks is not feasible, such as in the detection of network intruders, email filtering, etc. Some of the primary approaches to machine learning include decision tree learning, artificial neural network learning algorithm, deep learning and association rule learning, besides others. Applications of machine learning can extend into the domains of agriculture, bioinformatics, linguistics, marketing, economics, etc. This book elucidates the concepts and innovative models around prospective developments with respect to the field of machine learning. It aims to serve as a resource guide for students and experts alike and contribute to the growth of the discipline.

A short introduction to every chapter is written below to provide an overview of the content of the book:

Chapter 1- Machine learning falls under the domain of computer science. It uses statistical methods to induce learning in computer systems without explicit programming. This is an introductory chapter, which will discuss briefly all the significant aspects of machine learning such as supervised learning, unsupervised learning and reinforcement learning;

Chapter 2- Machine learning evolved from a study of computational learning theory and pattern recognition. It explores the development of algorithms for making data-driven decisions and predictions. This chapter has been carefully written to provide an easy understanding of the varied theories in machine learning, such as computational learning theory, statistical learning theory, adaptive resonance theory and Hebbian theory;

Chapter 3- In machine learning, any reduction in the number of random variables through obtaining a set of principal variables is known as dimensionality reduction. The aim of this chapter is to explore the fundamentals of dimensionality reduction, such as feature extraction, independent component analysis, feature selection, principal component analysis, etc.;

Chapter 4- Ensemble learning is the process that employs learning algorithms for obtaining improved predictive performance. This chapter discusses in detail the theories and methodologies related to ensemble learning, and includes vital topics such as bootstrap aggregating, boosting, AdaBoost, gradient boosting, etc.;

Chapter 5- In machine learning, statistical classification strives to understand the category to which a new observation belongs. An example of this is assigning a diagnosis to a patient based on the presence or absence of certain symptoms, or even identifying an email as spam or non-spam. The topics elaborated in this chapter, such as probabilistic classification, multiclass classification and linear classifier, will help in providing a better perspective about statistical classification;

Chapter 6- Reinforcement learning is concerned with the way a software agent takes an action to maximize some result. All the diverse principles of reinforcement learning have been carefully analyzed in this chapter. It includes vital topics such as Q-learning, state-action-reward-state-action and temporal difference learning, among others;

Chapter 7- Supervised learning is a learning task concerned with the mapping of an input to an output based on an analysis of different input-output pairs. The topics elaborated in this chapter on supervised, semi-supervised and similarity learning, structured prediction and support vector machine will help to provide an extensive understanding of the subject;

Chapter 8- Unsupervised learning refers to the learning task of identifying a function which describes the structure of data that is unlabeled or unclassified. This chapter includes a detailed discussion of competitive learning, vector quantization, generative adversarial network, generative topographic map, etc. which will be crucial for a comprehensive understanding of unsupervised learning.

I extend my sincere thanks to the publisher for considering me worthy of this task. Finally, I thank my family for being a source of support and help.

Margaret Nash

Machine Learning

Machine learning falls under the domain of computer science. It uses statistical methods to induce learning in computer systems without explicit programming. This is an introductory chapter, which will discuss briefly all the significant aspects of machine learning such as supervised learning, unsupervised learning and reinforcement learning.

Machine learning (ML) is a category of algorithm that allows software applications to become more accurate in predicting outcomes without being explicitly programmed. The basic premise of machine learning is to build algorithms that can receive input data and use statistical analysis to predict an output while updating outputs as new data becomes available.

The processes involved in machine learning are similar to that of data mining and predictive modeling. Both require searching through data to look for patterns and adjusting program actions accordingly. Many people are familiar with machine learning from shopping on the internet and being served ads related to their purchase. This happens because recommendation engines use machine learning to personalize online ad delivery in almost real time. Beyond personalized marketing, other common machine learning use cases include fraud detection, spam filtering, network security threat detection, predictive maintenance and building news feeds.

Working of Machine Learning

Machine learning algorithms are often categorized as supervised or unsupervised. Supervised algorithms require a data scientist or data analyst with machine learning skills to provide both input and desired output, in addition to furnishing feedback about the accuracy of predictions during algorithm training. Data scientists determine which variables, or features, the model should analyze and use to develop predictions. Once training is complete, the algorithm will apply what was learned to new data.

Unsupervised algorithms do not need to be trained with desired outcome data. Instead, they use an iterative approach called deep learning to review data and arrive at conclusions. Unsupervised learning algorithms -- also called neural networks -- are used for more complex processing tasks than supervised learning systems, including image recognition, speech-to-text and natural language generation. These neural networks work by combing through millions of examples of training data and automatically identifying often subtle correlations between many variables. Once trained, the algorithm can use its bank of associations to interpret new data. These algorithms have only become feasible in the age of big data, as they require massive amounts of training data.

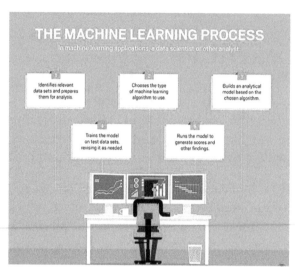

Examples of Machine Learning

Machine learning is being used in a wide range of applications today. One of the most well-known examples is Facebook's News Feed. The News Feed uses machine learning to personalize each member's feed. If a member frequently stops scrolling to read or like a particular friend's posts, the News Feed will start to show more of that friend's activity earlier in the feed. Behind the scenes, the software is simply using statistical analysis and predictive analytics to identify patterns in the user's data and use those patterns to populate the News Feed. Should the member no longer stop to read, like or comment on the friend's posts, that new data will be included in the data set and the News Feed will adjust accordingly.

Machine learning is also entering an array of enterprise applications. Customer relationship management (CRM) systems use learning models to analyze email and prompt sales team members to respond to the most important messages first. More advanced systems can even recommend potentially effective responses. Business intelligence (BI) and analytics vendors use machine learning in their software to help users automatically identify potentially important data points. Human resource (HR) systems use learning models to identify characteristics of effective employees and rely on this knowledge to find the best applicants for open positions.

Machine learning also plays an important role in self-driving cars. Deep learning neural networks are used to identify objects and determine optimal actions for safely steering a vehicle down the road.

Virtual assistant technology is also powered through machine learning. Smart assistants combine several deep learning models to interpret natural speech, bring in relevant context -- like a user's personal schedule or previously defined preferences -- and take an action, like booking a flight or pulling up driving directions.

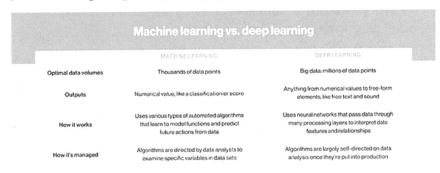

Machine learning vs. deep learning		
	MACHINE LEARNING	DEEP LEARNING
Optimal data volumes	Thousands of data points	Big data: millions of data points
Outputs	Numerical value, like a classification or score	Anything from numerical values to free-form elements, like free text and sound
How it works	Uses various types of automated algorithms that learn to model functions and predict future actions from data	Uses neural networks that pass data through many processing layers to interpret data features and relationships
How it's managed	Algorithms are directed by data analysts to examine specific variables in data sets	Algorithms are largely self-directed on data analysis once they're put into production

Types of Machine Learning Algorithms

Just as there are nearly limitless uses of machine learning, there is no shortage of machine learning algorithms. They range from the fairly simple to the highly complex. Here are a few of the most commonly used models:

- This class of machine learning algorithm involves identifying a correlation -- generally between two variables -- and using that correlation to make predictions about future data points.

- Decision trees: These models use observations about certain actions and identify an optimal path for arriving at a desired outcome.

- K-means clustering. This model groups a specified number of data points into a specific number of groupings based on like characteristics.

- Neural networks: These deep learning models utilize large amounts of training data to identify correlations between many variables to learn to process incoming data in the future.

- Reinforcement learning: This area of deep learning involves models iterating over many attempts to complete a process. Steps that produce favorable outcomes are rewarded and steps that produce undesired outcomes are penalized until the algorithm learns the optimal process.

The Future of Machine Learning

While machine learning algorithms have been around for decades, they've attained new popularity as artificial intelligence (AI) has grown in prominence. Deep learning models in particular power today's most advanced AI applications.

Machine learning platforms are among enterprise technology's most competitive realms, with most major vendors, including Amazon, Google, Microsoft, IBM and others, racing to sign customers up for platform services that cover the spectrum of machine learning activities, including data collection, data preparation, model building, training and application deployment. As machine learning continues to increase in importance to business operations and AI becomes ever more practical in enterprise settings, the machine learning platform wars will only intensify.

Continued research into deep learning and AI is increasingly focused on developing more general applications. Today's AI models require extensive training in order to produce an algorithm that is highly optimized to perform one task. But some researchers are exploring ways to make models more flexible and able to apply context learned from one task to future, different tasks.

Supervised Learning

The majority of practical machine learning uses supervised learning.

Supervised learning is where you have input variables (x) and an output variable (Y) and you use an algorithm to learn the mapping function from the input to the output.

$$Y = f(X)$$

The goal is to approximate the mapping function so well that when you have new input data (x) that you can predict the output variables (Y) for that data.

It is called supervised learning because the process of an algorithm learning from the training dataset can be thought of as a teacher supervising the learning process. We know the correct answers, the algorithm iteratively makes predictions on the training data and is corrected by the teacher. Learning stops when the algorithm achieves an acceptable level of performance.

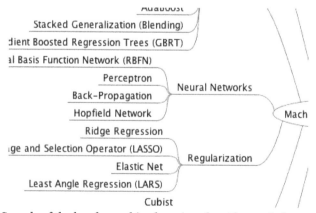

Sample of the handy machine learning algorithms mind map.

Supervised learning problems can be further grouped into regression and classification problems.

- Classification: A classification problem is when the output variable is a category, such as "red" or "blue" or "disease" and "no disease".

- Regression: A regression problem is when the output variable is a real value, such as "dollars" or "weight".

Some common types of problems built on top of classification and regression include recommendation and time series prediction respectively.

Some popular examples of supervised machine learning algorithms are:

- Linear regression for regression problems.

- Random forest for classification and regression problems.

- Support vector machines for classification problems.

Unsupervised Learning

Unsupervised learning is a type of machine learning algorithm used to draw inferences from datasets consisting of input data without labeled responses.

The most common unsupervised learning method is cluster analysis, which is used for exploratory data analysis to find hidden patterns or grouping in data. The clusters are modeled using a measure of similarity which is defined upon metrics such as Euclidean or probabilistic distance.

Common clustering algorithms include:

- Hierarchical clustering: builds a multilevel hierarchy of clusters by creating a cluster tree.

- k-Means clustering: partitions data into k distinct clusters based on distance to the centroid of a cluster.

- Gaussian mixture models: models clusters as a mixture of multivariate normal density components.

- Self-organizing maps: uses neural networks that learn the topology and distribution of the data.

- Hidden Markov models: uses observed data to recover the sequence of states.

Unsupervised learning methods are used in bioinformatics for sequence analysis and genetic clustering; in data mining for sequence and pattern mining; in medical imaging for image segmentation; and in computer vision for object recognition.

Reinforcement Learning

Reinforcement learning is an approach to machine learning that is inspired by behaviorist psychology. It is similar to how a child learns to perform a new task. Reinforcement learning contrasts with other machine learning approaches in that the algorithm is not explicitly told how to perform a task, but works through the problem on its own.

As an agent, which could be a self-driving car or a program playing chess, interacts with its environment, receives a reward state depending on how it performs, such as driving to destination safely or winning a game. Conversely, the agent receives a penalty for performing incorrectly, such as going off the road or being checkmated.

The agent over time makes decisions to maximize its reward and minimize its penalty using dynamic programming. The advantage of this approach to artificial intelligence is that it allows an AI program to learn without a programmer spelling out how an agent should perform the task.

Reinforcement learning, in the context of artificial intelligence, is a type of dynamic programming that trains algorithms using a system of reward and punishment.

There are three basic concepts in reinforcement learning: state, action, and reward. The state describes the current situation. For a robot that is learning to walk, the state is the position of its two legs. For a Go program, the state is the positions of all the pieces on the board.

Action is what an agent can do in each state. Given the state, or positions of its two legs, a robot can take steps within a certain distance. There are typically finite (or a fixed range of) actions an agent can take. For example, a robot stride can only be, say, 0.01 meter to 1 meter. The Go program can only put down its piece in one of 19 x 19 (that is 361) positions.

When a robot takes an action in a state, it receives a reward. Here the term "reward" is an abstract concept that describes feedback from the environment. A reward can be positive or negative. When the reward is positive, it is corresponding to our normal meaning of reward. When the reward is negative, it is corresponding to what we usually call "punishment."

Each of these concepts seems simple and straightforward: Once we know the state, we choose an action that (hopefully) leads to positive reward. But the reality is more complex.

Consider this example: a robot learns to go through a maze. When the robot takes one step to the right, it reaches an open location, but when it takes one step to the left, it also reaches an open location. After going left for three steps, the robot hits a wall. Looking back, taking the left step at location 1 is a bad idea (bad action). How would the robot use the reward at each location (state) to learn how to get through the maze?

References

- Machine-learning-ML: searchenterpriseai.techtarget.com, Retrieved 29 May 2018

- Supervised-and-unsupervised-machine-learning-algorithms: machinelearningmastery.com, Retrieved 31 March 2018

- Unsupervised-learning, discovery: mathworks.com, Retrieved 11 July 2018

- Reinforcement-learning-32055: techopedia.com, Retrieved 21 June 2018

- Reinforcement-learning-explained: oreilly.com, Retrieved 30 May 2018

Machine Learning Theories

Machine learning evolved from a study of computational learning theory and pattern recognition. It explores the development of algorithms for making data-driven decisions and predictions. This chapter has been carefully written to provide an easy understanding of the varied theories in machine learning, such as computational learning theory, statistical learning theory, adaptive resonance theory and Hebbian theory.

Computational Learning Theory

Computational learning theory is a branch of theoretical computer science that formally studies how to design computer programs that are capable of learning and identifies the computational limits of learning by machines Historically researchers in the artificial intelligence community have judged learning algorithms empirically according to their performance on sample problems While such evaluations provide much useful information and insight often it is hard using such evaluations to make meaningful comparisons among competing learning algorithms.

Computational learning theory provides a formal framework in which to precisely formulate and address questions regarding the performance of different learning algorithms so that careful comparisons of both the predictive power and the computational efficiency of alternative learning algorithms can be made Three key aspects that must be formalized are the way in which the learner interacts with its environment the definition of successfully completing the learning task and a formal definition of efficiency of both data usage sample complexityand processing time complexity It is important to remember that the theoretical learning models studied are abstractions from reallife problems Thus close connections with experimentalists are useful to help validate or modify these abstractions so that the theoretical results help to explain or predict empirical performance In this direction computational learning theory research has predict empirical performance In this direction computational learning theory research .

Theoretical results in machine learning mainly deal with a type of inductive learning called supervised learning. In supervised learning, an algorithm is given samples that are labeled in some useful way. For example, the samples might be descriptions of mushrooms, and the labels could be whether or not the mushrooms are edible. The algorithm takes these previously labeled samples and uses them to induce a classifier. This classifier is a function that assigns labels to samples including samples that have never been previously seen by the algorithm. The goal of the supervised learning algorithm is to optimize some measure of performance such as minimizing the number of mistakes made on new samples.

In addition to performance bounds, computational learning theory studies the time complexity and feasibility of learning.. In computational learning theory, a computation is considered feasible if it can be done in polynomial time. There are two kinds of time complexity results:

- Positive results – Showing that a certain class of functions is learnable in polynomial time.

- Negative results – Showing that certain classes cannot be learned in polynomial time.

Negative results often rely on commonly believed, but yet unproven assumptions, such as:

- Computational complexity – P ≠ NP (the P versus NP problem);

- Cryptographic – One-way functions exist.

There are several different approaches to computational learning theory. These differences are based on making assumptions about the inference principles used to generalize from limited data. This includes different definitions of probability and different assumptions on the generation of samples. The different approaches include:

- Exact learning, proposed by Dana Angluin;

- Probably approximately correct learning (PAC learning), proposed by Leslie Valiant;

- VC theory, proposed by Vladimir Vapnik and Alexey Chervonenkis;

- Bayesian inference;

- Algorithmic learning theory, from the work of E. Mark Gold;

- Online machine learning, from the work of Nick Littlestone.

Computational learning theory has led to several practical algorithms. For example, PAC theory inspired boosting, VC theory led to support vector machines, and Bayesian inference led to belief networks (by Judea Pearl).

Statistical Learning Theory

The main goal of statistical learning theory is to provide a framework for studying the problem of inference, that is of gaining knowledge, making predictions, making decisions or constructing models from a set of data. This is studied in a statistical framework that is there are assumptions of statistical nature about the underlying phenomena.

Indeed, a theory of inference should be able to give a formal definition of words like learning, generalization, over fitting, and also to characterize the performance of learning algorithms so that, ultimately, it may help design better learning algorithms.

There are thus two goals: make things more precise and derive new or improved algorithms.

Learning and Inference

What is under study here is the process of inductive inference which can roughly be summarized as the following steps:

1. Observe a phenomenon.

2. Construct a model of that phenomenon.

3. Make predictions using this model.

Of course, this definition is very general and could be taken more or less as the goal of Natural Sciences. The goal of Machine Learning is to actually automate this process and the goal of Learning Theory is to formalize it.

We consider a special case of the above process, which is the supervised learning framework for pattern recognition. In this framework, the data consists of instance-label pairs, where the label is either +1 or −1. Given a set of such pairs, a learning algorithm constructs a function mapping instances to labels. This function should be such that it makes few mistakes when predicting the label of unseen instances.

Of course, given some training data, it is always possible to build a function that fits exactly the data. But, in the presence of noise, this may not be the best thing to do as it would lead to a poor performance on unseen instances (this is usually referred to as over fitting).

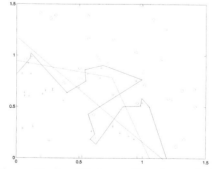

Figure: Trade-off between fit and complexity

The general idea behind the design of learning algorithms is thus to look for regularities (in a sense to be defined later) in the observed phenomenon (i.e. training data). These can then be generalized from the observed past to the future. Typically, one would look, in a collection of possible models, for one which fits well the data, but at the same time is as simple as possible. This immediately raises the question of how to measure and quantify simplicity of a model (i.e. a $\{-1, +1\}$-valued function).

It turns out that there are many ways to do so, but no best one. For example in Physics, people tend to prefer models which have a small number of constants and that correspond to simple mathematical formulas. Often, the length of description of a model in a coding language can be an indication of its complexity. In classical statistics, the number of free parameters of a model is usually a measure of its complexity. Surprisingly as it may seem, there is no universal way of measuring simplicity (or its counterpart complexity) and the choice of a specific measure inherently depends on the problem at hand. It is actually in this choice that the designer of the learning algorithm introduces knowledge about the specific phenomenon under study.

This lack of universally best choice can actually be formalized in what is called the No Free Lunch theorem, which in essence says that, if there is no assumption on how the past (i.e. training data) is related to the future (i.e. test data), prediction is impossible. Even more, if there is no a priori restriction on the possible phenomena that are expected, it is impossible to generalize and there is thus no better algorithm (any algorithm would be beaten by another one on some phenomenon).

Hence the need to make assumptions, like the fact that the phenomenon we observe can be explained by a simple model. However, as we said, simplicity is not an absolute notion, and this leads to the statement that data cannot replace knowledge, or in pseudo-mathematical terms:

Generalization = Data + Knowledge.

We assume that data are an i.i.d. sample of n pairs $\{(X_t, Y_t)\}_{t=1}^{n} \in (X \times Y)^n$. A learning algorithm (or, a prediction rule) is a mapping $\hat{Y}: (X \times Y)^n \to D$,, where $D = y^X$ is the space of all measurable functions $x \to y$. We either write $\hat{y}(x; X^n, Y^n)$ to make the dependence on data explicit, or simply $\hat{y}(x)$ if the dependence is understood. Let P denote the set of all distributions on $x \times y$ Consider the case of regression with squared loss. For the distribution-free setting of Statistical Learning Theory, define the minimax value is:

$$vx^{iid,sq}(F,n) \triangleq \inf_{\hat{y}} \sup_{P \in p} \left\{ \mathbb{E}\left(\hat{y}(x) - y\right)^2 - \inf_{f \in F} \mathbb{E}\left(f(x) - y\right)^2 \right\}$$

$$= \inf_{\hat{y}} \sup_{P \in p, f \in F} \left\{ \mathbb{E}\left(\hat{y}(x) - y\right) - \mathbb{E}\left(f(x) - y\right)^2 \right\}$$

where the expected value in the first term is over n + 1 i.i.d. random variables (X1,

Y1),..., (Xn, Yn), (X, Y). Note that the supremum ranges over all distributions on X × Y. The minimax objective $vx^{iid,sq}(F,n)$ is defined above in terms of predictive risk relative to the risk of a reference class F. Alternatively, it can be re-written as follows:

$$v^{iid,sq}(F,n) \triangleq \inf_{\hat{y}} \sup_{P \in p} \left\{ \mathbb{E}\|\hat{y}-f_P\|^2 - \inf_{f \in F}\|f-f_P\|^2 \right\}$$

$$= \inf_{\hat{y}} \sup_{P \in p, f \in F} \left\{ \mathbb{E}\|\hat{y}-f_P\|^2 - \|f-f_P\|^2 \right\}$$

Where $f_P(a) = \mathbb{E}[Y|X=a]$ is the mean function associated with P, and the norm $\|.\| = \|.\|_{L_2}(P_X)$. Recalling that $\|g\|^2_{L_2(P_X)} = \int g^2(x)P_X(dx) = \mathbb{E}g^2(X)$, we can easily verify the equivalence of (5.7) and (5.8). For absolute loss, let us define the analogue of (5.7) as

$$vx^{iid,sq}(F,n) \triangleq \inf_{\hat{y}} \sup_{P \in p} \left\{ \mathbb{E}|\hat{y}(x)-y| - \inf_{f \in F} \mathbb{E}|f(x)-y| \right\}$$

and for general losses as

$$v^{iid}(F,n) \triangleq \inf_{\hat{y}} \sup_{P \in p} \left\{ \mathbb{E}l(\hat{y}(x,y)) - \inf_{f \in F} \mathbb{E}l(f,(x,y)) \right\}$$

Let us now consider the distribution-dependent PAC framework for classification and write down its minimax value:

$$v^{pac}(F,n) \triangleq \inf_{\hat{y}} \sup_{P_f} P(\hat{y}(x) \neq f(x)) = \inf_{\hat{y}} \sup_{P_f} \mathbb{E}|\hat{y}(x)-f(x)|$$

Where P_f ranges over distributions given by $P_X \times P^f_{Y|X}$ with $P_X \times P^f_{Y|X=a} = \delta_{f(a)}$ for $f \in F$ a class of {0, 1}-valued functions. In the label noise scenario, the distribution $P^f_{Y|X=a}$ a puts some mass on 1− f (a).

As we go forward, it is important to think of $v(F,n)$ as a measure of complexity of F. If F = {f} contains only one function, the values defined above are zero since we can simply set $\hat{y} = f$. On the opposite end of the spectrum, the complexity V(Y X, n) of the set of all possible functions is, in general, impossible to make small. One goal of this course is to understand how this value fares for function classes between these two extremes, and to understand what other (easier-to-grasp) measures of complexity of F are related to V(F, n).

Adaptive Resonance Theory

This network was developed by Stephen Grossberg and Gail Carpenter in 1987. It is based on competition and uses unsupervised learning model. Adaptive Resonance Theory (ART) networks, as the name suggests, is always open to new learning (adaptive) without losing the old patterns (resonance). Basically, ART network is a vector classifier which accepts an input vector and classifies it into one of the categories depending upon which of the stored pattern it resembles the most.

Operating Principal

The main operation of ART classification can be divided into the following phases –

- Recognition phase – The input vector is compared with the classification presented at every node in the output layer. The output of the neuron becomes "1" if it best matches with the classification applied, otherwise it becomes "0".

- Comparison phase – In this phase, a comparison of the input vector to the comparison layer vector is done. The condition for reset is that the degree of similarity would be less than vigilance parameter.

- Search phase – In this phase, the network will search for reset as well as the match done in the above phases. Hence, if there would be no reset and the match is quite good, then the classification is over. Otherwise, the process would be repeated and the other stored pattern must be sent to find the correct match.

ART1

It is a type of ART, which is designed to cluster binary vectors. We can understand about this with the architecture of it.

Architecture of ART1

It consists of the following two units –

Computational Unit

Components of computational units are as follows –

- Input unit (F1 layer) – It further has the following two portions –
  - F1(a) layer (Input portion) – In ART1, there would be no processing in this portion rather than having the input vectors only. It is connected to F1(b) layer (interface portion).
  - F1(b) layer (Interface portion) – This portion combines the signal from the input portion with that of F2 layer. F1(b) layer is connected to F2 layer through bottom up weights bij and F2layer is connected to F1(b) layer through top down weights tji.
- Cluster Unit (F2 layer) – This is a competitive layer. The unit having the largest net input is selected to learn the input pattern. The activation of all other cluster unit are set to 0.

- Reset Mechanism – The work of this mechanism is based upon the similarity between the top-down weight and the input vector. Now, if the degree of this similarity is less than the vigilance parameter, then the cluster is not allowed to learn the pattern and a rest would happen.

Supplement Unit

Actually the issue with Reset mechanism is that the layer F2 must have to be inhibited under certain conditions and must also be available when some learning happens. That is why two supplemental units namely, G1 and G2 are added along with reset unit, R. They are called gain control units. These units receive and send signals to the other units present in the network. '+' indicates an excitatory signal, while '−' indicates an inhibitory signal.

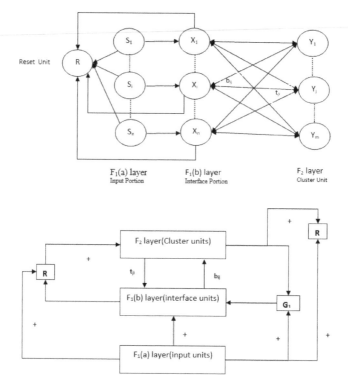

Parameters used

Following parameters are used –

- n – Number of components in the input vector
- m – Maximum number of clusters that can be formed
- bij – Weight from F1(b) to F2 layer, i.e. bottom-up weights
- tji – Weight from F2 to F1(b) layer, i.e. top-down weights

- ρ – Vigilance parameter
- ||x|| – Norm of vector x

Algorithm

Step 1 – Initialize the learning rate, the vigilance parameter, and the weights as follows –

$$\alpha > 1 \text{ and } 0 < \rho \leq 1$$

$$0 < b_{ij}(0) < \frac{\alpha}{\alpha - 1 + n} \text{ and } t_{ij}(0) = 1$$

Step 2 – Continue step 3-9, when the stopping condition is not true.

Step 3 – Continue step 4-6 for every training input.

Step 4 – Set activations of all F1(a) and F1 units as follows

$$F2 = 0 \text{ and } F1(a) = \text{input vectors}$$

Step 5 – Input signal from F1(a) to F1(b) layer must be sent like

$$s_i = x_i$$

Step 6 – For every inhibited F2 node

$$y_j = \sum_i b_{ij} x_i \text{ the condition is yj} \neq -1$$

Step 7 – Perform step 8-10, when the reset is true.

Step 8 – Find J for yJ ≥ yj for all nodes j

Step 9 – Again calculate the activation on F1(b) as follows

$$x_i = sitJi$$

Step 10 – Now, after calculating the norm of vector x and vector s, we need to check the reset condition as follows –

If ||x||/ ||s|| < vigilance parameter ρ, then inhibit node J and go to step 7

Else If ||x||/ ||s|| ≥ vigilance parameter ρ, then proceed further.

Step 11 – Weight updating for node J can be done as follows –

$$b_{ij}(new) = \frac{\alpha x_i}{\alpha - 1 + ü\,x\ |}$$

$$t_{ij}(new) = x_i$$

Step 12 – The stopping condition for algorithm must be checked and it may be as follows –

- Do not have any change in weight.

- Reset is not performed for units.

- Maximum number of epochs reached.

Hebbian Theory

Hebbian theory is a theoretical type of cell activation model in artificial neural networks that assesses the concept of "synaptic plasticity" or dynamic strengthening or weakening of synapses over time according to input factors.

Hebbian theory is also known as Hebbian learning, Hebb's rule or Hebb's postulate.

Hebbian theory is named after Donald Hebb, a neuroscientist from Nova Scotia who wrote "The Organization of Behavior" in 1949, which has been part of the basis for the development of artificial neural networks.

When someone learns something new, the neurons within the brain begin to adapt to the processes that are required. This is a basic mechanism of synaptic plasticity, which is described through the Hebbian theory.

How neurons operate and link together creates a trend that begins the skill-building process within the brain. When they fire, then they tend to be wired together in some way. Through the Hebbian theory, that wiring is described as a process of causality. Many neurons will fire simultaneously during the learning process.

These connections form to become engrams. Those engrams become patterns of learning. Those patterns will then eventually turn into practical knowledge that can be used for multiple purposes.

Mirror Neurons and the Hebbian Theory

The learning process that is described through Hebbian theory and the synaptic plasticity involved is also the foundation of how mirror neurons are able to form within the engrams that are eventually created by the patterns of firing. A mirror neuron fires when an action must be performed or when an individual hears or sees a similar action being taken that is similar.

These neurons show how the "learning by osmosis" skill, or watching and then doing, can develop within living beings. The neurons activate by seeing the skill being performed, then activate once again when the skills are being observed. This process reinforces the building patterns of the engrams, establishing information additions in various conditions.

It is possible for all 5 traditional senses to create their own engrams that interlock with each other, creating mirror neurons that fire in different ways, based on the perspective of the individual sense. Watching someone perform a skill would be different from hearing someone perform a skill, for example.

And when individuals perform the skill on their own, the sense of touch reflects the movements being performed and continues to build neuron "neighborhoods" that help the information be retained for future reference.

Hopfield Model

Hopfield model is an associative memory model using the Hebb's rule for all possible pairs ij with binary units. The state variable xi of the neuron i takes on either on of the two possible values: 1 or -1, which corresponds to the firing state or not firing state, respectively.

$$S_i(t+1) := \text{sgn}\left(\sum_j w_{ij} S_i(t) - \mu_i\right)$$

Where sgn is the sign function defined as follows:

$$\text{sgn}(x) = \begin{cases} 1 & \text{if } x \geq 0 \\ -1 & \text{if } x < 0 \end{cases}$$

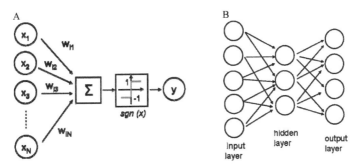

Figure: The schematic diagram of neural network. (A) Hopfield neuron. The unit fires if the weighted sum Σ_j wijSj of the inputs reaches or exceeds the threshold μi. (B) An example of three layer perceptron.

Drawbacks of Hebb's Rule

Though being simple, the classical Hebb's rule has some disadvantages. Depending the application area of neural network, some drawbacks are tolerable but some need improvement. Generally speaking, for the purpose of data processing and statistical analysis, the speed and power of computation are valued more than the resemblance between the model and the physiological realism. On the other hand, for unraveling the memory formation mechanism and harvesting the emerging properties of biological network, the models need to be built upon a certain degree of biophysical basis.

Stability of Hebbian Network

For classical Hebb's rule, there is no algorithm for synapses to get weaker and no upper bound that limits how strong the connectivity can get. Therefore, it is intrinsically unstable. To overcome the stability problem, Bienenstock, Cooper, and Munro proposed an omega shaped learning rule called BCM rule. The general BCM improves Hebb's rule and takes the following form:

$$\frac{dw_{ij}}{dt} = \varphi(x_i).x_j - k_w.w_{ij}$$

There are two main differences between these two rules: the decay of synaptic weight with a rate constant kw and the nonlinear dependence of synaptic weight with respect to postsynaptic activities. The nonlinearity was described by the postsynaptic activation function, $\varphi(x)$. As shown in figure, the activation function is negative for xi under threshold value θw but grows positive once the postsynaptic activity becomes larger than θw

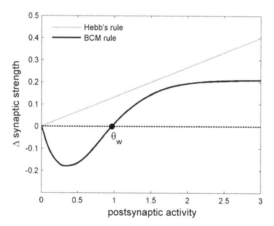

Figure: The activation function of synaptic strength with respect to postsynaptic activity. Hebb's rule poses linear dependence of synaptic strength on postsynaptic activity while BCM rule sets nonlinear omega-shaped dependence. The x-axis corresponds to postsynaptic activity, xi and the y-axis represents the activation function, $\varphi(x)$

The Simplification of Neuronal Activities

Under external stimulation, neurons fire and emit a series of pulses instead of a simple output level. In Hebb's rule, only a single value xi is assigned to the neuron i to represent its activity. Yet the simplification results into the loss of information such as the threshold and tendency of firing as well as the detailed change in the short-term and the long-term plasticity.

The variety and emerging properties may be the results of differentiated neurons. The network of these specialized neurons with individual attributes gives rise to bountiful functionality.

The Inability to Model Spike Timing Dependence

It has been experimentally shown that the change in synaptic plasticity depends upon the relative spike timing between presynaptic and postsynaptic neurons. Spike timing dependence has become an important experimental protocol in eliciting change in synaptic plasticity since its discovery. Although the role of temporal order was suggested in the original statement of Hebb's rule, the time window requirement is not incorporated in the equations.

Statistical Classification

In machine learning, statistical classification strives to understand the category to which a new observation belongs. An example of this is assigning a diagnosis to a patient based on the presence or absence of certain symptoms, or even identifying an email as spam or non-spam. The topics elaborated in this chapter, such as probabilistic classification, multiclass classification and linear classifier, will help in providing a better perspective about statistical classification.

Statistical classification is the division of data into meaningful categories for analysis. It is possible to apply statistical formulas to data to do this automatically, allowing for large scale data processing in preparation for analysis. Some standardized systems exist for common types of data like results from medical imaging studies. This allows multiple entities to evaluate data with the same metrics so they can compare and exchange information easily.

As researchers and other parties collect data, they can assign it to loose categories on the basis of similar characteristics. They can also develop formulas to classify their data as it comes in, automatically dividing it into specific statistical classifications. As they collect information, researchers may not know very much about their data, which makes it difficult to classify. Formulas can identify important features to use as potential category identifiers.

Processing data requires statistical classification to separate out different kinds of information for analysis and comparison. For instance, in a census, workers should be able to explore multiple parameters to provide a meaningful assessment of the data they collect. Using declarations on census forms, a statistical classification algorithm can separate out different types of households and individuals on the basis of information like age, household configuration, average income, and so forth.

The data collected must be quantitative in nature for statistical analysis to work. Qualitative information can be too subjective. As a result, researchers need to design data collection methods carefully to get information they can actually use. For example, in a clinical trial, observers filling out forms during follow-up examinations could use a scoring rubric to assess patient health. Instead of a qualitative assessment like "the patient looks good," the researcher could assign a score of seven on a scale, which a formula could use to process the data.

Classification is of two types:

- Binary Classification: When we have to categorize given data into 2 distinct classes. Example – On the basis of given health conditions of a person, we have to determine whether the person has a certain disease or not.

- Multiclass Classification: The number of classes is more than 2. For Example – On the basis of data about different species of flowers, we have to determine which specie does our observation belong to.

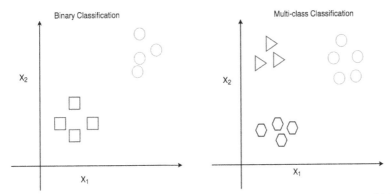

Figure: Binary and Multiclass Classification. Here x1 and x2 are our variables upon which the class is predicted.

Working of Classification

Suppose we have to predict whether a given patient has a certain disease or not, on the basis of 3 variables, called features.

Which means there are two possible outcomes:

1. The patient has the said disease. Basically a result labelled "Yes" or "True".

2. The patient is disease free. A result labelled "No" or "False".

This is a binary classification problem.

We have a set of observations called training data set, which comprises of sample data with actual classification results. We train a model, called Classifier on this data set, and use that model to predict whether a certain patient will have the disease or not.

The outcome, thus now depends upon:

1. How well these features are able to "map" to the outcome.

2. The quality of our data set. By quality I refer to statistical and Mathematical qualities.

3. How well our Classifier generalizes this relationship between the features and the outcome.

4. The values of the x1 and x2.

Following is the generalized block diagram of the classification task.

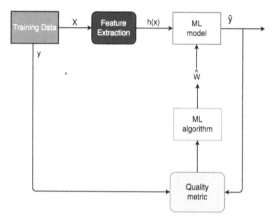

Generalized Classification Block Diagram

1. X: pre-classified data, in the form of a N*M matrix. N is the no. of observations and M is the number of features

2. y: An N-d vector corresponding to predicted classes for each of the N observations.

3. Feature Extraction: Extracting valuable information from input X using a series of transforms.

4. ML Model: The "Classifier" we'll train.

5. y': Labels predicted by the Classifier.

6. Quality Metric: Metric used for measuring the performance of the model.

7. ML Algorithm: The algorithm that is used to update weights w', which update the model and "learns" iteratively.

Types of Classifiers (Algorithms)

There are various types of classifiers. Some of them are:

- Linear Classifiers: Logistic Regression

- Tree Based Classifiers: Decision Tree Classifier

- Support Vector Machines

- Artificial Neural Networks

- Bayesian Regression

- Gaussian Naive Bayes Classifiers

- Stochastic Gradient Descent (SGD) Classifier

- Ensemble Methods : Random Forests, AdaBoost, Bagging Classifier, Voting Classifier, ExtraTrees Classifier

Frequentist Procedures

Early work on statistical classification was undertaken by Fisher, in the context of two-group problems, leading to Fisher's linear discriminant function as the rule for assigning a group to a new observation. This early work assumed that data-values within each of the two groups had a multivariate normal distribution. The extension of this same context to more than two-groups has also been considered with a restriction imposed that the classification rule should be linear. Later work for the multivariate normal distribution allowed the classifier to be nonlinear: several classification rules can be derived based on slight different adjustments of the Mahalanobis distance, with a new observation being assigned to the group whose center has the lowest adjusted distance from the observation.

Bayesian Procedures

Unlike frequentist procedures, Bayesian classification procedures provide a natural way of taking into account any available information about the relative sizes of the sub-populations associated with the different groups within the overall population. Bayesian procedures tend to be computationally expensive and, in the days before Markov chain Monte Carlo computations were developed, approximations for Bayesian clustering rules were devised.

Some Bayesian procedures involve the calculation of group membership probabilities: these can be viewed as providing a more and more informative outcome of a data analysis than a simple attribution of a single group-label to each new observation.

Feature Vectors

Most algorithms describe an individual instance whose category is to be predicted using a feature vector of individual, measurable properties of the instance. Each property is termed a feature, also known in statistics as an explanatory variable (or independent variable, although features may or may not be statistically independent). Features may variously be binary (e.g. "on" or "off"); categorical (e.g. "A", "B", "AB" or "O", for blood type); ordinal (e.g. "large", "medium" or "small"); integer-valued (e.g. the number of occurrences of a particular word in an email); or real-valued (e.g. a measurement of blood pressure). If the instance is an image, the feature values might correspond to the pixels of an image; if the instance is a piece of text, the feature values might be occurrence frequencies of different words. Some algorithms work only in terms of discrete data and require that real-valued or integer-valued data be *discretized* into groups (e.g. less than 5, between 5 and 10, or greater than 10).

Linear Classifiers

A large number of algorithms for classification can be phrased in terms of a linear function that assigns a score to each possible category k by combining the feature vector of an instance with a vector of weights, using a dot product. The predicted category is the one with the highest score. This type of score function is known as a linear predictor function and has the following general form:

$$\text{score}(\mathbf{X}_i, k) = \beta_k \cdot \mathbf{X}_i,$$

where X_i is the feature vector for instance i, β_k is the vector of weights corresponding to category k, and score(X_i, k) is the score associated with assigning instance i to category k. In discrete choice theory, where instances represent people and categories represent choices, the score is considered the utility associated with person i choosing category k.

Algorithms with this basic setup are known as linear classifiers. What distinguishes them is the procedure for determining (training) the optimal weights/coefficients and the way that the score is interpreted.

Examples of such algorithms are

- Logistic regression and Multinomial logistic regression.
- Probit regression.
- The perceptron algorithm.
- Support vector machines.
- Linear discriminant analysis.

Practical Applications of Classification

1. Google's self driving car uses deep learning enabled classification techniques which enables it to detect and classify obstacles.

2. Spam E-mail filtering is one of the most widespread and well recognized uses of Classification techniques.

3. Detecting Health Problems, Facial Recognition, Speech Recognition, Object Detection, Sentiment Analysis all use Classification at their core.

Probabilistic Classification

Probabilistic classifiers and, in particular, the archetypical naive Bayes classifier, are among the most popular classifiers used in the machine learning community and increasingly in many applications. These classifiers are derived from generative probability models which provide a principled way to the study of statistical classification in complex domains such as natural language and visual processing.

The study of probabilistic classification is the study of approximating a joint distribution with a product distribution. Bayes rule is used to estimate the conditional probability of a class label, and then assumptions are made on the model, to decompose this probability into a product of conditional probabilities.

$$Pr\left(y|x\right) = Pr\left(y|x^1, x^2, ...x^n\right) = \prod_{i=1}^{n} Pr\left(x^i|x^1, ...x^{i-1}, y\right) \frac{Pr\left(y\right)}{Pr\left(x\right)} = \prod_{j=1}^{n'} Pr\left(y^j|y\right) \frac{Pr\left(y\right)}{Pr\left(x\right)},$$

where $x = \left(x^1, ..., x^n\right)$ is the observation and the $y^j = g_j\left(x^1, ..x^{i-1}, x^i\right)$, for some function g_j, are independent given the class label y.

While the use of Bayes rule is harmless, the final decomposition step introduces independence assumptions, which may not hold in the data. The functions g_j encode the probabilistic assumptions and allow the representation of any Bayesian network, e.g., a Markov model. The most common model used in classification, however, is the naive Bayes model in which $\forall_j, g_j\left(x^1, ...x^{i-1}, x^i\right) \equiv x^i$. That is, the original attributes are assumed to be independent given the class label.

Although the naive Bayes algorithm makes some unrealistic probabilistic assumptions it has been found to work remarkably well in practice. Roth develops a partial answer to this unexpected behavior using techniques from learning theory. It is shown that naive Bayes and other probabilistic classifiers are all "Linear Statistical Query" classifiers; thus, PAC type guarantees can be given on the performance of the classifier on future, previously unseen data, as a function of its performance on the training data, independently of the probabilistic assumptions made when deriving the classifier.

We consider the standard binary classification problem in a probabilistic setting. In this model one assumes that data elements (x, y) are sampled according to some arbitrary distribution P on $\chi \times \{0,1\}. \chi \left(e.g., \chi = \Re^M\right)$ is the instance space and $y \in \{0,1\}$ is the label. The goal of the learner is to determine, given a new example $x \in \chi, ,$ its most likely corresponding label $y(x)$, which is chosen as follows:

$$y(x) = \arg \max_{i \in \{0,1\}} P\left(y = i|x\right) = \arg \max_{i \in \{0,1\}} P\left(x|y = i\right) \frac{P\left(y = i\right)}{P\left(x\right)}.$$

We define the following distributions over $\chi: P_0 = P\left(x|y = 0\right)$ and $P_1 = P\left(x|y = 1\right)$. With this notation, the Bayesian classifier predicts $y = 0$ iff $P_0\left(x\right) > P_1\left(x\right)$.

Types of Classification

Formally, an "ordinary" classifier is some rule, or function, that assigns to a sample x a class label $\hat{y}$:

$$\hat{y} = f(x)$$

The samples come from some set X (e.g., the set of all documents, or the set of all images), while the class labels form a finite set Y defined prior to training.

Probabilistic classifiers generalize this notion of classifiers: instead of functions, they are conditional distributions $\Pr(Y \mid X)$, meaning that for a given $x \in X$, they assign probabilities to all $y \in Y$ (and these probabilities sum to one). "Hard" classification can then be done using the optimal decision rule.

$$\hat{y} = \arg\max_y \Pr(Y = y \mid X)$$

or, in English, the predicted class is that which has the highest probability.

Binary probabilistic classifiers are also called binomial regression models in statistics. In econometrics, probabilistic classification in general is called discrete choice.

Some classification models, such as naive Bayes, logistic regression and multilayer perceptrons (when trained under an appropriate loss function) are naturally probabilistic. Other models such as support vector machines are not, but methods exist to turn them into probabilistic classifiers.

Generative and Conditional Training

Some models, such as logistic regression, are conditionally trained: they optimize the conditional probability $\Pr(Y \mid X)$ directly on a training set. Other classifiers, such as naive Bayes, are trained generatively: at training time, the class-conditional distribution $\Pr(X \mid Y)$ and the class prior $\Pr(Y)$ are found, and the conditional distribution $\Pr(Y \mid X)$ is derived using Bayes' rule.

Probability Calibration

When performing classification you often want not only to predict the class label, but also obtain a probability of the respective label. This probability gives you some kind of confidence on the prediction. Some models can give you poor estimates of the class probabilities and some even do not support probability prediction. The calibration module allows you to better calibrate the probabilities of a given model, or to add support for probability prediction.

Well calibrated classifiers are probabilistic classifiers for which the output of the predict_proba method can be directly interpreted as a confidence level. For instance, a well calibrated (binary) classifier should classify the samples such that among the samples to which it gave a predict_proba value close to 0.8, approximately 80% actually belong to the positive class. The following plot compares how well the probabilistic predictions of different classifiers are calibrated:

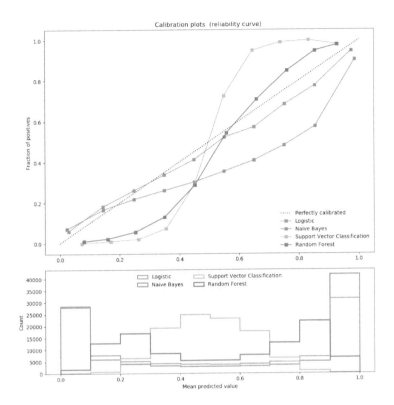

Logistic Regression returns well calibrated predictions by default as it directly optimizes log-loss. In contrast, the other methods return biased probabilities; with different biases per method:

- GaussianNB tends to push probabilities to 0 or 1 (note the counts in the histograms). This is mainly because it makes the assumption that features are conditionally independent given the class, which is not the case in this dataset which contains 2 redundant features.

- Random Forest Classifier shows the opposite behavior: the histograms show peaks at approximately 0.2 and 0.9 probability, while probabilities close to 0 or 1 are very rare. An explanation for this is given by Niculescu-Mizil and Caruana. "Methods such as bagging and random forests that average predictions from a base set of models can have difficulty making predictions near 0 and 1 because variance in the underlying base models will bias predictions that should be near zero or one away from these values. Because predictions are restricted to the interval [0,1], errors caused by variance tend to be one-sided near zero and one. For example, if a model should predict p = 0 for a case, the only way bagging can achieve this is if all bagged trees predict zero. If we add noise to the trees that bagging is averaging over, this noise will cause some trees to predict values larger than 0 for this case, thus moving the average prediction of the bagged ensemble away from 0. We observe this effect most strongly with random forests because the base-level trees trained with random forests have relatively high variance due to feature sub setting." As a result, the calibration curve also referred to as the reliability diagram shows a characteristic sigmoid shape, indicating that the classifier could trust its "intuition" more and return probabilities closer to 0 or 1 typically.

- Linear Support Vector Classification (LinearSVC) shows an even more sigmoid curve as the RandomForestClassifier, which is typical for maximum-margin methods, which focus on hard samples that are close to the decision boundary (the support vectors).

Two approaches for performing calibration of probabilistic predictions are provided: a parametric approach based on Platt's sigmoid model and a non-parametric approach based on isotonic regression (sklearn.isotonic). Probability calibration should be done on new data not used for model fitting. The class CalibratedClassifierCV uses a cross-validation generator and estimates for each split the model parameter on the train samples and the calibration of the test samples. The probabilities predicted for the folds are then averaged. Already fitted classifiers can be calibrated by CalibratedClassifierCV via the parameter cv="prefit". In this case, the user has to take care manually that data for model fitting and calibration are disjoint.

The following images demonstrate the benefit of probability calibration. The first image present a dataset with 2 classes and 3 blobs of data. The blob in the middle contains random samples of each class. The probability for the samples in this blob should be 0.5.

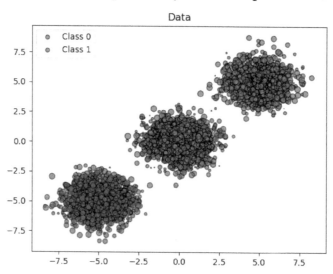

The following image shows on the data above the estimated probability using a Gaussian naive Bayes classifier without calibration, with a sigmoid calibration and with a non-parametric isotonic calibration. One can observe that the non-parametric model provides the most accurate probability estimates for samples in the middle, i.e., 0.5.

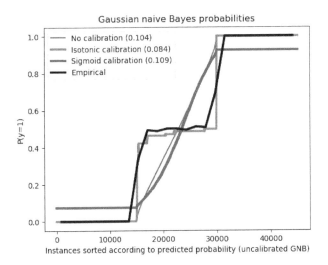

The following experiment is performed on an artificial dataset for binary classification with 100.000 samples (1.000 of them are used for model fitting) with 20 features. Of the 20 features, only 2 are informative and 10 are redundant. The figure shows the estimated probabilities obtained with logistic regression, a linear support-vector classifier (SVC), and linear SVC with both isotonic calibration and sigmoid calibration. The calibration performance is evaluated with Brier score brier_score_loss, reported in the legend (the smaller the better).

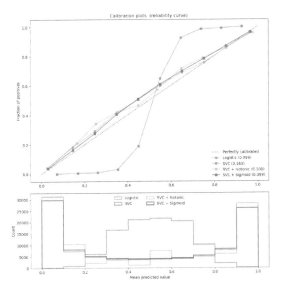

One can observe here that logistic regression is well calibrated as its curve is nearly diagonal. Linear SVC's calibration curve or reliability diagram has a sigmoid curve, which is typical for an under-confident classifier. In the case of LinearSVC, this is caused by the margin property of the hinge loss, which lets the model focus on hard samples that are close to the decision boundary (the support vectors). Both kinds of calibration can fix this issue and yield nearly identical results. The next figure shows the calibration curve of Gaussian naive Bayes on the same data, with both kinds of calibration and also without calibration.

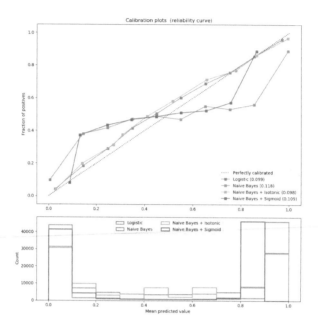

One can see that Gaussian naive Bayes performs very badly but does so in an other way than linear SVC: While linear SVC exhibited a sigmoid calibration curve, Gaussian naive Bayes' calibration curve has a transposed-sigmoid shape. This is typical for an over-confident classifier. In this case, the classifier's overconfidence is caused by the redundant features which violate the naive Bayes assumption of feature-independence.

Calibration of the probabilities of Gaussian naive Bayes with isotonic regression can fix this issue as can be seen from the nearly diagonal calibration curve. Sigmoid calibration also improves the brier score slightly, albeit not as strongly as the non-parametric isotonic calibration. This is an intrinsic limitation of sigmoid calibration, whose parametric form assumes a sigmoid rather than a transposed-sigmoid curve. The non-parametric isotonic calibration model, however, makes no such strong assumptions and can deal with either shape, provided that there is sufficient calibration data. In general, sigmoid calibration is preferable in cases where the calibration curve is sigmoid and where there is limited calibration data, while isotonic calibration is preferable for non-sigmoid calibration curves and in situations where large amounts of data are available for calibration.

Calibrated Classifier CV can also deal with classification tasks that involve more than two classes if the base estimator can do so. In this case, the classifier is calibrated first for each class separately in an one-vs-rest fashion. When predicting probabilities for unseen data, the calibrated probabilities for each class are predicted separately. As those probabilities do not necessarily sum to one, a post processing is performed to normalize them.

The next image illustrates how sigmoid calibration changes predicted probabilities for a 3-class classification problem. Illustrated is the standard 2-simplex, where the three corners correspond to the three classes. Arrows point from the probability vectors predicted by an uncalibrated classifier to the probability vectors predicted by the same classifier after sigmoid calibration on a hold-out validation set. Colors indicate the true class of an instance (red: class 1, green: class 2, blue: class 3).

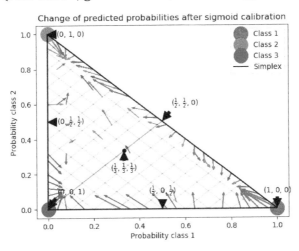

The base classifier is a random forest classifier with 25 base estimators (trees). If this classifier is trained on all 800 training data points, it is overly confident in its predictions and thus incurs a large log-loss. Calibrating an identical classifier, which was trained on 600 data points, with method='sigmoid' on the remaining 200 data points reduces the confidence of the predictions, i.e., moves the probability vectors from the edges of the simplex towards the center:

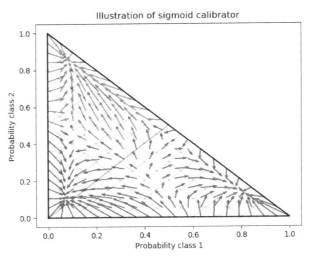

This calibration results in a lower log-loss. An alternative would have been to increase the number of base estimators which would have resulted in a similar decrease in log-loss.

Naive Bayes Classifier

Naive Bayes classifiers are a collection of classification algorithms based on Bayes' Theorem. It is not a single algorithm but a family of algorithms where all of them share a common principle, i.e. every pair of features being classified is independent of each other.

To start with, let us consider a dataset.

Consider a fictional dataset that describes the weather conditions for playing a game of golf. Given the weather conditions, each tuple classifies the conditions as fit("Yes") or unfit("No") for planning golf.

Here is a tabular representation of our dataset.

	OUTLOOK	TEMPERATURE	HUMIDITY	WINDY	PLAY GOLF
0	Rainy	Hot	High	False	No
1	Rainy	Hot	High	True	No
2	Overcast	Hot	High	False	Yes
3	Sunny	Mild	High	False	Yes
4	Sunny	Cool	Normal	False	Yes
5	Sunny	Cool	Normal	True	No
6	Overcast	Cool	Normal	True	Yes
7	Rainy	Mild	High	False	No
8	Rainy	Cool	Normal	False	Yes
9	Sunny	Mild	Normal	False	Yes
10	Rainy	Mild	Normal	True	Yes
11	Overcast	Mild	High	True	Yes
12	Overcast	Hot	Normal	False	Yes
13	Sunny	Mild	High	True	No

The dataset is divided into two parts, namely, feature matrix and the response vector.

- Feature matrix contains all the vectors (rows) of dataset in which each vector consists of the value of dependent features. In above dataset, features are 'Outlook', 'Temperature', 'Humidity' and 'Windy'.

- Response vector contains the value of class variable (prediction or output) for each row of feature matrix. In above dataset, the class variable name is 'Play golf'.

Assumption

The fundamental Naive Bayes assumption is that each feature makes an:

- Independent

- Equal

contribution to the outcome.

With relation to our dataset, this concept can be understood as:

- We assume that no pair of features are dependent. For example, the temperature being 'Hot' has nothing to do with the humidity or the outlook being 'Rainy' has no effect on the winds. Hence, the features are assumed to be independent.

- Secondly, each feature is given the same weight (or importance). For example, knowing only temperature and humidity alone can't predict the outcome accurately. None of the attributes is irrelevant and assumed to be contributing equally to the outcome.

Note: The assumptions made by Naive Bayes are not generally correct in real-world situations. In-fact, the independence assumption is never correct but often works well in practice.

Now, before moving to the formula for Naive Bayes, it is important to know about Bayes' theorem.

Bayes' Theorem

Bayes' Theorem finds the probability of an event occurring given the probability of another event that has already occurred. Bayes' theorem is stated mathematically as the following equation:

$$P(A \mid B) = \frac{P(B \mid A)P(A)}{P(B)}$$

where A and B are events and P(B) ? 0.

- Basically, we are trying to find probability of event A, given the event B is true. Event B is also termed as evidence.

- P (A) is the priori of A (the prior probability, i.e. Probability of event before evidence is seen). The evidence is an attribute value of an unknown instance (here, it is event B).

- P (A|B) is a posteriori probability of B, i.e. probability of event after evidence is seen.

Now, with regards to our dataset, we can apply Bayes' theorem in following way:

$$P(y \mid X) = \frac{P(X \mid y)P(y)}{P(X)}$$

where, y is class variable and X is a dependent feature vector (of size n) where:

$$X = (x_1, x_2, x_3, \ldots, x_n)$$

Just to clear, an example of a feature vector and corresponding class variable can be: (refer 1st row of dataset)

X = (Rainy, Hot, High, False)

y = No

So basically, P (X|y) here means, the probability of "Not playing golf" given that the weather conditions are "Rainy outlook", "Temperature is hot", "high humidity" and "no wind".

Naive Assumption

Now, its time to put a naive assumption to the Bayes' theorem, which is independence among the features. So now, we split evidence into the independent parts.

Now, if any two events A and B are independent, then,

P(A,B) = P(A)P(B)

Hence, we reach to the result:

$$P(y \mid x_1,...,x_n) = \frac{P(x_1 \mid y)P(x_2 \mid y)...P(x_n \mid y)P(y)}{P(x_1)P(x_2)...P(x_n)}$$

which can be expressed as:

$$P(y \mid x_1,...,x_n) = \frac{P(y)\prod_{i=1}^{n} P(x_i \mid y)}{P(x_1)P(x_2)...P(x_n)}$$

Now, as the denominator remains constant for a given input, we can remove that term:

$$P(y \mid x_1,...,x_n) \propto P(y)\prod_{i=1}^{n} P(x_i \mid y)$$.

Now, we need to create a classifier model. For this, we find the probability of given set of inputs for all possible values of the class variable y and pick up the output with maximum probability. This can be expressed mathematically as:

$$y = argmax_y P(y)\prod_{i=1}^{n} P(x_i \mid y)$$

So, finally, we are left with the task of calculating P(y) and P(x_i | y).

Please note that P (y) is also called class probability and P(xi | y) is called conditional probability.

The different naive Bayes classifiers differ mainly by the assumptions they make regarding the distribution of P (x_i | y).

Let us try to apply the above formula manually on our weather dataset. For this, we need to do some pre computations on our dataset.

We need to find P (x_i | y_j) for each x_i in X and y_j in y. All these calculations have been demonstrated in the tables below:

Outlook

	Yes	No	P(yes)	P(no)
Sunny	2	3	2/9	3/5
Overcast	4	0	4/9	0/5
Rainy	3	2	3/9	2/5
Total	9	5	100%	100%

Temperature

	Yes	No	P(yes)	P(no)
Hot	2	2	2/9	2/5
Mild	4	2	4/9	2/5
Cool	3	1	3/9	1/5
Total	9	5	100%	100%

Humidity

	Yes	No	P(yes)	P(no)
High	3	4	3/9	4/5
Normal	6	1	6/9	1/5
Total	9	5	100%	100%

Wind

	Yes	No	P(yes)	P(no)
False	6	2	6/9	2/5
True	3	3	3/9	3/5
Total	9	5	100%	100%

Play		P(Yes)/P(No)
Yes	9	9/14
No	5	5/14
Total	14	100%

So, in the figure above, we have calculated P (x_i | y_j) for each x_i in X and y_j in y manually in the tables 1-4. For example, probability of playing golf given that the temperature is cool, i.e P (temp. = cool | play golf = Yes) = 3/9.

Also, we need to find class probabilities (P(y)) which has been calculated in the table 5. For example, P (play golf = Yes) = 9/14.

So now, we are done with our pre-computations and the classifier is ready!

Let us test it on a new set of features (let us call it today):

today = (Sunny, Hot, Normal, False)

So, probability of playing golf is given by:

$$P(Yes|today) = \frac{P(Sunny\ Outlook\,|\,Yes)P(Hot\,Temperature\,|\,Yes)P(Normal\,Humidity\,|\,Yes)P(No\,Wind\,|\,Yes)P(Yes)}{P(today)}$$

and probability to not play golf is given by:

$$P(No|today) = \frac{P(Sunny\ Outlook\,|\,No)P(Hot\,Temperature\,|\,No)P(Normal\,Humidity\,|\,No)P(No\,Wind\,|\,No)P(No)}{P(today)}$$

Since, P (today) is common in both probabilities, we can ignore P(today) and find proportional probabilities as:

$$P(Yes|today) \propto \frac{2}{9}.\frac{2}{9}.\frac{6}{9}.\frac{6}{9}.\frac{9}{14} \approx 0.0141$$

and

$$P(No \mid today) \propto \frac{3}{5}.\frac{2}{5}.\frac{1}{5}.\frac{2}{5}.\frac{5}{14} \approx 0.0068$$

Now, since

$$P(Yes \mid today) + P(No \mid today) = 1$$

These numbers can be converted into a probability by making the sum equal to 1 (normalization):

$$P(Yes \mid today) = \frac{0.0141}{0.0141 + 0.0068} = 0.67$$

and

$$P(No \mid today) = \frac{0.0068}{0.0141 + 0.0068} = 0.33$$

Since

$$P(Yes \mid today) > P(No \mid today)$$

So, prediction that golf would be played is 'Yes'.

The method that we discussed above is applicable for discrete data. In case of continuous data, we need to make some assumptions regarding the distribution of values of each feature. The different naive Bayes classifiers differ mainly by the assumptions they make regarding the distribution of $P(x_i \mid y)$.

Now, we discuss one of such classifiers here.

Gaussian Naive Bayes Classifier

In Gaussian Naive Bayes, continuous values associated with each feature are assumed to be distributed according to a Gaussian distribution. A Gaussian distribution is also called Normal distribution. When plotted, it gives a bell shaped curve which is symmetric about the mean of the feature values as shown below:

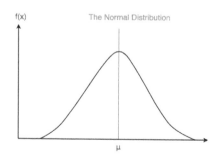

The likelihood of the features is assumed to be Gaussian, hence, conditional probability is given by:

$$P(x_i|y) = \frac{1}{\sqrt{2\pi\sigma_y^2}} \exp\left(-\frac{(x_i - \mu y)^2}{2\sigma_y^2}\right)$$

Now, we look at an implementation of Gaussian Naive Bayes classifier using scikit-learn.

```
# load the iris dataset
from sklearn.datasets import load_iris
iris = load_iris()


# store the feature matrix (X) and response vector (y)
X = iris.data
y = iris.target


# splitting X and y into training and testing sets
from sklearn.model_selection import train_test_split
X_train, X_test, y_train, y_test = train_test_split(X, y, test_size=0.4,
random_state=1)


# training the model on training set
from sklearn.naive_bayes import GaussianNB
gnb = GaussianNB()
gnb.fit(X_train, y_train)


# making predictions on the testing set
y_pred = gnb.predict(X_test)


# comparing actual response values (y_test) with predicted response
values (y_pred)
from sklearn import metrics
```

```
print("Gaussian Naive Bayes model accuracy(in %):", metrics.accura-
cy_score(y_test, y_pred)*100)
```

Run on IDE

Output

Gaussian Naive Bayes model accuracy(in %): 95.0

Other popular Naive Bayes classifiers are:

- Multinomial Naive Bayes: Feature vectors represent the frequencies with which certain events have been generated by a multinomial distribution. This is the event model typically used for document classification.

- Bernoulli Naive Bayes: In the multivariate Bernoulli event model, features are independent booleans (binary variables) describing inputs. Like the multinomial model, this model is popular for document classification tasks, where binary term occurrence (i.e. a word occurs in a document or not) features are used rather than term frequencies (i.e. frequency of a word in the document).

Multiclass Classification

In multiclass classification, each record belongs to one of three or more classes, and the algorithm's goal is to construct a function which, given a new data point, will correctly identify into which class the new data point falls.

For example, a multiclass algorithm can determine which parental guideline rating a movie is likely to receive – "PG," "TV-14," "R," "G," etc. – based on patterns it learns from this sample movie dataset:

Title	Rating	Tags	Release Year	User Rating Score
Hannah Montana: The Movie	G	[General Audiences], Suitable for all ages]	2009	56
Hannah Montana: The Movie	G	[General Audiences], Suitable for all ages]	2009	56
Chicken Little	G	[General Audiences], Suitable for all ages]	2005	95
The Smurfs and the Magic Flute	G	[General Audiences], Suitable for all ages]	1976	NA
Zootopia	PG	[Mild thematic elements], [ruude humor], [action]	2016	97
Finding Dory	PG	[Mild thematic elements], [ruude humor], [action]	2016	98
Pete's Dragon	PG	[action], [peril], [brief language]	2016	93
Kubo and the Two Strings	PG	[Thematic elements], [Scary images], [action], [peril]	2016	96
Sherlock	TV-14	[Parents strongly cautioned]	2016	95
Death Note	TV-14	[Parents strongly cautioned]	2006	77
Arrow	TV-14	[Parents strongly cautioned]	2015	96

The movies have also been tagged with descriptions – "General Audience," "Suitable for all ages," etc. This is different than the rating system in that each movie can be described by one or more of the tag categories, which is known as a multi-label classification problem.

Binary to Multiclass

There are multiple ways to decompose the multiclass prediction into multiple binary decisions.

One-versus-all

Let's assume that our black-box algorithm is a linear classifier, and each class can be separated from all the rest labels. If we do this, we are basically decomposing the task to learning k independent binary classifiers, and we know how to do this.

Formally, let D be the set of training examples. For any label I, take elements of D with label I as positive examples and all other elements of D as negative examples. Then, construct a binary classification problem for I. This is a binary learning problem that we can solve. Since there are k possible labels, we are producing k binary classifiers $w_1, w_2, ..., w_k$. Once we have learned the k classifiers, the decision is made by winner takes all (WTA) strategy, such that $f(x) = \arg\max_i w_i^T x$. The "score" $w_i^T x$ (the sigmoid function can be applied on it) can be thought of as the probability that x has label i.

Graphically, consider the data set with three color labels shown in the figure below. Using binary classifiers, we separated the black from the rest, blue from the rest, and green from the rest. Easy.

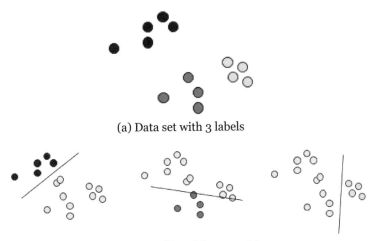

(a) Data set with 3 labels

(b) Decomposed into binary problems

The only caveat is that when some points with a certain label are not linearly separable from the other, like shown in the figure below, this scheme cannot be used. Basically, we are concerned about the expressivity of this paradigm.

Figure: Red points are not linearly separable from other points

It is not always possible to learn, because it is not always separable in the way we want. Even though it works well and is the commonly used method, there is no theoretical justification for it.

All-versus-all

Assume that there is a separation between every pair of classes using a binary classifier in the hypothesis space. Then, we can look at all pairs of labels $\left(\binom{k}{2}\right.$ of them)), and for each pair, define a binary learning problem. In each case, for pair (i, j), the positive examples are all examples with label i, and negative examples are those with label j. Now instead of k classifiers as in OvA, we have $\binom{k}{2}$ classifier.

In this case each label gets k_1 votes, and the decision is more involved, because output of binary classifiers may not cohere. To make a decision, an option is to classify example x to take label i if i wins on x more often than any $j = 1, ...,k,$. Alternatively, we can do a tournament. Starting with n/2 pairs, continue with the winners and go down iteratively. Either way, there are potential issues. However, overall, it is a good method.

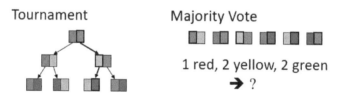

Figure: Tournament and majority vote

One-versus-all VS all-versus-all

There is a trade-off between OvA and AvA paradigms. Computationally, to apply AvA, a quadratic number of classifiers have to be trained, while OvA requires linear number of classifiers. AvA has more expressivity, but less examples to learn from. In terms of number of examples, AvA has smaller learning problems. And it makes AvA preferable when ran in dual.

Extension from Binary

This topic discusses strategies of extending the existing binary classifiers to solve multi-class classification problems. Several algorithms have been developed based on neural networks, decision trees, k-nearest neighbors, naive Bayes, support vector machines and Extreme Learning Machines to address multi-class classification problems. These types of techniques can also be called as algorithm adaptation techniques.

Neural Networks

Multilayer perceptrons provide a natural extension to the multi-class problem. Instead of just having one neuron in the output layer, with binary output, one could have N binary neurons leading to multi-class classification. In practice, the last layer of a neural network is usually a softmax function layer, which is the algebraic simplification of N logistic classifiers, normalized per class by the sum of the N-1 other logistic classifiers.

Extreme Learning Machines

Extreme Learning Machines (ELM) is a special case of single hidden layer feed-forward neural networks (SLFNs) where in the input weights and the hidden node biases can be chosen at random. Many variants and developments are made to the ELM for multiclass classification.

k-nearest Neighbours

k-nearest neighbors kNN is considered among the oldest non-parametric classification algorithms. To classify an unknown example, the distance from that example to every other training example is measured. The k smallest distances are identified, and the most represented class by these k nearest neighbors is considered the output class label.

Naive Bayes

Naive Bayes is a successful classifier based upon the principle of maximum a posteriori (MAP). This approach is naturally extensible to the case of having more than two classes, and was shown to perform well in spite of the underlying simplifying assumption of conditional independence.

Decision Trees

Decision trees are a powerful classification technique. The tree tries to infer a split of the training data based on the values of the available features to produce a good generalization. The algorithm can naturally handle binary or multiclass classification problems. The leaf nodes can refer to either of the K classes concerned.

Support Vector Machines

Support vector machines are based upon the idea of maximizing the margin i.e. maximizing the minimum distance from the separating hyper plane to the nearest example.

The basic SVM supports only binary classification, but extensions have been proposed to handle the multiclass classification case as well. In these extensions, additional parameters and constraints are added to the optimization problem to handle the separation of the different classes.

Hierarchical Classification

Hierarchical classification tackles the multi-class classification problem by dividing the output space i.e. into a tree. Each parent node is divided into multiple child nodes and the process is continued until each child node represents only one class. Several methods have been proposed based on hierarchical classification.

Learning Paradigms

Based on learning paradigms, the existing multi-class classification techniques can be classified into batch learning and online learning. Batch learning algorithms require all the data samples to be available beforehand. It trains the model using the entire training data and then predicts the test sample using the found relationship. The online learning algorithms, on the other hand, incrementally build their models in sequential iterations. In iteration t, an online algorithm receives a sample, x_t and predicts its label $\hat{y}_t$ using the current model; the algorithm then receives y_t, the true label of x_t and updates its model based on the sample-label pair: (x_t, y_t). Recently, a new learning paradigm called progressive learning technique has been developed. The progressive learning technique is capable of not only learning from new samples but also capable of learning new classes of data and yet retain the knowledge learnt thus far.

Linear Classifier

A linear classifier does classification decision based on the value of a linear combination of the characteristics. Imagine that the linear classifier will merge into its weights all the characteristics that define a particular class. (Like merge all samples of the class cars together)

This type of classifier works better when the problem is linear separable.

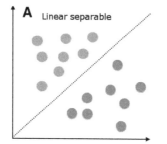

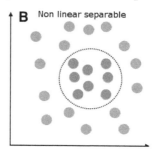

$$f(\vec{x}, \vec{W}, \vec{b}) = \sum j(Wjx_j) + b$$

x: input vector

W: Weight matrix

b: Bias vector

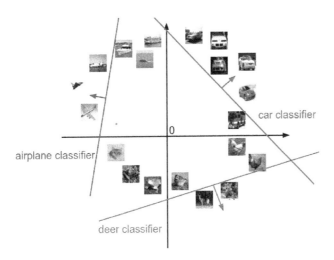

The weight matrix will have one row for every class that needs to be classified, and one column for ever element (feature) of x. On the picture above each line will be represented by a row in our weight matrix.

Weight and Bias Effect

The effect of changing the weight will change the line angle, while changing the bias, will move the line left/right

Parametric Approach

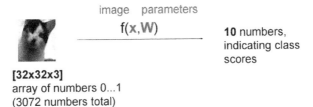

The idea is that out hypothesis/model have parameters that will aid the mapping between the input vectors to a specific class score. The parametric model has two important components:

- Score Function: Is a function f (x,W,b) that will map our raw input vector to a score vector.

- Loss Function: Quantifies how well our current set of weights maps some input x to a expected output y, the loss function is used during training time.

On this approach, the training phase will find us a set of parameters that will change the hypothesis/model to map some input, to some of the output class.

During the training phase, which consist as a optimization problem, the weights (W) and bias (b) are the only thing that we can change.

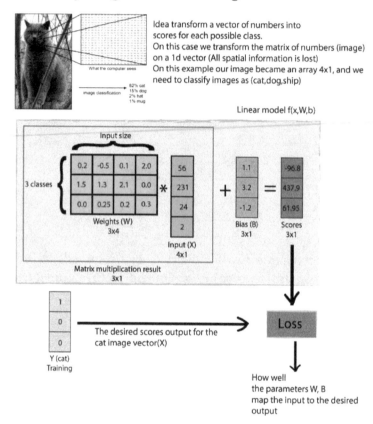

Now some topics that is important on the diagram above:

1. The input image x is stretched to a single dimension vector, this loose spatial information.

2. The weight matrix will have one column for every element on the input.

3. The weight matrix will have one row for every element of the output (on this case 3 labels).

4. The bias will have one row for every element of the output (on this case 3 labels).

5. The loss will receive the current scores and the expected output for it's current input X.

Consider each row of W a kind of pattern match for a specified class. The score for each class is calculated by doing a inner product between the input vector X and the specific row for that class. Ex:

$$score_{cat} = [0.2(56) - 0.5(231) + 0.1(24) + 2(2)] + 1.1 = -96.8$$

Example on Matlab

```
>> W = [0.2 -0.5 0.1 2; 1.5 1.3 2.1 0; 0 0.25 0.2 0.3]

W =

    0.2000   -0.5000    0.1000    2.0000
    1.5000    1.3000    2.1000         0
         0    0.2500    0.2000    0.3000

>> X = [56 231 24 2]'

X =

    56
   231
    24
     2

>> B = [1.1 3.2 -1.2]

B =

    1.1000    3.2000   -1.2000

>> scores = (W*X)+B'

scores =

  -96.8000
  437.9000
   61.9500
```

The image below reshape back the weights to an image, we can see by this image that the training try to compress on each row of W all the variants of the same class.

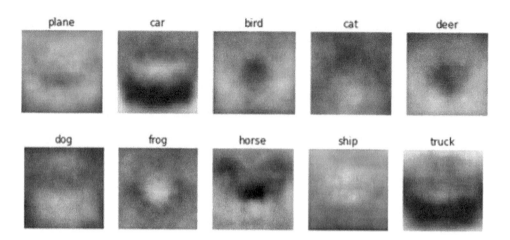

Bias Trick

Some learning libraries implementations, does a trick to consider the bias as part of the weight matrix, the advantage of this approach is that we can solve the linear classification with a single matrix multiplication.

$$f(x,W) = W.x$$

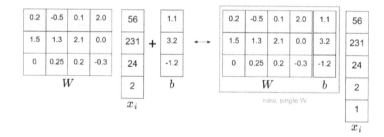

Basically you add an extra row at the end of the input vector, and concatenate a column on the W matrix.

Input and Features

The input vector sometimes called feature vector, is your input data that is sent to the classifier. As the linear classifier does not handle non-linear problems, it is the responsibility of the engineer, process this data and presents it in a form that is separable to the classifier.

The best case scenario is that you have a large number of features, and each of them has a high correlation to the desired output and low correlation between them.

Generative Models vs. Discriminative Models

There are two broad classes of methods for determining the parameters of a linear classifier . They can be generative and discriminative models. Methods of the first class model conditional density functions $P(\vec{x} \mid \text{class})$. Examples of such algorithms include:

- Linear Discriminant Analysis (or Fisher's linear discriminant) (LDA)—assumes Gaussian conditional density models.

- Naive Bayes classifier with multinomial or multivariate Bernoulli event models.

The second set of methods includes discriminative models, which attempt to maximize the quality of the output on a training set. Additional terms in the training cost function can easily perform regularization of the final model. Examples of discriminative training of linear classifiers include:

- Logistic regression—maximum likelihood estimation of $P(\vec{x} \mid \text{class})$ assuming that the observed training set was generated by a binomial model that depends on the output of the classifier.

- Perceptron—an algorithm that attempts to fix all errors encountered in the training set.

- Support vector machine—an algorithm that maximizes the margin between the decision hyper plane and the examples in the training set.

Despite its name, LDA does not belong to the class of discriminative models in this taxonomy. However, its name makes sense when we compare LDA to the other main linear dimensionality reduction algorithm: principal components analysis (PCA). LDA is a supervised learning algorithm that utilizes the labels of the data, while PCA is an unsupervised learning algorithm that ignores the labels. To summarize, the name is a historical artifact.

Discriminative training often yields higher accuracy than modeling the conditional density functions. However, handling missing data is often easier with conditional density models.

All of the linear classifier algorithms listed above can be converted into non-linear algorithms operating on a different input space $\varphi(\vec{x})$, using the kernel trick.

Discriminative Training

Discriminative training of linear classifiers usually proceeds in a supervised way, by means of an optimization algorithm that is given a training set with desired outputs and a loss function that measures the discrepancy between the classifier's outputs and the desired outputs. Thus, the learning algorithm solves an optimization problem of the form

$$\underset{\mathbf{w}}{\text{argmin}}\ R(\mathbf{w}) + C \sum_{i=1}^{N} L(y_i, \mathbf{w}^\mathsf{T} \mathbf{x}_i)$$

where

- w is a vector of classifier parameters,

- $L(y_i, w^T x_i)$ is a loss function that measures the discrepancy between the classifier's prediction and the true output y_i for the i'th training example,

- $R(w)$ is a regularization function that prevents the parameters from getting too large (causing overfitting), and

- C is a scalar constant (set by the user of the learning algorithm) that controls the balance between the regularization and the loss function.

Popular loss functions include the hinge loss (for linear SVMs) and the log loss (for linear logistic regression). If the regularization function R is convex, then the above is a convex problem. Many algorithms exist for solving such problems; popular ones for linear classification include (stochastic) gradient descent, L-BFGS, coordinate descent and Newton methods.

Perceptron

A perceptron is a simple model of a biological neuron in an artificial neural network. Perceptron is also the name of an early algorithm for supervised learning of binary classifiers.

The perceptron algorithm was designed to classify visual inputs, categorizing subjects into one of two types and separating groups with a line. Classification is an important part of machine learning and image processing. Machine learning algorithms find and classify patterns by many different means. The perceptron algorithm classifies patterns and groups by finding the linear separation between different objects and patterns that are received through numeric or visual input.

The perceptron algorithm was developed at Cornell Aeronautical Laboratory in 1957, funded by the United States Office of Naval Research. The algorithm was the first step planned for a machine implementation for image recognition. The machine, called Mark 1 Perceptron, was physically made up of an array of 400 photocells connected to perceptrons whose weights were recorded in potentiometers, as adjusted by electric motors. The machine was one of the first artificial neural networks ever created.

At the time, the perceptron was expected to be very significant for the development of artificial intelligence (AI). While high hopes surrounded the initial perceptron, technical limitations were soon demonstrated. Single-layer perceptrons can only separate classes if they are linearly separable. Later on, it was discovered that by using multiple layers, perceptrons can classify groups that are not linearly separable, allowing them to solve problems single layer algorithms can't solve.

References

- Har-Peled, S., Roth, D., Zimak, D. (2003) "Constraint Classification for Multiclass Classification and Ranking." In: Becker, B., Thrun, S., Obermayer, K. (Eds) Advances in Neural Information Processing Systems 15: Proceedings of the 2002 Conference, MIT Press. ISBN 0-262-02550-7

- What-is-statistical-classification: wisegeek.com, Retrieved 29 April 2018

- Peter Mills (2011). "Efficient statistical classification of satellite measurements". International Journal of Remote Sensing. arXiv:1202.2194. doi:10.1080/01431161.2010.507795

- Getting-started-with-classification: geeksforgeeks.org, Retrieved 22 March 2018

- Venkatesan, Rajasekar; Meng Joo, Er (2016). "A novel progressive learning technique for multiclass classification". Neurocomputing. 207: 310–321. arXiv:1609.00085. doi:10.1016/j.neucom.2016.05.006

- Naive-bayes-classifiers: geeksforgeeks.org, Retrieved 14 July 2018

Unsupervised Learning

Unsupervised learning refers to the learning task of identifying a function which describes the structure of data that is unlabeled or unclassified. This chapter includes a detailed discussion of competitive learning, vector quantization, generative adversarial network, generative topographic map, etc. which will be crucial for a comprehensive understanding of unsupervised learning.

Unsupervised learning is the training of an artificial intelligence (AI) algorithm using information that is neither classified nor labeled and allowing the algorithm to act on that information without guidance.

In unsupervised learning, an AI system may group unsorted information according to similarities and differences even though there are no categories provided. AI systems capable of unsupervised learning are often associated with generative learning models, although they may also use a retrieval-based approach (which is most often associated with supervised learning). Chatbots, self-driving cars, facial recognition programs, expert systems and robots are among the systems that may use either supervised or unsupervised learning approaches.

In unsupervised learning, an AI system is presented with unlabeled, uncategorized data and the system's algorithms act on the data without prior training. The output is dependent upon the coded algorithms. Subjecting a system to unsupervised learning is one way of testing AI.

Unsupervised learning algorithms can perform more complex processing tasks than supervised learning systems. However, unsupervised learning can be more unpredictable than the alternate model. While an unsupervised learning AI system might, for example, figure out on its own how to sort cats from dogs, it might also add unforeseen and undesired categories to deal with unusual breeds, creating clutter instead of order.

Types of Unsupervised learning

Clustering

"Clustering" is the process of grouping similar entities together. The goal of this unsupervised machine learning technique is to find similarities in the data point and group similar data points together.

Grouping similar entities together help profile the attributes of different groups. In other words, this will give us insight into underlying patterns of different groups. There are many applications of grouping unlabeled data, for example, you can identify different groups/segments of customers and market each group in a different way to maximize the revenue. Another example is grouping documents together, which belong to the similar topics etc.

Clustering is also used to reduces the dimensionality of the data when you are dealing with a copious number of variables.

There are a few different types of clustering you can utilize:

K-mean Clustering

1. It starts with K as the input, which is how many clusters you want to find. Place K centroids in random locations in your space.

2. Now, using the euclidean distance between data points and centroids, assign each data point to the cluster, which is close to it.

3. Recalculate the cluster centers as a mean of data points assigned to it.

4. Repeat 2 and 3 until no further changes occur.

One of the methods is called "Elbow" method can be used to decide an optimal number of clusters. Here you would run K-mean clustering on a range of K values and plot the *"percentage of variance explained"* on the Y-axis and *"K"* on X-axis.

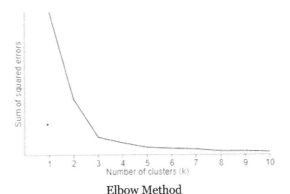

Elbow Method

In the picture below you would notice that as we add more clusters after 3 it doesn't give much better modeling on the data. The first cluster adds much information, but at some point, the marginal gain will start dropping.

Hierarchical Clustering

Unlike K-mean clustering *Hierarchical* clustering starts by assigning all data points as their own cluster. As the name suggests it builds the hierarchy and in the next step, it combines the two nearest data point and merges it together to one cluster.

1. Assign each data point to its own cluster.

2. Find closest pair of cluster using euclidean distance and merge them in to single cluster.

3. Calculate distance between two nearest clusters and combine until all items are clustered in to a single cluster.

In this technique, you can decide the optimal number of clusters by noticing which vertical lines can be cut by horizontal line without intersecting a cluster and covers the maximum distance.

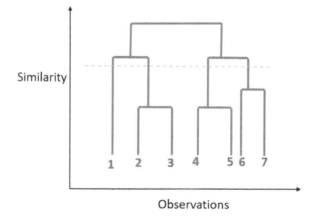

Probabilistic Clustering

Clustering your data points into clusters on a probabilistic scale. K-Means is a special case where the probabilities are always either 0 or 1. This is also sometimes called Fuzzy K-Means.

These variations on the same fundamental concept might look something like this in code:

```
#Import the KMeans package from Scikit Learn

from sklearn.cluster import KMeans
```

```
#Grab the training data

x = os.path('train')

#Set the desired number of clusters

k = 5

#Run the KMeans algorithm

kmeans = KMeans(n_clusters=k).fit(x)

#Show the resulting labels

kmeans.labels_
```

Any clustering algorithm will typically output all of your data points and the respective clusters to which they belong.

Data Compression

Even with major advances over the past decade in computing power and storage costs, it still makes sense to keep your data sets as small and efficient as possible. That means only running algorithms on necessary data and not training on too much. Unsupervised learning can help with that through a process called dimensionality reduction.

Dimensionality reduction (dimensions = how many columns are in your dataset) relies on many of the same concepts as Information Theory: it assumes that a lot of data is redundant, and that you can represent most of the information in a data set with only a fraction of the actual content. In practice, this means combining parts of your data in unique ways to convey meaning. There are a couple of popular algorithms commonly used to reduce dimensionality:

- *Principal Component Analysis (PCA)* – finds the linear combinations that communicate most of the variance in your data.

- *Singular-Value Decomposition (SVD)* – factorizes your data into the product of 3 other, smaller matrices.

These methods as well as some of their more complex cousins all rely on concepts from Linear Algebra to break down a matrix into more digestible and informatory pieces.

Unsupervised Deep Learning

Unsurprisingly, unsupervised learning has also been extended to Neural Nets and Deep Learning. This area is still nascent, but one popular application of Deep Learning in an unsupervised fashion is called an Autoencoder.

Autoencoders follow the same philosophy as the data compression algorithms above—— using a smaller subset of features to represent our original data. Like a Neural Net, an Autoencoder uses weights to try and mold the input values into a desired output; but the clever twist here is that the output is the same thing as the input! In other words, the Autoencoder tries to figure out how to best represent our input data as itself, using a smaller amount of data than the original.

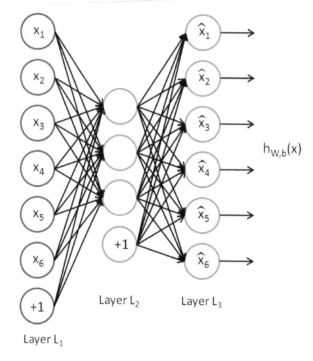

Autoencoders have proven useful in computer vision applications like object recognition, and are being researched and extended to domains like audio and speech.

Competitive Learning

Competitive learning is a type of unsupervised learning model used in machine learning and artificial intelligence systems.

In a competitive learning model, there are hierarchical sets of units in the network with inhibitory and excitatory connections. The excitatory connections are between individual layers and the inhibitory connections are between units in layered clusters. Units in a cluster are either active or inactive.

Scientists explain that the configuration of active units represents an input pattern to be sent to the next level. In processes like vector quantization, professionals can see the principles of competitive learning at work. Competitive learning also exists alongside other learning models such as ensemble learning, where more than one learning unit works together in a dedicated effort toward a result.

Mathematical Formulation

Following are the three important factors for mathematical formulation of this learning rule:

- Condition to be a winner

  Suppose if a neuron y_k wants to be the winner, then there would be the following condition

  $$y_k = \begin{cases} 1 & if\ v_k > v_j\ for\ all\ j,\ j \neq k \\ 0 & otherwise \end{cases}$$

  It means that if any neuron, say, y_k wants to win, then its induced local field (the output of the summation unit), say v_k, must be the largest among all the other neurons in the network.

- Condition of the sum total of weight

  Another constraint over the competitive learning rule is the sum total of weights to a particular output neuron is going to be 1. For example, if we consider neuron k then

  $$\sum_k w_{kj} = 1 \quad for\ all\ k$$

- Change of weight for the winner

  If a neuron does not respond to the input pattern, then no learning takes place in that neuron. However, if a particular neuron wins, then the corresponding weights are adjusted as follows:

  $$\Delta w_{kj} = \begin{cases} -\alpha\left(x_j - w_{kj}\right), & if\ neuron\ k\ wins \\ 0 & if\ neuron\ k\ losses \end{cases}$$

  Here α is the learning rate.

This clearly shows that we are favoring the winning neuron by adjusting its weight and if a neuron is lost, then we need not bother to re-adjust its weight.

Competitive Learning Algorithms

The k-means Algorithm

The standard k-means algorithm calculates the distance between the input vector and the centers vector. The distance may be of different types, but usually the Euclidian norm is used:

$$\left\| x(n) - c_i(n) \right\| = \sqrt{x_1(n) - c_{1i}(n)]^2 + \cdots + [x_m(n) - c_{mi}(n)]^2},$$

where $x(n)$ is the input vector, c_i is the center vector i, m is the vectors dimension and N is the number of the centers. The center j with a minimum distance is declared winner:

$$j = \operatorname{argmin} \left\| x(n) - c_i(n) \right\| \quad i = 1,\dots,N.$$

The winning center is moved with a fraction η towards the input

$$c_i(n+1) = c_i(n) - \eta \left[x(n) - c_i(n) \right].$$

The learning rate η may be constant or descendant with a fraction, for example:

$$\eta(n+1) = \eta(n) - \frac{1}{N},$$

where N represents the centers number.

The weights are randomly initialized, usually at the input vector values. Equations $j = \operatorname{argmin} \left\| x(n) - c_i(n) \right\| \quad i = 1,\dots,N.$ and $c_i(n+1) = c_i(n) - \eta \left[x(n) - c_i(n) \right].$ are than applied iteratively until the algorithm converges or freezes as the number of iterations reaches a specified value, respectively the descending learning rate becomes zero or a very small value.

The classical k-means algorithm has the "dead units" problem. That is, if a center is initialized far away from the input data set in comparison with other centers, it may never win the competition, so it may never update, becoming a dead unit.

The Frequency Sensitive Competitive Algorithm

To solve the "dead units" problem it has been introduced the so called "frequency sensitive competitive learning" algorithm or competitive algorithm "with conscience". Each center counts the number of times when it has won the competition and reduces its learning rate consequently. If a center has won too often "it feels guilty" and it pulls itself out of the competition. The FSCL algorithm is an extension of k-means algorithm, obtained by modifying relation (2) according to the following one:

$$j = \operatorname{argmin} y_i \|x(n) - c_i(n)\| \quad i = 1,...,N.$$

with the relative winning frequency y_i of the center c_i defined as

$$y_i = \frac{s_i}{\sum\limits_{i=1}^{N} s_i},$$

where s_i is the number of times when the center c_i was declared winner in the past. So the centers that have won the competition during the past have a reduced chance to win again, proportional with their frequency term y. After selecting out the winner, the FSCL algorithm updates the winner with equation $c_i(n+1) = c_i(n) - \eta \left[x(n) - c_i(n) \right]$. in the same way as the k-means algorithm, and meanwhile adjusting the corresponding s_i with the following relation:

$$s_i(n+1) = s_i(n) + 1.$$

The FSCL algorithm can almost always successfully distribute the N centres into the input data set without the "dead units problem", but only when the clusters number is known.

The Rival Penalized Competitive Learning Algorithm

The rival penalized competitive algorithm performs appropriate clustering without knowing the clusters number. It determines not only the winning center j but also the second winning center r, named rival

$$j = \operatorname{argmin} y_i \|x(n) - c_i(n)\| \quad i = 1,...,N \quad i \neq j.$$

The second winning center will move away its center from the input with a ratio β, called the de-learning rate. All the other centers vectors will not change. So the learning law can be synthesized in the following relation:

$$c_i(n+1) = \begin{cases} c_i(n) + \eta \left[x(n) - c_i(n) \right] & if\ i = j \\ c_i(n) - \beta \left[x(n) - c_i(n) \right] & if\ i = r \\ c_i(n) & if\ i = j\ and\ i \neq r \end{cases}$$

If the learning speed η is chosen much greater than β, with at least one order of magnitude, the number of the output data classes will be automatically found. In other words, suppose that the number of classes is unknown and the centers number N is greater than the clusters number, than the centers vectors will converge towards the centroids of the input data classes. The RPCL will move away the rival, in each iteration, converging much faster than the k-means and the FSCL algorithms. The number of extra seed points, respectively the difference between N and the number k of classes will be driven away from the data set. If N is smaller than the number of input data classes, than the network will oscillate during training, indicating that the clusters number must be increased.

The Dynamically Penalized Rival Competitive Learning Algorithm

The DRPCL is a variant of the RPCL algorithm. It determines not only the winning neuron, but also the second winning neuron, the first rival. Comparative to the RPCL algorithm, the DRPCL algorithm applies a new mechanism to dynamically control the rival penalization. For this it introduces a new term, the penalization strength:

$$p\big(c_i(n)\big) = \frac{min\big(\|x(n)-c_w\|,\|c_w-c_r\|\big)}{\|c_w-c_r\|},$$

where c_w and c_r are the center of the winner, respectively of the rival. With this factor the de-learning rate β in equation becomes:

$$\beta = \eta\, p\big(c_i(n)\big).$$

It can be noticed that the value of p(ci) in relation is always between 0 and 1, which can be therefore regarded as the probability of rival penalization. If the condition $\|x(n)-c_w\| \geq \|c_w-c_r\|$ is satisfied, than the rival will be fully penalized with the learning rate η. Otherwise, the rival will be penalized with the de-learning rate η p(ci(n), which is gradually attenuated as the distance between the winner and its rival increases. So, the DRPCL algorithm is actually a generalization of the RPCL algorithm, which moves away the undesired centers much faster than the RPCL algorithm, because its de-learning rate is greater.

Vector Quantization

Vector quantization (VQ) is an efficient coding technique to quantize signal vectors. It has been widely used in signal and image processing, such as pattern recognition and speech and image coding. A VQ compression procedure has two main steps: codebook training (sometimes also referred to as codebook generation) and coding (i.e., code vector matching). In the training step, similar vectors in a training sequence are grouped into clusters, and each cluster is assigned to a single representative vector called a code vector. In the coding step, each input vector is then compressed by replacing it with the nearest code vector referenced by a simple cluster index. The index (or address) of the matched code vector in the codebook is then transmitted to the decoder over a channel and is used by the decoder to retrieve the same code vector from an identical codebook. This is the reconstructed reproduction of the corresponding input vector. Compression is thus obtained by transmitting the index of the code vector rather than the entire code vector itself.

Vector Quantizer Encoder System Object

The Vector Quantizer Encoder object performs vector quantization encoding. The object finds the nearest code word by computing a distortion based on Euclidean or weighted Euclidean distance.

To perform vector quantization encoding:

1. Create the dsp.VectorQuantizerEncoder object and set its properties.

2. Call the object with arguments, as if it were a function.

Creation

Syntax

```
vqenc = dsp.VectorQuantizerEncoder

vqenc = dsp.VectorQuantizerEncoder(Name,Value)
```

Description

```
vqenc = dsp.VectorQuantizerEncoder returns a vector quan-
tizer encoder System object™, vqenc. This object finds a ze-
ro-based index of the nearest codeword for each given input
column vector.

vqenc = dsp.VectorQuantizerEncoder(Name,Value) returns a vec-
tor quantizer encoder System object, vqenc, with each speci-
fied property set to the specified value.
```

Properties

Unless otherwise indicated, properties are *nontunable*, which means you cannot change their values after calling the object. Objects lock when you call them, and the release function unlocks them.

If a property is *tunable*, you can change its value at any time.

For more information on changing property values,

Code Book Source — Source of Code Book Values

Property (default) | Input port

Specify how to determine the codebook values as Property or Input port.

Code book — Matrix of Code Words

[1.5 13.3 136.4 6.8; 2.5 14.3 137.4 7.8; 3.5 15.3 138.4 8.8] (default) | matrix

Specify the codebook to which the input column vector or matrix is compared, as a k-by-N matrix. Each column of the codebook matrix is a code word, and each code word corresponds to an index value. The code word vectors must have the same number of rows as the input. The first code word vector corresponds to an index value of 0, the second code word vector corresponds to an index value of 1, and so on. The default is:

$$\begin{bmatrix} 1.5 & 13.3 & 136.4 & 6.8 \\ 2.5 & 14.3 & 137.4 & 7.8 \\ 3.5 & 15.3 & 138.4 & 8.8 \end{bmatrix}$$

Tunable: Yes

Dependencies

This property applies when you set the Codebook Source property to Property.

Data Types: single | double | int8 | int16 | int32 | int64 | uint8 | uint16 | uint32 | uint64

Distortion Measure — Distortion Calculation Method

Squared error (default) | Weighted squared error

Specify how to calculate the distortion as Squared error or Weighted squared error. If you set this property to Squared error, the object calculates the distortion by evaluating the Euclidean distance between the input column vector and each code word in the codebook. If you set this property to weighted squared error, the object calculates the distortion by evaluating a weighted Euclidean distance using a weighting factor to emphasize or deemphasize certain input values.

Weights Source — Source of Weighting Factor

Property (default) | Input port

Specify how to determine weighting factor as Property or Input port.

Dependencies

This property applies when you set the Distortion Measure property to weighted squared error.

Weights — Weighting Factor

[1 1 1] (default) | vector

Specify the weighting factor as a vector of length equal to the number of rows of the input.

Tunable: Yes

Dependencies

This property applies when you set the distortion measure property to weighted squared error and weights Source property is property.

Data Types: single | double | int8 | int16 | int32 | int64 | uint8 | uint16 | uint32 | uint64

Tie Breaker Rule — Behavior when Input Column Vector is Equidistant from Two Code Words

Choose the lower index (default) | Choose the higher index

Specify whether to represent the input column vector by the lower index valued code word or higher indexed valued code word when an input column vector is equidistant from two code words. You can set this property to Choose the lower index or choose the higher index.

Code word Output Port — Enable output of Code Word Value

false (default) | true

Set this property to true to output the code word vectors nearest to the input column vectors.

Quantization Error Output Port — Enable Output of Quantization Error

false (default) | true

Set this property to true to output the quantization error value that results when the object represents the input column vector by the nearest code word.

Output Index Data Type — Data Type of Index Output

int32 (default) | int8 | uint8 | int16 | uint16 | uint32

Specify the data type of the index output as: `int8`, `uint8`, `int16`, `uint16`, `int32`, `uint32`.

Fixed-Point Properties

Rounding Method — Rounding method for fixed-point operations

Floor (default) | Ceiling | Convergent | Nearest | Round | Simplest | Zero

Specify the rounding method as Ceiling, Convergent, Floor, Nearest, Round, Simplest or Zero.

Overflow Action — Overflow action for fixed-point operations

Wrap (default) | Saturate

Specify the overflow action as Wrap or Saturate.

Product Data Type — Source of product word and fraction lengths

Same as input (default) | Custom

Specify the product fixed-point data type as same as input or Custom.

Custom Product Data Type — Product word and fraction lengths

numerictype([],16,15) (default) | numerictype

Specify the product fixed-point type as a scaled numeric type object with a signedness of Auto.

Dependencies

This property applies when you set the Product Data Type property to Custom.

Accumulator Data Type — Source of accumulator word and fraction lengths

Same as product (default) | Same as input | Custom

Specify the accumulator fixed-point data type as Same as product, Same as input, or Custom.

Custom Accumulator Data Type — Accumulator word and fraction lengths

numerictype([],16,15) (default) | numerictype

Specify the accumulator fixed-point type as a scaled numeric type object with a signedness of Auto.

Dependencies

This property applies when you set the Accumulator Data Type property to Custom.

Usage

For versions earlier than R2016b, use the step function to run the System object algorithm. The arguments to step are the object you created, followed by the arguments shown here.

For example, `y = step(obj,x)` and `y = obj(x)` perform equivalent operations.

Syntax

```
Index = vqenc(Input)

Index = vqenc(Input,Codebook)

Index = vqenc(___,Weights)

[Index,Codeword] = vqenc(___)

[Index,Qerr] = vqenc(___)
```

Description

`Index = vqenc (Input)` returns Index, a scalar or column vector representing the quantization region(s) to which Input belongs.

`Index = vqenc (Input, Codebook)` uses the codebook given in input Codebook, a k-by-N matrix with N code words each of length k. This option is available when the Code book Source property is Input port.

`Index = vqenc (___,Weights)` uses the input vector Weights to emphasize or de-emphasize certain input values when calculating the distortion measure. Weights must be a vector of length equal to the number of rows of Input. This option is available when the Distortion Measure property is weighted squared error and the Weights Source property is Input port.

`[Index,Codeword] = vqenc (___)` outputs the Code word values that correspond to each index value when the Code word Output Port property is true. This syntax can be used with any of the previous input syntaxes.

`[Index,Qerr] = vqenc (___)` outputs the quantization error Qerr for each input value when the Quantization Error Output Port property is true.

Input Arguments

Input — Data Input

column vector | matrix

Data input, specified as a column vector of size k-by-1 or a matrix of size k-by-M, where k is the length of each code word in the codebook.

The number of rows in the data input, the length of the Weights vector, and the length of the code word vector must all be the same value. All inputs to the object must have the same data type.

Data Types: `single` | `double` | `int8` | `int16` | `int32` | `int64` | fi

Code Book — Code Book Values

column vector | matrix

Codebook values, specified as a column vector of size k-by-1 or a matrix of size k-by-N, where k is the length of each code word and N is the number of code words.

The length of the code word vector, the number of rows in the data input, and the length of the Weights vector must all be the same value. All inputs to the object must have the same data type.

Dependencies

This input applies when the Code book Source property is Input port.

Data Types: `single` | `double` | `int8` | `int16` | `int32` | `int64` | fi

Weights — Measure of Emphasis

vector

The object uses the weights vector to emphasize or de-emphasize certain input values when calculating the distortion measure.

The length of the Weights vector must equal the number of rows in the data input and the length of the code word. All inputs to the object must have the same data type.

Dependencies

This input applies when the Distortion Measure property is weighted squared error and the Weights Source property is Input port.

Data Types: single | double | int8 | int16 | int32 | int64 | fi

Output Arguments

Index — Indices of Nearest Code Word Vectors

scalar | row vector

Indices of the nearest code word vectors, returned as a scalar or a row vector. The object compares each input column vector to the code word vectors in the codebook matrix. Each column of this codebook matrix is a code word. The object finds the code word vector nearest to the input column vector and returns its zero-based index. When the input is a matrix, the indices of the nearest code word vectors are horizontally concatenated.

The object finds the nearest code word by calculating the distortion using the method specified in Distortion Measure property.

Data Types: int32

Code Word — Code Word

column vector | matrix

Code word values that correspond to each index value, returned as a column vector or a matrix. When the input is a matrix, the corresponding code word vectors are horizontally concatenated into a matrix.

Dependencies

This output is enabled when the Code word Output Port property is set to true.

Data Types: `single` | `double` | `int8` | `int16` | `int32` | `int64` | fi

Qerr — Quantization Error

scalar | row vector

Quantization error, returned as a scalar or a row vector. The quantization error results when the object represents the input column vector by its nearest code word. When the input is a matrix, the quantization error values are horizontally concatenated.

Dependencies

This output is enabled when the Quantization Error Output Port property is set to true.

Data Types: `single` | `double` | `int8` | `int16` | `int32` | `int64` | fi

Object Functions

To use an object function, specify the System object as the first input argument. For example, to release system resources of a System object named obj, use this syntax:

```
release(obj)
```

Common to All System Objects

step	Run System object algorithm
release	Release resources and allow changes to System object property values and input characteristics
reset	Reset internal states of System object

Vector Quantization Example

Face, a 1024 x 768 size image of a raccoon face, is used here to illustrate how k-means is used for vector quantization.

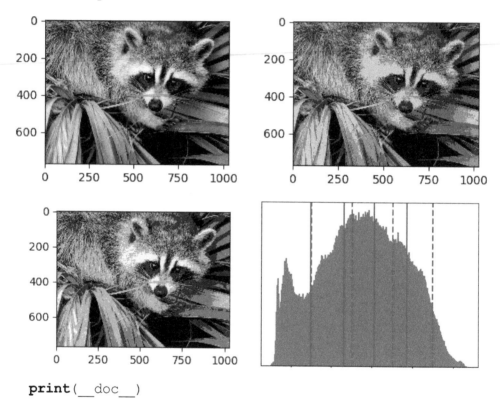

```
print(__doc__)
```

```
# Code source: Gaël Varoquaux
# Modified for documentation by Jaques Grobler
# License: BSD 3 clause


import numpy as np
import scipy as sp
```

```python
import matplotlib.pyplot as plt

from sklearn import cluster


try:    # SciPy >= 0.16 have face in misc
    from scipy.misc import face
    face = face(gray=True)
except ImportError:
    face = sp.face(gray=True)


n_clusters = 5
np.random.seed(0)


X = face.reshape((-1, 1))  # We need an (n_sample, n_feature)
array
k_means = cluster.KMeans(n_clusters=n_clusters, n_init=4)
k_means.fit(X)
values = k_means.cluster_centers_.squeeze()
labels = k_means.labels_


# create an array from labels and values
face_compressed = np.choose(labels, values)
face_compressed.shape = face.shape


vmin = face.min()
vmax = face.max()


# original face
plt.figure(above, figsize=(3, 2.2))
```

```
plt.imshow(face, cmap=plt.cm.gray, vmin=vmin, vmax=256)


# compressed face
plt.figure(above, figsize=(3, 2.2))
plt.imshow(face_compressed, cmap=plt.cm.gray, vmin=vmin,
vmax=vmax)


# equal bins face
regular_values = np.linspace(0, 256, n_clusters + 1)
regular_labels = np.searchsorted(regular_values, face) - 1
regular_values = .5 * (regular_values[1:] + regular_val-
ues[:-1])   # mean
regular_face = np.choose(regular_labels.ravel(), regular_
values, mode="clip")
regular_face.shape = face.shape
plt.figure(above, figsize=(3, 2.2))
plt.imshow(regular_face, cmap=plt.cm.gray, vmin=vmin, vmax-
=vmax)


# histogram
plt.figure(above, figsize=(3, 2.2))
plt.clf()
plt.axes([.01, .01, .98, .98])
plt.hist(X, bins=256, color='.5', edgecolor='.5')
plt.yticks(())
plt.xticks(regular_values)
values = np.sort(values)
for center_1, center_2 in zip(values[:-1], values[1:]):
    plt.axvline(.5 * (center_1 + center_2), color='b')


for center_1, center_2 in zip(regular_values[:-1], regular_
values[1:]):
```

```
    plt.axvline(.5 * (center_1 + center_2), color='b', lin-
estyle='--')


plt.show()
```

Generative Adversarial Network

A generative adversarial network (GAN) is a type of construct in neural network technology that offers a lot of potential in the world of artificial intelligence. A generative adversarial network is composed of two neural networks: a generative network and a discriminative network. These work together to provide high-level simulation of conceptual tasks.

In a generative adversarial network, the generative network constructs results from input, and "shows" them to the discriminative network. The discriminative network is supposed to distinguish between authentic and synthetic results given by the generative network.

Experts sometimes describe this as the generative network trying to "fool" the discriminative network, which has to be trained to recognize particular sets of patterns and models. The use of generative adversarial networks is somewhat common in image processing, and in the development of new deep stubborn networks that move toward more high-level simulation of human cognitive tasks. Scientists are looking at the potential that generative adversarial networks have to advance the power of neural networks and their ability to "think" in human ways.

Working of GAN

As we saw, there are two main components of a GAN – Generator Neural Network and Discriminator Neural Network.

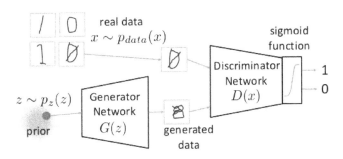

The Generator Network takes an random input and tries to generate a sample of data. In the above image, we can see that generator G(z) takes a input z from p(z), where z is a sample from probability distribution p(z). It then generates a data which is then fed into a discriminator network D(x). The task of Discriminator Network is to take input either from the real data or from the generator and try to predict whether the input is real or generated. It takes an input x from $p_{data}(x)$ where $p_{data}(x)$ is our real data distribution. D(x) then solves a binary classification problem using sigmoid function giving output in the range 0 to 1.

Let us define the notations we will be using to formalize our GAN,

Pdata(x) -> the distribution of real data

X -> sample from pdata(x)

P(z) -> distribution of generator

Z -> sample from p(z)

G(z) -> Generator Network

D(x) -> Discriminator Network

Now the training of GAN is done (as we saw above) as a fight between generator and discriminator. This can be represented mathematically as:

$$\min_{G} \max_{D} V(D,G)$$

$$V(D,G) = E_{x \sim pdata(x)} \Big[\log D(x) \Big] + E_{z \sim p_z (z)} \Big[\log \big(1 - D \big(G(z) \big) \big) \Big]$$

In our function V (D, G) the first term is entropy that the data from real distribution ($p_{data}(x)$) passes through the discriminator (aka best case scenario). The discriminator tries to maximize this to 1. The second term is entropy that the data from random input (p(z)) passes through the generator, which then generates a fake sample which is then passed through the discriminator to identify the fakeness (aka worst case scenario). In this term, discriminator tries to maximize it to 0 (i.e. the log probability that the data from generated is fake is equal to 0). So overall, the discriminator is trying to maximize our function V.

On the other hand, the task of generator is exactly opposite, i.e. it tries to minimize the function V so that the differentiation between real and fake data is bare minimum. This, in other words is a cat and mouse game between generator and discriminator.

Parts of Training GAN

So broadly a training phase has two main subparts and they are done sequentially

- Pass 1: Train discriminator and freeze generator (freezing means setting training as false. The network does only forward pass and no back propagation is applied)

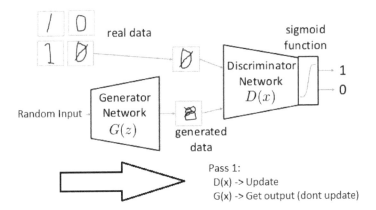

Pass 1:
D(x) -> Update
G(x) -> Get output (dont update)

- Pass 2: Train generator and freeze discriminator

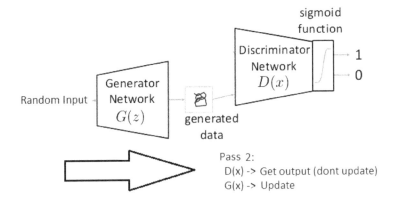

Pass 2:
D(x) -> Get output (dont update)
G(x) -> Update

Steps to Train a GAN

Step 1: Define the problem: Do you want to generate fake images or fake text. Here you should completely define the problem and collect data for it.

Step 2: Define architecture of GAN: Define how your GAN should look like. Should both your generator and discriminator be multi layer perceptrons, or convolutional neural networks? This step will depend on what problem you are trying to solve.

Step 3: Train Discriminator on real data for n epochs: Get the data you want to generate fake on and train the discriminator to correctly predict them as real. Here value n can be any natural number between 1 and infinity.

Step 4: Generate fake inputs for generator and train discriminator on fake data: Get generated data and let the discriminator correctly predict them as fake.

Step 5: Train generator with the output of discriminator: Now when the discriminator is trained, you can get its predictions and use it as an objective for training the generator. Train the generator to fool the discriminator.

Step 6: Repeat step 3 to step 5 for a few epochs.

Step 7: Check if the fake data manually if it seems legit. If it seems appropriate, stop training, else go to step 3: This is a bit of a manual task, as hand evaluating the data is the best way to check the fakeness. When this step is over, you can evaluate whether the GAN is performing well enough.

Implementing a Toy GAN

Lets see a toy implementation of GAN to strengthen our theory. We will try to generate digits by training a GAN on Identify the Digits dataset. A bit about the dataset; the dataset contains 28×28 images, which are black and white. All the images are in ".png" format. For our task, we will only work on the training set.

You also need to setup the libraries, namely

- Numpy

- Pandas

- Tensorflow

- Keras

- Keras_adversarial

Before starting with the code, let us understand the internal working through pseudo code. A pseudo code of GAN training can be thought out as follows

For number of training iterations do

  For k steps do check equation link 112

- Sample minibatch of m noise samples $\left\{z^{(1)},...,z^{(m)}\right\}$ from noise prior $p_g(z)$

- Sample minibatch of m examples $\left\{x^{(1)},...,x^{(m)}\right\}$ from data generating distribution $p_{data(x)}$

- Update the discriminator by ascending its stochastic gradient:

$$\nabla_{\theta_d}\frac{1}{m}\sum_{i=1}^{m}\left[\log D\left(x^{(i)}\right)+\log\left(1-D\left(G\left(z^{(i)}\right)\right)\right)\right].$$

End for

- Sample minibatch of m noise samples $\left\{z^{(1)},...,z^{(m)}\right\}$ from noise prior $p_g(z)$

- Update the generator by descending its stochastic gradient:

$$\nabla_{\theta_d} \frac{1}{m} \sum_{i=1}^{m} \log\left(1 - D\left(G\left(z^{(i)}\right)\right)\right).$$

End for

This is the first implementation of GAN that was published in the paper. Numerous improvements/updates in the pseudo code can be seen in the recent papers such as adding batch normalization in the generator and discrimination network, training generator k times etc.

Now lets start with the code.

Let us first import all the modules

```
# import modules
%pylab inline


import os
import numpy as np
import pandas as pd
from scipy.misc import imread


import keras
from keras.models import Sequential
from keras.layers import Dense, Flatten, Reshape, InputLayer
from keras.regularizers import L1L2
```

To have a deterministic randomness, we set a seed value

```
# to stop potential randomness
seed = 128
rng = np.random.RandomState(seed)
We set the path of our data and working directory
# set path
root_dir = os.path.abspath('.')
data_dir = os.path.join(root_dir, 'Data')
```

Let us load our data

```
# load data
train = pd.read_csv(os.path.join(data_dir, 'Train', 'train.csv'))

test = pd.read_csv(os.path.join(data_dir, 'test.csv'))


temp = []

for img_name in train.filename:
    image_path = os.path.join(data_dir, 'Train', 'Images', 'train', img_name)

    img = imread(image_path, flatten=True)

    img = img.astype('float32')

    temp.append(img)


train_x = np.stack(temp)


train_x = train_x / 255.
```

To visualize what our data looks like, let us plot one of the image

```
# print image
img_name = rng.choice(train.filename)

filepath = os.path.join(data_dir, 'Train', 'Images', 'train', img_name)


img = imread(filepath, flatten=True)


pylab.imshow(img, cmap='gray')

pylab.axis('off')

pylab.show()
```

Define variables, which we will be using later

```
# define variables

# define vars g_input_shape = 100 d_input_shape = (28, 28)
hidden_1_num_units = 500 hidden_2_num_units = 500 g_output_
num_units = 784 d_output_num_units = 1 epochs = 25 batch_size
= 128
```

Now define our generator and discriminator networks

```
# generator

model_1 = Sequential([

    Dense(units=hidden_1_num_units, input_dim=g_input_shape,
activation='relu', kernel_regularizer=L1L2(1e-5, 1e-5)),


    Dense(units=hidden_2_num_units, activation='relu', ker-
nel_regularizer=L1L2(1e-5, 1e-5)),


    Dense(units=g_output_num_units, activation='sigmoid',
kernel_regularizer=L1L2(1e-5, 1e-5)),


    Reshape(d_input_shape),

])


# discriminator

model_2 = Sequential([

    InputLayer(input_shape=d_input_shape),


    Flatten(),


    Dense(units=hidden_1_num_units, activation='relu', ker-
nel_regularizer=L1L2(1e-5, 1e-5)),


    Dense(units=hidden_2_num_units, activation='relu', ker-
nel_regularizer=L1L2(1e-5, 1e-5)),
```

```
     Dense(units=d_output_num_units,  activation='sigmoid',
kernel_regularizer=L1L2(1e-5, 1e-5)),

])
```

Here is the architecture of our networks

```
In [9]:  model_1.summary()
```

Layer (type)	Output Shape	Param #
dense_1 (Dense)	(None, 500)	50500
dense_2 (Dense)	(None, 500)	250500
dense_3 (Dense)	(None, 784)	392784
reshape_1 (Reshape)	(None, 28, 28)	0

```
Total params: 693,784
Trainable params: 693,784
Non-trainable params: 0
```

```
In [10]:  model_2.summary()
```

Layer (type)	Output Shape	Param #
input_1 (InputLayer)	(None, 28, 28)	0
flatten_1 (Flatten)	(None, 784)	0
dense_4 (Dense)	(None, 500)	392500
dense_5 (Dense)	(None, 500)	250500
dense_6 (Dense)	(None, 1)	501

```
Total params: 643,501
Trainable params: 643,501
Non-trainable params: 0
```

We will then define our GAN, for that we will first import a few important modules

```
from keras_adversarial import AdversarialModel, simple_gan,
gan_targets
```

```
from keras_adversarial import AdversarialOptimizerSimultane-
ous, normal_latent_sampling
```

Let us compile our GAN and start the training

```
gan  =  simple_gan(model_1,  model_2,  normal_latent_sam-
pling((100,)))
```

```
model = AdversarialModel(base_model=gan,player_params=[mod-
el_1.trainable_weights, model_2.trainable_weights])
```

```
model.adversarial_compile(adversarial_optimizer=Adver-
sarialOptimizerSimultaneous(),     player_optimizers=['adam',
'adam'], loss='binary_crossentropy')
```

```
history = model.fit(x=train_x, y=gan_targets(train_x.shape),
epochs=10, batch_size=batch_size)
```

Here's how our GAN would look like,

```
In [13]: gan.summary()
```

Layer (type)	Output Shape	Param #	Connected to
input_1 (InputLayer)	(None, 28, 28)	0	
lambda_1 (Lambda)	(None, 100)	0	input_1[0][0]
gan (Model)	[(None, 1), (None, 1)	1337285	lambda_1[0][0] input_1[0][0]
yfake (Activation)	(None, 1)	0	gan[1][0]
yreal (Activation)	(None, 1)	0	gan[1][1]

```
Total params: 1,337,285
Trainable params: 1,337,285
Non-trainable params: 0
```

We get a graph like after training for 10 epochs.

```
plt.plot(history.history['player_0_loss'])

plt.plot(history.history['player_1_loss'])

plt.plot(history.history['loss'])
```

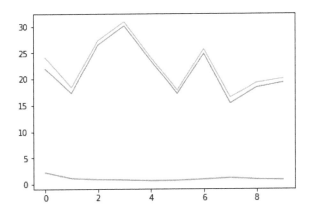

After training for 100 epochs, I got the following generated images

```
zsamples = np.random.normal(size=(10, 100))

pred = model_1.predict(zsamples)

for i in range(pred.shape):
```

```
plt.imshow(pred[i, :], cmap='gray')

plt.show()
```

You have built your first generative model!

Applications of GAN

- Predicting the next frame in a video: You train a GAN on video sequences and let it predict what would occur next

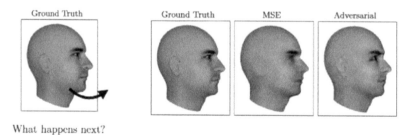

- Increasing Resolution of an image: Generate a high resolution photo from a comparatively low resolution.

Fig.: From left to right: bicubic interpolation, deep residual network optimized for MSE, deep residual generative adversarial network optimized for a loss more senstive to human perception, orignal HR image. Corresponding PSNR and SSIM are shown in brackets. (4x upscaling)

- Interactive Image Generation: Draw simple strokes and let the GAN draw an impressive picture for you.

- Image to Image Translation: Generate an image from another image. For example, given on the left, you have labels of a street scene and you can generate a real looking photo with GAN. On the right, you give a simple drawing of a handbag and you get a real looking drawing of a handbag.

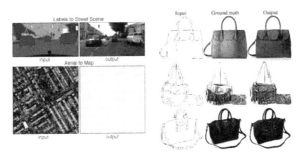

- Text to Image Generation: Just say to your GAN what you want to see and get a realistic photo of the target.

This bird has a yellow belly and tarsus, grey back, wings, and brown throat, nape with a black face

Self-organizing Map

Self Organizing Map (SOM) by Teuvo Kohonen provides a data visualization technique which helps to understand high dimensional data by reducing the dimensions of data to a map. SOM also represents clustering concept by grouping similar data together. Therefore it can be said that SOM reduces data dimensions and displays similarities among data.

With SOM, clustering is performed by having several units compete for the current object. Once the data have been entered into the system, the network of artificial neurons is trained by providing information about inputs. The weight vector of the unit is closest to the current object becomes the winning or active unit. During the training stage, the values for the input variables are gradually adjusted in an attempt to preserve neighborhood relationships that exist within the input data set. As it gets closer to the input object, the weights of the winning unit are adjusted as well as its neighbors.

The SOM is a new, effective software tool for the visualization of high-dimensional data. It converts complex, nonlinear statistical relationships between high-dimensional data items into simple geometric relationships on a low-dimensional display.

As it thereby compresses information while preserving the most important topological and metric relationships of the primary data items on the display, it may also be thought to produce some kind of abstractions.

Reducing Data Dimensions

Unlike other learning technique in neural networks, training a SOM requires no target vector. A SOM learns to classify the training data without any external supervision.

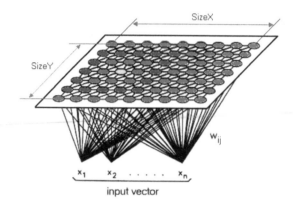

Data Similarity

Getting the Best Matching Unit is done by running through all wright vectors and calculating the distance from each weight to the sample vector. The weight with the shortest distance is the winner. There are numerous ways to determine the distance, however, the most commonly used method is the *Euclidean Distance* and/or *Cosine Distance*.

SOM Algorithm

Each data from data set recognizes themselves by competeting for representation. SOM mapping steps starts from initializing the weight vectors. From there a sample vector is selected randomly and the map of weight vectors is searched to find which weight best represents that sample. Each weight vector has neighboring weights that are close to it. The weight that is chosen is rewarded by being able to become more like that randomly selected sample vector. The neighbors of that weight are also rewarded by being able to become more like the chosen sample vector. From this step the number of neighbors and how much each weight can learn decreases over time. This whole process is repeated a large number of times, usually more than 1000 times.

In sum, learning occurs in several steps and over many iterations:

1. Each node's weights are initialized.

2. A vector is chosen at random from the set of training data.

3. Every node is examined to calculate which one's weights are most like the input vector. The winning node is commonly known as the Best Matching Unit (BMU).

4. Then the neighborhood of the BMU is calculated. The amount of neighbors decreases over time.

5. The winning weight is rewarded with becoming more like the sample vector. The neighbors also become more like the sample vector. The closer a node is to the BMU, the more its weights get altered and the farther away the neighbor is from the BMU, the less it learns.

6. Repeat step 2 for N iterations.

Result Interpretation

An example of the result of a self organizing map is shown below:

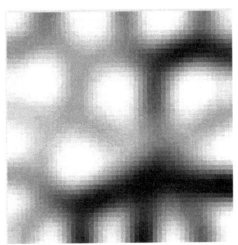

If the average distance is high, then the surrounding weights are very different and a dark color is assigned to the location of the weight. If the average distance is low, a lighter color is assigned. The resulting map shows that black is not similar to the white parts because there are lines of black representing no similarity between white parts. Looking at the map it clearly represents that the two not very similar by having black in between. It can be said that the white parts represent different clusters and the black lines represent the division of the clusters.

Learning Algorithm

The goal of learning in the self-organizing map is to cause different parts of the network to respond similarly to certain input patterns. This is partly motivated by how visual, auditory or other sensory information is handled in separate parts of the cerebral cortex in the human brain.

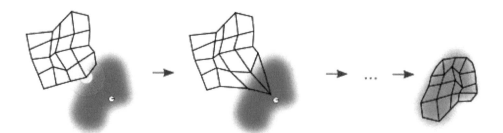

An illustration of the training of a self-organizing map. The blue blob is the distribution of the training data, and the small white disc is the current training datum drawn from that distribution. At first (left) the SOM nodes are arbitrarily positioned in the data space. The node (highlighted in yellow) which is nearest to the training datum is selected. It is moved towards the training datum, as (to a lesser extent) are its neighbors on the grid. After many iterations the grid tends to approximate the data distribution (right).

The weights of the neurons are initialized either to small random values or sampled evenly from the subspace spanned by the two largest principal component eigenvectors. With the latter alternative, learning is much faster because the initial weights already give a good approximation of SOM weights.

The network must be fed a large number of example vectors that represent, as close as possible, the kinds of vectors expected during mapping. The examples are usually administered several times as iterations.

The training utilizes competitive learning. When a training example is fed to the network, its Euclidean distance to all weight vectors is computed. The neuron whose weight vector is most similar to the input is called the best matching unit (BMU). The weights of the BMU and neurons close to it in the SOM grid are adjusted towards the input vector. The magnitude of the change decreases with time and with the grid-distance from the BMU. The update formula for a neuron v with weight vector $W_v(s)$ is

$$W_v(s+1) = W_v(s) + \Theta(u,v,s) \cdot \alpha(s) \cdot (D(t) - W_v(s)),$$

where s is the step index, t an index into the training sample, u is the index of the BMU for D(t), $\alpha(s)$ is a monotonically decreasing learning coefficient and D(t) is the input vector; $\Theta(u, v, s)$ is the neighborhood function which gives the distance between the neuron u and the neuron v in step s. Depending on the implementations, t can scan the training data set systematically (t is 0, 1, 2...T-1, then repeat, T being the training sample's size), be randomly drawn from the data set (bootstrap sampling), or implement some other sampling method (such as jackknifing).

The neighborhood function $\Theta(u, v, s)$ depends on the grid-distance between the BMU (neuron $u)$ and neuron v. In the simplest form it is 1 for all neurons close enough to BMU and o for others, but a Gaussian function is a common choice, too. Regardless of the functional form, the neighborhood function shrinks with time. At the beginning when the neighborhood is broad, the self-organizing takes place on the global scale. When the neighborhood has shrunk to just a couple of neurons, the weights are converging to local estimates. In some implementations the learning coefficient Θ and the neighborhood function Θ decrease steadily with increasing s, in others (in particular those where t scans the training data set) they decrease in step-wise fashion, once every T steps.

This process is repeated for each input vector for a (usually large) number of cycles λ. The network winds up associating output nodes with groups or patterns in the input data set. If these patterns can be named, the names can be attached to the associated nodes in the trained net.

During mapping, there will be one single *winning* neuron: the neuron whose weight vector lies closest to the input vector. This can be simply determined by calculating the Euclidean distance between input vector and weight vector.

While representing input data as vectors has been emphasized, it should be noted that any kind of object which can be represented digitally, which has an appropriate distance measure associated with it, and in which the necessary operations for training are possible can be used to construct a self-organizing map. This includes matrices, continuous functions or even other self-organizing maps.

Variables

These are the variables needed, with vectors in bold,

- s is the current iteration.
- λ is the iteration limit.
- t is the index of the target input data vector in the input data set **D**.
- $D(t)$ is a target input data vector.
- v is the index of the node in the map.
- W_v is the current weight vector of node v.
- u is the index of the best matching unit (BMU) in the map.
- $\theta(u,v,s)$ is a restraint due to distance from BMU, usually called the neighborhood function, and
- $\alpha(s)$ is a learning restraint due to iteration progress.

Algorithm

1. Randomize the node weight vectors in a map.

2. Randomly pick an input vector $D(t)$.

3. Traverse each node in the map.

   - Use the Euclidean distance formula to find the similarity between the input vector and the map's node's weight vector.

   - Track the node that produces the smallest distance (this node is the best matching unit, BMU).

4. Update the weight vectors of the nodes in the neighborhood of the BMU (including the BMU itself) by pulling them closer to the input vector.

   - $W_v(s+1) = W_v(s) + \theta(u,v,s) \cdot \alpha(s) \cdot (D(t) - W_v(s))$.

5. Increase s and repeat from step 2 while $s < \lambda$.

A variant algorithm:

1. Randomize the map's nodes' weight vectors.

2. Traverse each input vector in the input data set.

   - Traverse each node in the map.

     o Use the Euclidean distance formula to find the similarity between the input vector and the map's node's weight vector.

     o Track the node that produces the smallest distance (this node is the best matching unit, BMU).

   - Update the nodes in the neighborhood of the BMU (including the BMU itself) by pulling them closer to the input vector.

     o $W_v(s+1) = W_v(s) + \theta(u,v,s) \cdot \alpha(s) \cdot (D(t) - W_v(s))$.

3. Increase s and repeat from step 2 while $s < \lambda$.

SOM Initialization

Selection of a good initial approximation is a well-known problem for all iterative methods of learning neural networks. Kohonen used random initiation of SOM weights. Recently, principal component initialization, in which initial map weights are chosen from the space of the first principal components, has become popular due to the exact reproducibility of the results.

Careful comparison of the random initiation approach to principal component initialization for one-dimensional SOM (models of principal curves) demonstrated that the advantages of principal component SOM initialization are not universal. The best initialization method depends on the geometry of the specific dataset. Principal component initialization is preferable (in dimension one) if the principal curve approximating the dataset can be univalently and linearly projected on the first principal component (quasilinear sets). For nonlinear datasets, however, random initiation performs better.

Examples

Fisher's Iris Flower Data

Consider an $n \times m$ array of nodes, each of which contains a weight vector and is aware of its location in the array. Each weight vector is of the same dimension as the node's input vector. The weights may initially be set to random values.

Now we need input to feed the map. Colors can be represented by their red, green, and blue components. Consequently, we will represent colors as vectors in the unit cube of the free vector space over R generated by the basis:

$R = <255, 0, 0>$

$G = <0, 255, 0>$

$B = <0, 0, 255>$

The diagram shown

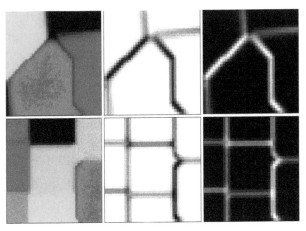

Self organizing maps (SOM) of three and eight colors with U-Matrix.

compares the results of training on the data sets

Three Colors = [255, 0, 0], [0, 255, 0], [0, 0, 255]

Eight Colors = [0, 0, 0], [255, 0, 0], [0, 255, 0], [0, 0, 255], [255, 255, 0], [0, 255, 255], [255, 0, 255], [255, 255, 255];

and the original images. Note the striking resemblance between the two.

Similarly, after training a 40×40 grid of neurons for 250 iterations with a learning rate of 0.1 on Fisher's Iris, the map can already detect the main differences between species.

Alternatives

- The generative topographic map (GTM) is a potential alternative to SOMs. In the sense that a GTM explicitly requires a smooth and continuous mapping from the input space to the map space, it is topology preserving. However, in a practical sense, this measure of topological preservation is lacking.

- The time adaptive self-organizing map (TASOM) network is an extension of the basic SOM. The TASOM employs adaptive learning rates and neighborhood functions. It also includes a scaling parameter to make the network invariant to scaling, translation and rotation of the input space. The TASOM and its variants have been used in several applications including adaptive clustering, multilevel thresholding, input space approximation, and active contour modeling. Moreover, a Binary Tree TASOM or BTASOM, resembling a binary natural tree having nodes composed of TASOM networks has been proposed where the number of its levels and the number of its nodes are adaptive with its environment.

- The growing self-organizing map (GSOM) is a growing variant of the self-organizing map. The GSOM was developed to address the issue of identifying a suitable map size in the SOM. It starts with a minimal number of nodes (usually four) and grows new nodes on the boundary based on a heuristic. By using a value called the spread factor, the data analyst has the ability to control the growth of the GSOM.

- The elastic maps approach borrows from the spline interpolation the idea of minimization of the elastic energy. In learning, it minimizes the sum of quadratic bending and stretching energy with the least squares approximation error.

- The conformal approach that uses conformal mapping to interpolate each training sample between grid nodes in a continuous surface. A one-to-one smooth mapping is possible in this approach.

Applications

- Meteorology and oceanography.
- Project prioritization and selection.
- Seismic facies analysis for oil and gas exploration.
- Failure Mode and Effect Analysis.
- Creation of artwork.

Generative Topographic Map

Generative Topographic mapping (GTM) is a novel non-linear latent variable model. It seeks an explanation to the behavior of a number of data variables in terms of a smaller number of latent variables. GTM allows for a non-linear relationship between latent and observed variables.

The GTM defines a non-linear, parametric mapping $y(x; W)$ from an L-dimensional latent space $\left(x \in \mathfrak{R}^L\right)$ to a D-dimensional data space $\left(y \in \mathfrak{R}^L\right)$ where normally $L < D$. $y(x, W)$ could e.g. be a multi-layer perceptron, in which case W would denote its weights and biases; as we shall see later, by making a careful choice of how we implement $y(x, W)$, significant savings can be made in terms of computation. For now, we just de ne it to be continuous and differentiable. $y(x, W)$ maps every point in the latent space to a point in the data space. Since the latent space is L-dimensional, these points will be confined to an L-dimensional manifold non-linearly embedded in the D-dimensional data space. Figure showed a schematic illustration where a 2-dimensional latent space was mapped to a 3-dimensional data space.

If we define a probability distribution over the latent space, $p(x)$, this will induce a corresponding probability distribution in the data space. Strictly confined to the L-dimensional manifold, this distribution would be singular, so we convolve it with an isotropic Gaussian noise distribution, given by

$$p\left(t|x,\ W,\ \beta\right) = N\left(y\left(x,\ W\right),\beta\right)$$

$$= \left(\frac{\beta}{2\pi}\right)^{-D/2} \exp\left\{-\frac{\beta}{2}\sum_{d}^{D}\left(t_d - y_d\left(x,\ W\right)\right)^2\right\}$$

where t is a point in the data space and β^{-1} denotes the noise variance. This can be thought of as smearing out the manifold, giving it a bit of volume, and corresponds to the residual variance of

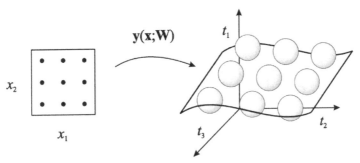

Figure: The basic idea of the GTM - points on a regular grid in the low-dimensional latent space (left) are mapped, using a parameterized, non-linear mapping y(x, W), to corresponding centers of Gaussians (right). These centers will lie in the low-dimensional manifold, defined by the mapping y(x, W), embedded in the (potentially) high-dimensional data space.

The PPCA model - it allows for some variance in the observed variables that is not explained by the latent variables.

By integrating out the latent variable, we get the probability distribution in the data space expressed as a function of the parameters β and W,

$$p(t|W, \beta) = \int p(t|x, W, \beta) p(x) dx.$$

This integral is generally not analytically tractable. However, by choosing $p(x)$ to have a particular form, a set of K equally weighted delta functions on a regular grid,

$$p(x) = \frac{1}{K} \sum_{k}^{K} \delta(x - x_k),$$

the integral in $p(\ |W, \beta)$ $\int p(t|x, \ , \beta) p(x) dx$ turns into a sum

$$p(t|W, \beta) = \frac{1}{K} \sum_{k}^{K} p(t|x_k, W, \beta).$$

An alternative approach is to approximate $p(x)$ with a Monte Carlo sample. If $p(x)$ is taken to be uniform over a finite interval, this becomes similar to
$$p(t|W, \beta) = \frac{1}{K} \sum_{k}^{K} p(t|x_k, W, \beta).$$

Now we have a model where each delta function center (we will from now on refer to these as latent points) maps to the center of a Gaussian, which lies in the manifold embedded in the data space, as illustrated in figure. Note that as long as $y(x; W)$ is continuous, the ordering of the latent points will be reflected in the ordering of the centers of Gaussians in the data space. What we have is a constrained mixture of Gaussians, since the centers of the mixture components cannot move independently of each other, but all depend on the mapping $y(x, W)$. Moreover, all components of the mixture share the same variance, β^{-1}, and the mixing coefficients are all fixed to $1/K$.

Given a finite set of i.i.d. data points, $\{t_1, ..., t_N\}$, we can write down the likelihood function for this model,

$$L = \prod_{n}^{N} p(t|W, \beta) = \prod_{n}^{N} \left[\frac{1}{K} \sum_{k}^{K} p(t_n|x_k, W, \beta) \right],$$

and maximize it with respect to W and β However, it is normally more convenient to work with the log-likelihood function,

$$l = \sum_{k}^{K} \ln \left(\frac{1}{K} \sum_{k}^{K} p(t_n|x_k, W, \beta) \right)$$

We could employ any standard non-linear optimization technique for the maximiza-tion, but having noted that we are working with a mixture of Gaussians, we may instead use the EM algorithm. An EM-algorithm could be used to fit a factor analysis model to a data set, where the key step was to compute the expectations of sufficient statistics of the latent variables, the values of which were missing. When fitting a mixture of Gaussians, which is maybe the most common example of the application of the EM-al-gorithm, the problem would be easily solved if we knew which data point was generated by which mixture component; unfortunately, this is usually not the case and so we treat these `labels' as missing variables.

An EM Algorithm for the GTM

Given some initial values for W and β, the E-step for the GTM is the same as for a gen-eral Gaussian mixture model, computing the responsibilities,

$$r_{kn} = p\left(\mathbf{x}_k | t_n, \mathbf{W}, \beta\right) = \frac{p\left(t_n | \mathbf{x}_k, \mathbf{W}, \beta\right)p\left(\mathbf{x}_k\right)}{\sum_{k'} p\left(t_n | \mathbf{x}_{k'}, \mathbf{W}, \beta\right)p\left(\mathbf{x}_{k'}\right)}$$

assumed by the kth component of the Gaussian mixture for the nth data point, for each possible pair of k and n. r_{kn} corresponds to the posterior probability that the nth data point was generated by the kth component. As the prior probabilities, $p(\mathbf{x}_k)$, were de-fined to be fixed and equal ($1/K$), these will cancel. Since the mixture components cor-respond to points in the latent space, the distribution of responsibilities over mixture components correspond to a distribution over the latent space, forming a connection to the EM-algorithm for FA. In the M-step, these responsibilities will act as weights in the update equations for W and β. In essence, we will try to move each component of the mixture towards data points for which it is most responsible.

So far, we have not specified the form for y(x, W), but only stated that it could be any parametric, non-linear model. For the GTM, we normally choose a generalized linear regression model, where y is a linear combination of a set of fixed basis functions,

$$y_d\left(x, \mathbf{W}\right) = \sum_m^M \phi_m\left(\mathbf{x}\right)w_{md},$$

We could consider a wide range of basis function, but for the rest of this thesis, we will use a combination of

- M_{NL} non-linear basis functions, in the form of non-normalized, Gaussian basis functions,

- L linear basis functions, for capturing linear trends in the data, and

- One fixed basis function, that allows the corresponding weights to act as biases.

Thus, we get

$$
\phi_m(x) = \begin{cases} \exp\left\{-\dfrac{\|x-\mu_m\|^2}{2\sigma^2}\right\} & \text{if } m \le M_{NL}, \\[2mm] x^l & \text{if } m = M_{NL} + l, \ l = 1,\ldots,L \\[2mm] 1 & \text{if } m = M_{NL} + L + 1 = M, \end{cases}
$$

Where μ_m, $m = 1,\ldots,M_{NL}$, denotes the centers of the Gaussian basis functions and σ their common width, and x^l denotes the lth element of x. Note that, throughout the rest of the this thesis, the GTM models used in experiments are understood to have linear and bias basis functions, and these will not be explicitly mentioned. It will be convenient to write in matrix form as:

$$
Y = \Phi W,
$$

where Y is a $K \times D$ matrix of mixture component centers Φ is a $K \times M$ matrix with element $\Phi_{km} = \phi_m(x_k)$, and W is a M D matrix containing the weight and bias parameters.

We now derive the M-step for this model as follows: using
$p(t|x,W,\beta) = N(y(x,W),\beta)$

$$
= \left(\frac{\beta}{2\pi}\right)^{-D/2} \exp\left\{-\frac{\beta}{2}\sum_d^D t_d - y_d(x,W))^2\right\},
$$

$r_{kn} = p(x_k|t_n,W,\beta) = \dfrac{p(t_n|x_k,W,\beta)p(x_k)}{\sum_{k'} p(t_n|x_{k'},W,\beta)p(x_{k'})}$ and $y_d(x,W) = \sum_m^M \phi_m(x)w_{md}$, we can calculate the derivatives of $l = \sum_k^K \ln\left(\dfrac{1}{K}\sum_k^K p(t_n|x_k,W,\beta)\right)$ with respect to w_{md}, yielding

$$
\frac{\partial l}{w_{md}} = \sum_{n,k}^{N,K} r_{kn\beta}\left(\sum_{m'}^M \phi_{m'}(x_k)w_{m'd} - t_{nd}\right)\phi_m(x_k),
$$

where r_{kn} are the responsibilities computed in the preceding E-step, and setting these derivatives to zero we obtain an update formula for W. A detailed derivation is found in appendix A. Similarly, calculating the derivatives of $l = \sum_k \ln\left(\dfrac{1}{K}\sum_k^K p(t_n|x_k,W,\beta)\right)$ with respect to β and setting these to zero, we obtain;

$$
\frac{1}{\beta} = \frac{1}{ND}\sum_n^N\sum_k^K r_{kn}\left\|y\left(x_k,\tilde{W}\right)\right\|^2.
$$

Here, $\tilde{W}$ corresponds to the updated weights, which means that we must first maximize with respect to the weights, then with respect to β. The update formula for β is the same as for general Gaussian mixtures and has an intuitive meaning. We set β^{-1}, which is the common variance of the Gaussian mixture, to the average weighted distance between mixture components and data points, where the weights are given by the responsibilities.

Using $Y = \Phi W$, the M-step for W can be written on matrix form as

$$\Phi^T G \Phi W = \Phi^T RT$$

where T is the $N \times D$ matrix containing the data points, R is the $K \times N$ responsibility matrix with elements defined in $r_{kn} = p\left(x_k | t_n, W, \beta\right) = \dfrac{p\left(t_n | x_k, W, \beta\right) p\left(x_k\right)}{\sum_{k'} p\left(t_n | x_{k'}, W, \beta\right) p\left(x_{k'}\right)}$, and G is an $K \times K$ diagonal matrix with entries:

$$g_{kk} = \sum_{n}^{N} r_{kn}.$$

$\Phi^T G \Phi W = \Phi^T RT$ can be seen as a form of generalized least squares. To draw the parallel with the *M*-step for the factor analysis model, we are setting W to map the weighted, non-linear representation of the latent variables, $G\Phi$, to the targets formed by the weighted combination of data points, RT.

We can now also see the advantages of having chosen a generalized linear regression model, as this part of the M-step is reduced to a matrix inversion and a few matrix multiplications. A different model, where the log-likelihood depended non-quadratically on the adjustable parameters, would have required non-linear, iterative maximization, at each iteration computing a new log-likelihood, which is generally the most costly part of the algorithm. Since $\Phi^T G\Phi$ is symmetric and often positive definite, we can utilize fast Cholesky decomposition for the matrix inversion, with the option of resorting to singular value decomposition (SVD), if the matrix proves to be singular. There are two possible ways this can happen: G may contain one or more zeros along its diagonal, which means that the corresponding mixture components take no responsibility at all. This is very unlikely to happen as long there are significantly less mixture components than data points. The second possible cause is rank deficiency in Φ which may occur if we choose the basis functions very broad or very narrow, or use more basis functions than latent points. Normally, there will be no difficulty avoiding such choices of basis functions and the rank of Φ can be checked prior to fitting the GTM to data.

In addition, we could impose a degree of weight regularization, leading to the equation:

$$\left(\Phi^T G\Phi + \lambda I\right)W = \Phi^T RT$$

Where λ is the regularization parameter and I is an identity matrix of the same dimensions as $\Phi^T G\Phi$. This correspond to specifying an isotropic Gaussian prior distribution over W,

$$p(W) = \left(\frac{\alpha}{2\pi}\right)^{W/2} \exp\left(-\frac{\alpha}{2}\|W\|^2\right),$$

with zero mean and variance α^{-1}, where W denotes the total number of elements in W. From $\frac{\partial l}{W_{md}} = \sum_{n,k}^{N,K} r_{kn\beta}\left(\sum_{m'}^{M} \phi_{m'}(x_k)W_{m'd} - t_{nd}\right)\phi_m(x_k),$ and $p(W) = \left(\frac{\alpha}{2\pi}\right)^{W/2} \exp\left(-\frac{\alpha}{2}\|W\|^2\right),$ it follows that $\lambda = \alpha/\beta$. Apart from ensuring a fast matrix inversion, the use of weight regularization gives us one handle on the model complexity through the real valued parameter α.

Initialization

The only remaining issue is to choose appropriate initial values for W and β. For W, one possibility is to use random samples drawn from a Gaussian distribution, $N(0, \varsigma)$, where ς is chosen so that the expected variance over y equals the variance of the training data. An alternative, which is often better, is to initialize the weights so that the L latent variables map to the L-dimensional hyper plane spanned by the L first principal components of the data set we are trying to model. A PCA initialization only requires the weight of the linear basis functions, so weights of the non-linear basis functions can be set to zero, or alternatively, to very small random values, resulting in a `semi-random' initialization. Whether we use random or PCA-based initialization, it is reasonable to initialize the weight vector corresponding to the bias basis function so as to match the mean of the training data. For β, our choice to some extent depends on how we choose W. If W is initialized randomly β is set to the reciprocal of the average squared distance between the centers of the resulting Gaussian mixture and the points in our data set, which correspond to the update formula in $\frac{1}{\beta} = \frac{1}{ND}\sum_{n}^{N}\sum_{k}^{K} r_{kn}\left\|y\left(x_k, \tilde{W}\right)\right\|^2.$ with all responsibilities being equal. If, on the other hand, W is initialized using PCA, β is set so that its inverse (the variance in the data space) equals the larger of:

- The length of the $(L + 1)^{th}$ principal component, i.e. the largest variance orthogonal to the L-dimensional hyper-plane to which the Gaussian mixture is initially mapped.

- Half the average minimal distance between the mixture component.

This is motivated by the idea that the initial β should be small enough to explain the variance orthogonal to, as well as the variance within, the initial manifold.

References

- Haykin, Simon (1999). "9. Self-organizing maps". Neural networks - A comprehensive foundation (2nd ed.). Prentice-Hall. ISBN 0-13-908385-5

- Unsupervised-learning: techtarget.com, Retrieved 22 July 2018

- Introductory-generative-adversarial-networks-gans: analyticsvidhya.com, Retrieved 16 May 2018

- Liu, Yonggang; Weisberg, Robert H.; Mooers, Christopher N. K. (2006). "Performance Evaluation of the Self-Organizing Map for Feature Extraction". Journal of Geophysical Research. 111: C05018. Bibcode:2006JGRC..111.5018L. doi:10.1029/2005jc003117

- Introduction-to-unsupervised-learning: algorithmia.com, Retrieved 16 April 2018

- Kaski, Samuel (1997). "Data Exploration Using Self-Organizing Maps". Acta Polytechnica Scandinavica. Mathematics, Computing and Management in Engineering Series No. 82. Espoo, Finland: Finnish Academy of Technology. ISBN 952-5148-13-0

- Competitive-learning-33277: techopedia.com, Retrieved 19 March 2018

- Chang, Wui Lee; Pang, Lie Meng; Tay, Kai Meng (March 2017). "Application of Self-Organizing Map to Failure Modes and Effects Analysis Methodology". Neurocomputing. PP: PP. doi:10.1016/j.neucom.2016.04.073

- Generative-adversarial-network-gan-32515: techopedia.com, Retrieved 31 March 2018

Supervised Learning

Supervised learning is a learning task concerned with the mapping of an input to an output based on an analysis of different input-output pairs. The topics elaborated in this chapter on supervised, semi-supervised and similarity learning, structured prediction and support vector machine will help to provide an extensive understanding of the subject.

The majority of practical machine learning uses supervised learning. Supervised learning is where you have input variables (x) and an output variable (Y) and you use an algorithm to learn the mapping function from the input to the output $Y = f(X)$. The goal is to approximate the mapping function so well that when you have new input data (x) that you can predict the output variables (Y) for that data.

Techniques of Supervised Machine Learning algorithms include linear and logistic regression, multi-class classification, Decision Trees and support vector machines.

Supervised learning requires that the data used to train the algorithm is already labeled with correct answers. For example, a classification algorithm will learn to identify animals after being trained on a dataset of images that are properly labeled with the species of the animal and some identifying characteristics.

Supervised learning problems can be further grouped into Regression and Classification problems. Both problems have as goal the construction of a succinct model that can predict the value of the dependent attribute from the attribute variables. The difference between the two tasks is the fact that the dependent attribute is numerical for regression and categorical for classification.

Regression

A regression problem is when the output variable is a real or continuous value, such as "salary" or "weight". Many different models can be used, the simplest is the linear regression. It tries to fit data with the best hyper-plane which goes through the points.

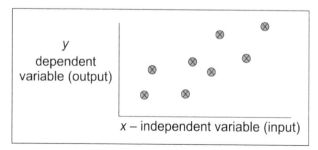

Types of Regression Models

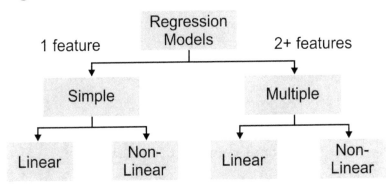

For examples: Which of the following is a regression task?

- Predicting age of a person.
- Predicting nationality of a person.
- Predicting whether stock price of a company will increase tomorrow.
- Predicting whether a document is related to sighting of UFOs?

Solution: Predicting age of a person (because it is a real value, predicting nationality is categorical, whether stock price will increase is discreet-yes/no answer, predicting whether a document is related to UFO is again discreet- a yes/no answer).

Let's take an example of linear regression. We have a Housing data set and we want to predict the price of the house. Following is the python code for it.

```python
# Python code to illustrate
# regression using data set
import matplotlib
matplotlib.use('GTKAgg')

import matplotlib.pyplot as plt
import numpy as np
from sklearn import datasets, linear_model
import pandas as pd

# Load CSV and columns
df = pd.read_csv("Housing.csv")
```

```
Y = df['price']
X = df['lotsize']


X=X.reshape(len(X),1)
Y=Y.reshape(len(Y),1)


# Split the data into training/testing sets
X_train = X[:-250]
X_test = X[-250:]


# Split the targets into training/testing sets
Y_train = Y[:-250]
Y_test = Y[-250:]


# Plot outputs
plt.scatter(X_test, Y_test,  color='black')
plt.title('Test Data')
plt.xlabel('Size')
plt.ylabel('Price')
plt.xticks(())
plt.yticks(())



# Create linear regression object
regr = linear_model.LinearRegression()

# Train the model using the training sets
regr.fit(X_train, Y_train)
```

```
# Plot outputs
plt.plot(X_test, regr.predict(X_test), color='red',linewidth=3)
plt.show()
```

Run on IDE

The output of the above code will be:

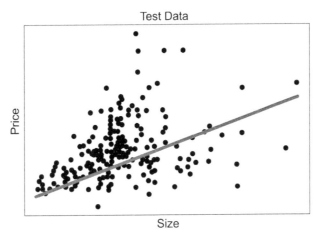

Here in this graph, we plot the test data. The red line indicates the best fit line for predicting the price. To make an individual prediction using the linear regression model:

```
print( str(round(regr.predict(5000))) )
```

Classification

A classification problem is when the output variable is a category, such as "red" or "blue" or "disease" and "no disease". A classification model attempts to draw some conclusion from observed values. Given one or more inputs a classification model will try to predict the value of one or more outcomes.

For example, when filtering emails "spam" or "not spam", when looking at transaction data, "fraudulent", or "authorized". In short Classification either predicts categorical class labels or classifies data (construct a model) based on the training set and the values (class labels) in classifying attributes and uses it in classifying new data. There are a number of classification models. Classification models include logistic regression, decision tree, random forest, gradient-boosted tree, multilayer perceptron, one-vs-rest, and Naive Bayes.

For example: Which of the following is/are classification problem(s)?

- Predicting the gender of a person by his/her handwriting style.
- Predicting house price based on area.

- Predicting whether monsoon will be normal next year.

- Predict the number of copies a music album will be sold next month.

Solution: Predicting the gender of a person Predicting whether monsoon will be normal next year. The other two are regression.

As we discussed classification with some examples. Now there is an example of classification in which we are performing classification on the iris dataset using *Random Forest Classifier* in python.

Dataset Description

```
Title: Iris Plants Database

Attribute Information:
        1. sepal length in cm
        2. sepal width in cm
        3. petal length in cm
        4. petal width in cm
        5. class:
          -- Iris Setosa
          -- Iris Versicolour
          -- Iris Virginica

Missing Attribute Values: None

Class Distribution: 33.3% for each of 3 classes

# Python code to illustrate

# classification using data set

#Importing the required library

import pandas as pd

from sklearn.cross_validation import train_test_split

from sklearn.ensemble import RandomForestClassifier

from sklearn.preprocessing import LabelEncoder

from sklearn.metrics import confusion_matrix

from sklearn.metrics import accuracy_score

from sklearn.metrics import classification_report
```

```
#Importing the dataset
dataset = pd.read_csv(
      'https://archive.ics.uci.edu/ml/machine-learning-'+
      'databases/iris/iris.data>,sep= ',', header= None)
data = dataset.iloc[:, :]

#checking for null values
print("Sum of NULL values in each column. ")
print(data.isnull().sum())

#seperating the predicting column from the whole dataset
X = data.iloc[:, :-1].values
y = dataset.iloc[:, 4].values

#Encoding the predicting variable
labelencoder_y = LabelEncoder()
y = labelencoder_y.fit_transform(y)

#Spliting the data into test and train dataset
X_train, X_test, y_train, y_test = train_test_split(
      X, y, test_size = 0.3, random_state = 0)

#Using the random forest classifier for the prediction
classifier=RandomForestClassifier()
classifier=classifier.fit(X_train,y_train)
predicted=classifier.predict(X_test)

#printing the results
print ('Confusion Matrix :')
```

```
print(confusion_matrix(y_test, predicted))
print ('Accuracy Score :',accuracy_score(y_test, predicted))
print ('Report : ')
print (classification_report(y_test, predicted))
```

Output

Sum of NULL values in each column.

```
    0    0
    1    0
    2    0
    3    0
    4    0
```

Confusion Matrix:

```
        [[16  0  0]
         [ 0 17  1]
         [ 0  0 11]]
```

Accuracy Score : 97.7

Report :

	precision	recall	f1-score	support
0	1.00	1.00	1.00	16
1	1.00	0.94	0.97	18
2	0.92	1.00	0.96	11
avg/total	0.98	0.98	0.98	45

The steps for supervised learning are:

- Prepare Data.
- Choose an Algorithm.
- Fit a Model.

- Choose a Validation Method.

- Examine Fit and Update Until Satisfied.

- Use Fitted Model for Predictions.

Prepare Data

All supervised learning methods start with an input data matrix, usually called X here. Each row of X represents one observation. Each column of X represents one variable, or predictor. Represent missing entries with NaNvalues in X. Statistics and Machine Learning Toolbox supervised learning algorithms can handle NaN values, either by ignoring them or by ignoring any row with a NaN value.

You can use various data types for response data Y. Each element in Y represents the response to the corresponding row of X. Observations with missing Y data are ignored.

- For regression, Y must be a numeric vector with the same number of elements as the number of rows of X.

- For classification, Y can be any of these data types. This table also contains the method of including missing entries.

Data Type	Missing Entry
Numeric vector	NaN
Categorical vector	<undefined>
Character array	Row of spaces
String array	<missing> or ""
Cell array of character vectors	''
Logical vector	(Cannot represent)

Choose an Algorithm

There are tradeoffs between several characteristics of algorithms, such as:

- Speed of training.

- Memory usage.

- Predictive accuracy on new data.

- Transparency or interpretability, meaning how easily you can understand the reasons an algorithm makes its predictions.

Fit a Model

The fitting function you use depends on the algorithm you choose.

Algorithm	Fitting Function
Classification Trees	`fitctree`
Regression Trees	`fitrtree`
Discriminant Analysis (classification)	`fitcdiscr`
k-Nearest Neighbors (classification)	`fitcknn`
Naive Bayes (classification)	`fitcnb`
Support Vector Machines (SVM) for classification	`fitcsvm`
SVM for regression	`fitrsvm`
Multiclass models for SVM or other classifiers	`fitcecoc`
Classification Ensembles	`fitcensemble`
Regression Ensembles	`fitrensemble`
Classification or Regression Tree Ensembles (e.g., Random Forests) in Parallel	`TreeBagger`

Choose a Validation Method

The three main methods to examine the accuracy of the resulting fitted model are:

- Examine the resubstitution error. For examples:
  o Classification Tree Resubstitution Error.
  o Cross Validate a Regression Tree.
  o Test Ensemble Quality.
  o Example: Resubstitution Error of a Discriminant Analysis Classifier.
- Examine the cross-validation error. For examples:
  o Cross Validate a Regression Tree.
  o Test Ensemble Quality.
  o Classification with Many Categorical Levels.
  o Cross Validating a Discriminant Analysis Classifier.
- Examine the out-of-bag error for bagged decision trees. For examples:
  o Test Ensemble Quality.
  o Regression of Insurance Risk Rating for Car Imports Using TreeBagger.
  o Classifying Radar Returns for Ionosphere Data Using TreeBagger.

Examine Fit and Update Until Satisfied

After validating the model, you might want to change it for better accuracy, better speed, or to use less memory.

- Change fitting parameters to try to get a more accurate model. For examples:
  - o Tune Robust Boost.
  - o Train Ensemble With Unequal Classification Costs.
  - o Improving Discriminant Analysis Models.
- Change fitting parameters to try to get a smaller model. This sometimes gives a model with more accuracy. For examples:
  - o Select Appropriate Tree Depth.
  - o Prune a Classification Tree.
  - o Surrogate Splits.
  - o Regularize a Regression Ensemble.
  - o Regression of Insurance Risk Rating for Car Imports Using TreeBagger.
  - o Classifying Radar Returns for Ionosphere Data Using TreeBagger.
- Try a different algorithm. For applicable choices:
  - o Characteristics of Classification Algorithms.
  - o Choose an Applicable Ensemble Aggregation Method.

When satisfied with a model of some types, you can trim it using the appropriate compact function (compact for classification trees, compact for regression trees, compact for discriminant analysis, compact for naive Bayes, compact for SVM, compact for ECOC models, compact for classification ensembles, and compact for regression ensembles). compact removes training data and other properties not required for prediction, e.g., pruning information for decision trees, from the model to reduce memory consumption. Because kNN classification models require all of the training data to predict labels, you cannot reduce the size of a Classification kNN model.

Use Fitted Model for Predictions

To predict classification or regression response for most fitted models, use the predict method:

```
Ypredicted = predict(obj,Xnew)
```

- obj is the fitted model or fitted compact model.

- Xnew is the new input data.

- Ypredicted is the predicted response, either classification or regression.

Bias–variance Tradeoff

The bias–variance tradeoff is a fundamental property of machine learning algorithms.

Bias

Bias is the tendancy of an estimator to pick a model for the data that is not structurally correct. A biased estimator is one that makes incorrect assumptions on the model level about the dataset. For example, suppose that we use a linear regression model on a cubic function. This model will be biased: it will structurally underestimate the true values in the dataset, always, no matter how many points we use.

Given points x, a true value , and a model $f(x)$, bias can be expressed mathematically as:

$$\text{Bias}[\hat{f}(x)] = E[\hat{f}(x) - f(x)]$$

Where E[·] is the expected value function (e.g. the mean value).

The key to understanding bias is to understand that, given enough "perfect" data points sampled from a compatible distribution which has no errors or variance in it (such as a line, in the case of linear regression), an unbiased model will fit every point exactly correctly.

Bias is also known as underfitting. Once we've selected a model bias becomes something that we want to, *within reason*, reduce.

Variance

Variance is error from sensitivity to small fluctuations in the training set. High variance can cause an algorithm to model the random noise in the training data, rather than the intended outputs (overfitting). It can expressed mathematically as:

$$Var(X) = E[X^2] - E[X]^2$$

Error due to Bias: The error due to bias is taken as the difference between the expected (or average) prediction of our model and the correct value which we are trying to predict. Of course you only have one model so talking about expected or average prediction values might seem a little strange. However, imagine you could repeat the whole model building process more than once: each time you gather new data and run a new analysis creating a new model. Due to randomness in the underlying data sets, the resulting models will have a range of predictions.

Error due to Variance: The error due to variance is taken as the variability of a model prediction for a given data point. Again, imagine you can repeat the entire model building process multiple times.

Graphical Definition

We can create a graphical visualization of bias and variance using a bulls-eye diagram. Imagine that the center of the target is a model that perfectly predicts the correct values. As we move away from the bulls-eye, our predictions get worse and worse. Imagine we can repeat our entire model building process to get a number of separate hits on the target. Each hit represents an individual realization of our model, given the chance variability in the training data we gather. Sometimes we will get a good distribution of training data so we predict very well and we are close to the bulls-eye, while sometimes our training data might be full of outliers or non-standard values resulting in poorer predictions. These different realizations result in a scatter of hits on the target.

We can plot four different cases representing combinations of both high and low bias and variance.

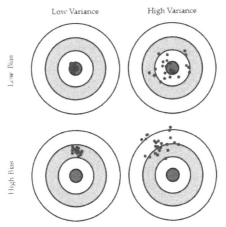

Graphical illustration of bias and variance.

Mathematical Definition

If we denote the variable we are trying to predict as Y and our covariates as X, we may assume that there is a relationship relating one to the other such as $Y = f(X) + \epsilon$ where the error term $\epsilon \in$ is normally distributed with a mean of zero like so $\epsilon \sim \mathcal{N}(0, \sigma_\delta)$.

We may estimate a model $\hat{f}(X)$ of $f(X)$ using linear regressions or another modeling technique. In this case, the expected squared prediction error at a point xx is:

$$Err(x) = E[(Y - \hat{f}(x))^2].$$

This error may then be decomposed into bias and variance components:

$$Err(x) = (E[\hat{f}(x)] - f(x))^2 + E[(\hat{f}(x) - E[\hat{f}(x)])^2] + \sigma_e^2$$
$$Err(x) = Bias^2 + Variance + Irreducible\ Error$$

That third term, irreducible error, is the noise term in the true relationship that cannot fundamentally be reduced by any model. Given the true model and infinite data to calibrate it, we should be able to reduce both the bias and variance terms to 0. However, in a world with imperfect models and finite data, there is a tradeoff between minimizing the bias and minimizing the variance.

Derivation

The derivation of the bias–variance decomposition for squared error proceeds as follows. For notational convenience, abbreviate $f = f(x)$ and $\hat{f} = \hat{f}(x)$. First, recall that, by definition, for any random variable X, we have

$$Var[X] = E[X^2] - (E[X])^2$$

Rearranging, we get:

$$E[X^2] = Var[X] + (E[X])^2$$

Since f is deterministic

$$E[f] = f.$$

This, given $y = f + \varepsilon$ and $E[\varepsilon] = 0$, implies $E[y] = E[f + \varepsilon] = E[f] = f$.

Also, since $Var[\varepsilon] = \sigma^2$,

$$Var[y] = E[(y - E[y])^2] = E[(y - f)^2] = E[(f + \varepsilon - f)^2] = E[\varepsilon^2] = Var[\varepsilon] + (E[\varepsilon])^2 = \sigma^2$$

Thus, since ε and $\hat{f}$ are independent, we can write

$$E\left[(y - \hat{f})^2\right] = E[y^2 + \hat{f}^2 - 2y\hat{f}]$$

$$= E[y^2] + E[\hat{f}^2] - E[2y\hat{f}]$$
$$= Var[y] + E[y]^2 + Var[\hat{f}] + (E[\hat{f}])^2 - 2f\,E[\hat{f}]$$
$$= Var[y] + Var[\hat{f}] + (f^2 - 2f\,E[\hat{f}] + (E[\hat{f}])^2)$$
$$= Var[y] + Var[\hat{f}] + (f - E[\hat{f}])^2$$
$$= \sigma^2 + Var[\hat{f}] + Bias[\hat{f}]^2$$

Application to Regression

The bias–variance decomposition forms the conceptual basis for regression regularization methods such as Lasso and ridge regression. Regularization methods introduce bias into the regression solution that can reduce variance considerably relative to the ordinary least squares (OLS) solution. Although the OLS solution provides non-biased regression estimates, the lower variance solutions produced by regularization techniques provide superior MSE performance.

Application to Classification

The bias–variance decomposition was originally formulated for least-squares regression. For the case of classification under the 0-1 loss (misclassification rate), it is possible to find a similar decomposition. Alternatively, if the classification problem can be phrased as probabilistic classification, then the expected squared error of the predicted probabilities with respect to the true probabilities can be decomposed as before.

Approaches

Dimensionality reduction and feature selection can decrease variance by simplifying models. Similarly, a larger training set tends to decrease variance. Adding features (predictors) tends to decrease bias, at the expense of introducing additional variance. Learning algorithms typically have some tunable parameters that control bias and variance; for example,

- Generalized linear models can be regularized to decrease their variance at the cost of increasing their bias.

- In artificial neural networks, the variance increases and the bias decreases with the number of hidden units increase. Like in GLMs, regularization is typically applied.

- In k-nearest neighbor models, a high value of k leads to high bias and low variance.

- In instance-based learning, regularization can be achieved varying the mixture of prototypes and exemplars.

- In decision trees, the depth of the tree determines the variance. Decision trees are commonly pruned to control variance.

One way of resolving the trade-off is to use mixture models and ensemble learning. For example, boosting combines many "weak" (high bias) models in an ensemble that has lower bias than the individual models, while bagging combines "strong" learners in a way that reduces their variance.

k-nearest Neighbors

In the case of k-nearest neighbors regression, a closed-form expression exists that relates the bias–variance decomposition to the parameter k:

$$E[(y - \hat{f}(x))^2 \mid X = x] = \left(f(x) - \frac{1}{k} \sum_{i=1}^{k} f(N_i(x)) \right)^2 + \frac{\sigma^2}{k} + \sigma^2$$

where $N_1(x), \ldots, N_k(x)$ sare the k nearest neighbors of x in the training set. The bias (first term) is a monotone rising function of k, while the variance (second term) drops off as k is increased. In fact, under "reasonable assumptions" the bias of the first-nearest neighbor (1-NN) estimator vanishes entirely as the size of the training set approaches infinity.

Application to Human Learning

While widely discussed in the context of machine learning, the bias-variance dilemma has been examined in the context of human cognition, most notably by Gerd Gigerenzer and co-workers in the context of learned heuristics. They have argued that the human brain resolves the dilemma in the case of the typically sparse, poorly-characterised training-sets provided by experience by adopting high-bias/low variance heuristics. This reflects the fact that a zero-bias approach has poor generalisability to new situations, and also unreasonably presumes precise knowledge of the true state of the world. The resulting heuristics are relatively simple, but produce better inferences in a wider variety of situations.

Geman argue that the bias-variance dilemma implies that abilities such as generic object recognition cannot be learned from scratch, but require a certain degree of "hard wiring" that is later tuned by experience. This is because model-free approaches to inference require impractically large training sets if they are to avoid high variance.

Generalization Error

The generalization error is often used as a means to measure a classifier's accuracy of generalization. Estimating the generalization error therefore becomes important in tuning as well as combining classifiers in order to maximize the accuracy of classification.

Estimating Generalization Error

For k-class classification, a classifier (learner) φ is trained via a training sample (X_i, Y_i) $n_i = 1$, independent and identically distributed according to an unknown $P(x, y)$, where φ maps from $\mathbb{R}^d \to \{0, \ldots, k-1\}$, with $k > 1$ and d is the dimension of X. To analyze a learning scenario, accuracy on inputs outside the training set is examined. This is performed through an error function that measures the ability of generalization, and is known as the generalization error (GE). For any classifier φ, GE is defined as

$$GE(\phi) = P(Y \neq \phi(X)) = E(I(Y \neq \phi(X))),$$

where $I(\cdot)$ is the indicator, (X, Y) is independent and identically distributed according to $P(x, y)$, and independent of $(Xi, Yi)^n_i = 1$. The empirical version of GE, called the empirical generalization error (EGE), is defined as

$$EGE(\phi) = \frac{1}{n} \sum_{i=1}^{n} I(Yi \neq \phi(X_i)).$$

In training, the classifier φ often involves a tuning parameter C, vector or scalar, whose value controls the trade-off between fitting and generalization. In what follows, we write φ as $\hat{\phi}c$ to indicate its dependency on $(Xi, Yi)^n_i = 1$ and C.

The quantity $GE(\hat{\phi}_c)$ compares classifiers indexed by different values of C. If $P(\cdot, \cdot)$ were known, we could select an optimal classifier by minimizing $GE(\hat{\phi}_c)$ over the range of tuning parameter C or, equivalently, over a class of classifiers. In practice, $P(\cdot, \cdot)$ is unknown, so $GE(\hat{\phi}_c)$ needs to be estimated from data.

Motivation-Binary Case

For motivation, we first examine the case with $Y \in \{0, 1\}$ and then generalize it to the multi category case. Our basic strategy of estimating $GE(\hat{\phi}_c)$ is to seek the optimal loss estimator in a class of candidate loss estimators that yields an approximately unbiased estimate of $GE(\hat{\phi}_c)$. Note that there does not exist an exact unbiased estimate of $GE(\hat{\phi}_c)$. Naturally, one might estimate $GE(\hat{\phi}_c)$ by $EGE(\hat{\phi}_c)$, the empirical version of $GE(\hat{\phi}_c)$. However, $EGE(\hat{\phi}_c)$ suffers from the problem of over fitting, in contrast to $GE(\hat{\phi}_c)$. This is evident from the fact that the tuning parameter C yielding the smallest training error usually does not give the optimal performance in generalization or prediction. To prevent over fitting from occurring, we introduce a class of candidate loss estimators of the form:

$$EGE(\hat{\phi}_c) + \lambda(X^n, \hat{\phi}_c),$$

where $X^n = \{X_i\}_{i=1}^{n}$ and λ is an overfitting penalty function that is to be determined optimally. For optimal estimation of $GE(\hat{\phi}_c)$, we choose to minimize the L2-distance between GE and ($EGE(\hat{\phi}_c) + \lambda(X^n, \hat{\phi}_c)$),

$$E\left[GE\left(\hat{\phi}_C\right)-\left(EGE\left(\hat{\phi}_C\right)+\lambda\left(X^n,\hat{\phi}_C\right)\right)\right]^2,$$

where the expectation E is taken with respect to $\left(X^n,Y^n\right)=\{X_i,Y_i\}_{i=1}^{n}$. Minimizing $(E\left[GE\left(\hat{\phi}_C\right)-\left(EGE\left(\hat{\phi}_C\right)+\lambda\left(X^n,\hat{\phi}_C\right)\right)\right]^2)$ with respect to $\lambda\left(X^n,\hat{\phi}_C\right)$ produces optimal $\lambda_0\left(X^n,\hat{\phi}_C\right)$ given expression in Theorem.

Theorem: The optimal $\lambda_0\left(X^n,\hat{\phi}_C\right)$ that minimizes $(E\left[GE\left(\hat{\phi}_C\right)-\left(EGE\left(\hat{\phi}_C\right)+\lambda\left(X^n,\hat{\phi}_C\right)\right)\right]^2)$ over $\lambda\left(X^n,\hat{\phi}_C\right)$ is

$$\lambda_0\left(X^n,\hat{\phi}_C\right)=2n^{-1}\sum_{i=1}^{n}\mathrm{Cov}\left(Yi,\ \hat{\phi}_C\left(X_i\right)|X^n\right)+D_{1n}\left(X^n,\hat{\phi}_C\right)+D_{2n}\left(X^n\right),$$

Where $D_{1n}\left(X^n,\hat{\phi}_C\right)=E(E\left(E(Y\mid X)-\hat{\phi}_C(X)\right)^2-n^{-1}\sum_i\left(E(Y_i\mid X_i)-\hat{\phi}_C(X_i)\right)^2\mid X^n)$, and $D_{2n}\left(X^n\right)=E\left(Var(Y\mid X)\right)-n^{-1}\sum_i Var(Y_i\mid X_i)$.

In $(\lambda_0\left(X^n,\hat{\phi}_C\right)=2n^{-1}\sum_{i=1}^{n}\mathrm{Cov}\left(Yi,\ \hat{\phi}_C\left(X_i\right)|X^n\right)+D_{1n}\left(X^n,\hat{\phi}_C\right)+D_{2n}\left(X^n\right))$, $n^{-1}\sum_i\mathrm{Cov}\left(Yi,\ \hat{\phi}_C\left(X_i\right)|X^n\right)$ is averaged over covariances between Y_i and its predicted value $\hat{\phi}_C\left(X_i\right)$ at each observation $\left(X_i,Y_i\right)$, which evaluates the accuracy of prediction of $\hat{\phi}_C$ on X^n. Note that $\mathrm{Cov}\left(Y_i,\ \hat{\phi}_C\left(X_i\right)|X^n\right)$ depends on the scale of Y_i. Thus the generalized degree of freedom of the classifier $\hat{\phi}$ is defined as $n\left(\sum_i Var(Y_i\mid X_i)\right)^{-1}\sum_i\mathrm{Cov}\left(Y_i,\ \hat{\phi}_C\left(X_i\right)|X^n\right)$, which measures the degree of freedom cost in classification as well as tuning and combining.

The term D_{1n} can be decomposed as a difference between the true model error $E\left(E(Y\mid X)-\hat{\phi}_C(X)\right)^2$ and its empirical version $n^{-1}\sum_i\left(E(Y_i\mid X_i)-\hat{\phi}_C(X)\right)^2$. The disparity between these two errors comes from potential randomness of X, when sampled from an unknown distribution. In the situation of fixed design, D_{1n} is identical to zero, since the empirical distribution X^n is the same as that of X. In the situation of random design, D_{1n} is usually non-zero and needs to be estimated, in view of the result of Breiman and Spector and Breiman in a different context.

The term D_{2n}, on the other hand, is independent of $\hat{\phi}_C$ or the purpose of comparison, it suffices to use the comparative GE, which is defined as $CGE\left(\hat{\phi}_C\right)=GE\left(\hat{\phi}_C\right)-D_{2n}\left(X^n\right)$ as opposed to the original GE. With GE replaced by CGE in $E\left[GE\left(\hat{\phi}_C\right)-\left(EGE\left(\hat{\phi}_C\right)\right.\right.$

$+ \lambda\left(X^{n}, \hat{\phi}_{C}\right)\Big)\Big]^{2}$, we find the optimal $\lambda_{o}\left(X^{n}, \hat{\phi}_{C}\right)$ for CGE to be $2n^{-1}\sum_{i}\text{Cov}\left(Yi, \hat{\phi}_{C}\left(X_{i}\right)\right.$

$\left.|X^{n}\right)+D_{1n}\left(X^{n}, \hat{\phi}_{C}\right).$

Estimation

Using ($EGE\left(\hat{\phi}_{C}\right) + \lambda\left(X^{n}, \hat{\phi}_{C}\right)$) and ($\lambda_{o}\left(X^{n}, \hat{\phi}_{C}\right)=2n^{-1}\sum_{i=1}^{n}\text{Cov}\left(Yi, \hat{\phi}_{C}\left(X_{i}\right)|X^{n}\right)+D_{1n}\left(X^{n},\right.$

$\left.\hat{\phi}_{C}\right)+D_{2n}\left(X^{n}\right)$) in Theorem, we propose to estimate $CGE\left(\hat{\phi}_{C}\right)$ by $\widehat{CGE}\left(\hat{\phi}_{C}\right) = EGE$

$\left(\hat{\phi}_{C}\right)+2n^{-1}\sum_{i=1}^{n}\widehat{\text{Cov}}\left(Y_{i},\hat{\phi}_{C}\left(X_{i}\right)|X^{n}\right)+\hat{D}1_{n}\left(X^{n}, \hat{\phi}_{C}\right)$, with $\widehat{\text{Cov}}$ the estimated covariance,

and $\hat{}$ the estimated D_{1n}. In the situation of fixed design, $D_{1n}\equiv 0$, and reduces to

$\widehat{CGE}\left(\hat{\phi}_{C}\right) = EGE\left(\hat{\phi}_{C}\right)+2n^{-1}\sum_{i}\widehat{\text{Cov}}\left(Y_{i},\hat{\phi}_{C}\left(X_{i}\right)|X^{n}\right).$

There are two major difficulties in estimating CGE in ($CGE\left(\hat{\phi}_{C}\right) = EGE\left(\hat{\phi}_{C}\right)+2n^{-1}$

$\sum_{i=1}^{n}\text{Cov}\left(Y_{i},\hat{\phi}_{C}\left(X_{i}\right)|X^{n}\right)+\hat{D}1_{n}\left(X^{n}, \hat{\phi}_{C}\right)$). First, there does not exist an exact unbiased

estimate of $\sum_{i}\text{Cov}\left(Y_{i},\hat{\phi}_{C}\left(X_{i}\right)|X^{n}\right)$ because Y_{i} follows a Bernoulli distribution.

Second, only one realization of data is available for estimating the unobserved

$\sum_{i}\text{Cov}\left(Y_{i},\hat{\phi}_{C}\left(X_{i}\right)|X^{n}\right)$ and D_{1n}. Consequently, a resampling method of some type is

required. However, it is known that the conventional bootstrap may not work when

classification involves tuning and combining with discontinuity.

To overcome these difficulties, we propose a novel data perturbation technique based on swapping values of inputs and outputs (labels) to estimate $\sum_{i}\text{Cov}\left(Y_{i},\hat{\phi}_{C}\left(X_{i}\right)|X^{n}\right)$ and D_{1n}. The learning accuracy of the classifier based on perturbed data estimates the sensitivity of classification, which yields an estimated GE.

First perturb $X_{i}, i = 1, \ldots, n$, via its empirical distribution $\hat{F}$ followed by flipping the corresponding label Y_{i} with a certain probability given the perturbed X_{i}. This generates perturbations for assessing accuracy of generalization of a classifier. More precisely, for $i = 1, \ldots, n$, let

$$X_{i}^{*} = \begin{cases} X_{i} \text{ with probability } 1-\tau, \\ \tilde{X}_{i} \text{ with probability } \tau, \end{cases}$$

where $\tilde{X}_{i}$ is sampled from $\hat{F}$. This step can given an X-fixed design. A perturbed Y_{i}^{*} is

$$Y_{i}^{*} = \begin{cases} Y_{i} \text{ with probability } 1-\tau, \\ \tilde{Y}_{i} \text{ with probability } \tau, \end{cases}$$

Where $0 \le \tau \le 1$ is the size of perturbation, and $\tilde{Y}_i \sim \text{Bin}\left(1, \hat{p}_i\left(X_i^*\right)\right)$, with $\hat{p}_i\left(X_i^*\right)$ an initial probability estimate of $E\left(Y_i \mid X_i^*\right)$, obtained via the same classification method that defines $\hat{\phi}_C$ or logistic regression if the classification method does not yield an probability estimate, such as in the case of support vector machine.

For simplicity, denote by E^*, Var^* and Cov^* the conditional mean, variance, and covariance with respect to $Y^{*n} = \{Y_i^*\}_{i=1}^n$, to $\left(X^{*n}, Y^n\right)$, with $X^{*n} = \{X_i^*\}_{i=1}^n$. The perturbed Y_i^* has the following properties:

(1) Its conditional mean $E^* Y_i^* = (1 - \tau)Y_i + \tau E\left(\tilde{Y}_i \mid X_i^*\right) = (1 - \tau)Y_i + \tau \hat{p}_i\left(X_i^*\right)$ and

(2) Its conditional variance

$$Var^*\left(Y_i^*\right) = E^*\left(Y_i^{*2}\right) - \left(E^*\left(Y_i^*\right)\right)^2 = \tau Var^*\left(\tilde{Y}_i\right) + \tau\left(1 - \tau\right)$$

$$\left(Y_i - E\left(\tilde{Y}_i \mid X_i^*\right)\right)^2 = \tau \hat{p}_i\left(X_i^*\right)\left(1 - \hat{p}_i\left(X_i^*\right)\right) + \tau\left(1 - \tau\right)\left(Y_i - \hat{p}_i\left(X_i^*\right)\right)^2$$

We now provide some heuristics for our proposed estimator. To estimate $\text{Cov}\left(Y_i, \hat{\phi}_C\right.$ $\left.\left(X_i\right) \mid X^n\right)$, note that it equals $\text{Var}\left(Y_i \mid X_i\right)\left[\text{Cov}\left(Y_i, \hat{\phi}_C\left(X_i\right) \mid X^n\right) / \left(Y_i \mid X_i\right)\right]$. Then we can estimate $\text{Cov}\left(Y_i, \hat{\phi}_C\left(X_i\right) \mid X^n\right) / \text{Var}\left(Y_i \mid X_i\right)$ Additionally, $\text{Var}\left(Y_i \mid X_i\right) / \text{Var}^*\left(Y_i^*\right)$ is estimated by $1 / K\left(Y_i, \hat{p}_i\left(X_i^*\right)\right)$ with $K\left(Y_i, \hat{p}_i\left(X_i^*\right)\right)$ When $\text{Var}\left(Y_i \mid X_i\right)$ is estimated by $\text{Var}^*\left(\tilde{Y}_i\right) = \hat{p}_i\left(X_i^*\right)\left(1 - \hat{p}_i\left(X_i^*\right)\right)$. This leads to our proposed estimator

$$\widehat{\text{Cov}}\left(Y_i, \hat{\phi}_C\left(X_i^*\right) \mid X^{*n}\right) = \frac{1}{K\left(Y_i, \hat{p}_i\left(X_i^*\right)\right)} \text{Cov}^*\left(Y_i^*, \hat{\phi}_C^*\left(X_i^*\right) \mid X^{*n}\right), i = 1, \ldots, n,$$

Where $\hat{\phi}_C^*$ is an estimated decision function via the same classification routine applied to $\left(X_i^*, Y_i^*\right)_{i=1}^n$.

To estimate D_{1n}, note that $E\left(E(Y \mid X) - \hat{\phi}_C^*(X)\right)^2$ can be estimated by $n^{-1} \sum_i \left(\hat{p}_i(X_i) - \hat{\phi}_C^*\right.$ $\left.(X_i)\right)^2$ when $E(Y \mid X) = p(X)$ is estimated by $\hat{p}_i(X)$, while $\left(E(Y_i \mid X_i) - \hat{\phi}(X_i)\right)^2$ may be estimated by $\left(\hat{p}_i\left(X_i^*\right) - \hat{\phi}_C^*\left(X_i^*\right)\right)^2$ when $E\left(Y_i \mid X_i\right)$ is replaced by $\hat{p}_i^*\left(X_i^*\right), i = 1, \ldots, n$. This leads to

$$\hat{D}_{1n}\left(X^n, \hat{\phi}_C\right)$$

$$= E^*\left(n^{-1} \sum_{i=1}^n \left(\hat{p}_i(X_i) - \hat{\phi}_C^*(X_i)\right)^2 - n^{-1} \sum_{i=1}^n \left(\hat{p}_i^*\left(X_i^*\right) - \hat{\phi}_C^*\left(X_i^*\right)\right)^2 \mid X^{*n}\right),$$

Where $\hat{\phi}_C^*$ is trained via $\left(X_i^*, Y_i^*\right)_{i=1}^n$ and $\hat{p}_i^*\left(X_i^*\right)$ is an estimated $E\left(Y_i^* \mid X_i^*\right)$.

Based on above equations, we obtain $\widehat{CGE}\left(\hat{\phi}_C\right)$ in equation. Note that the proposed estimator $\widehat{CGE}\left(\hat{\phi}_C\right)$ is constructed based on perturbed data, and can be generally computed via Monte Carlo (MC) approximation. In some situations, however, $\widehat{CGE}\left(\hat{\phi}_C\right)$ can be computed analytically without recourse to MC methods, permitting fast implementation, as in Fisher's linear discrimination. For problems considered in this topic, we use a MC numerical approximation for implementation. First, generate D perturbed samples $\left\{X_i^{*l}\right\}_{i=1}^n$ according to above equation, $l = 1, \ldots, D$. Second, for each sample $\left\{X_i^{*l}\right\}_{i=1}^n$ generate D perturbed samples $\left\{Y_i^{*lm}\right\}_{i=1}^n$ according to above equation, $m = 1, \ldots, D$. For $m = 1, \ldots, D, i = 1, \ldots, n$, compute $\widehat{Cov}\left(Y_i^*, \hat{\phi}_C^*\left(X_i^*\right) \mid X^n\right) = \left(D^2 - 1\right)\sum_{l,m}\hat{\phi}_C^{*lm}\left(X_i^{*l}\right)\left(Y_i^{*lm} - \bar{Y}_i^*\right)$, where $\hat{\phi}_C^{*lm}$ is trained via $\left(X_i^{*l}, Y_i^{*lm}\right)_{i=1}^n$, and $\bar{Y}_i^* = D^2\sum_{l,m}Y_i^{*lm}$. Now equation is approximated by the corresponding sample MC covariance, i.e.,

$$\widehat{Cov}\left(Y_i, \hat{\phi}_C\left(X_i\right) \mid X^n\right)$$

$$\approx \frac{1}{D^2 - 1}\sum_{l,m=1}^D \frac{1}{K\left(Y_i, \hat{p}_i\left(X_i^{*l}\right)\right)}\hat{\phi}_C^{*lm}\left(X_i^{*l}\right)\left(Y_i^{*lm} - \bar{Y}_i^*\right); \quad i = 1,\ldots,n,$$

while $= E^*\left(n^{-1}\sum_{i=1}^n\left(\hat{p}_i\left(X_i\right) - \hat{\phi}_C^*\left(X_i\right)\right)^2 - n^{-1}\sum_{i=1}^n\left(\hat{p}_i^*\left(X_i^*\right) - \hat{\phi}_C^*\left(X_i^*\right)\right)^2 \mid X^{*n}\right)$, is approximated as

$$\hat{D}_{1n}\left(X^n, \hat{\phi}_C\right)$$

$$\approx \frac{1}{n(D^2 - 1)}\sum_{i=1}^n\sum_{l,m=1}^D\left(\left(\hat{p}_i\left(X_i\right) - \hat{\phi}_C^{*lm}\left(X_i\right)\right)^2 - \left(\hat{p}_i^*\left(X_i^{*l}\right) - \hat{\phi}_C^{*lm}\left(X_i^{*l}\right)\right)^2\right).$$

The estimated CGE is now MC-approximated, with approximated Cod and $\hat{D}_{1n}$ given in ($\approx \frac{1}{D^2 - 1}\sum_{l,m=1}^D \frac{1}{K\left(Y_i, \hat{p}_i\left(X_i^{*l}\right)\right)}\hat{\phi}_C^{*lm}\left(X_i^{*l}\right)\left(Y_i^{*lm} - \bar{Y}_i^*\right); \quad i = 1,\ldots,n,$) and $\approx \frac{1}{n(D^2 - 1)}\sum_{i=1}^n\sum_{l,m=1}^D$ $\left(\left(\hat{p}_i\left(X_i\right) - \hat{\phi}_C^{*lm}\left(X_i\right)\right)^2 - \left(\hat{p}_i^*\left(X_i^{*l}\right) - \hat{\phi}_C^{*lm}\left(X_i^{*l}\right)\right)^2\right)$. By the Law of Large Numbers, $(E^*\left(n^{-1}\sum_{i=1}^n\right.$ $\left(\hat{p}_i\left(X_i\right) - \hat{\phi}_C^*\left(X_i\right)\right)^2 - n^{-1}\sum_{i=1}^n\left(\hat{p}_i^*\left(X_i^*\right) - \hat{\phi}_C^*\left(X_i^*\right)\right)^2 \mid X^{*n}$), and $\approx \frac{1}{D^2 - 1}\sum_{i=1}^n\sum_{l,m=1}^D\left(\left(\hat{p}_i\left(X_i\right) - \hat{\phi}_C^{*lm}\right.\right.$ $\left.\left(X_i\right)\right)^2 - \left(\hat{p}_i^*\left(X_i^{*l}\right) - \hat{\phi}_C^{*lm}\left(X_i^{*l}\right)\right)^2\right)$ converge and $= E^*\left(n^{-1}\sum_{i=1}^n\left(\hat{p}_i\left(X_i\right) - \hat{\phi}_C^*\left(X_i\right)\right)^2 - n^{-1}\sum_{i=1}^n\right.$ $\left(\hat{p}_i^*\left(X_i^*\right) - \hat{\phi}_C^*\left(X_i^*\right)\right)^2 \mid X^{*n}$), respectively, and hence MC-approximated CGE converges, as $D \to \infty$. In practice, we recommend that D be at least $n^{1/2}$ to ensure the precision of MC approximation.

Sensitivity with Respect to τ and Initial Probabilities

Our proposed estimator of CGE depends on the value of $0 < \tau < 1$, with $\tau = 0.5$ recommended in implementation based on our limited numerical experience. This dependency on τ can be removed by a data-driven selection routine that may be computationally intensive. One proposal is to employ CV, or our proposed method once again, to seek the optimal τ by minimizing CV with respect to $\tau \in (0, 1)$. For the problem considered in this topic, we fix $\tau = 0.5$ for simplicity and ease of computation.

The initial probability estimation for $p_i(x_i)$ and $p_i^*(x_i)$ may be also important. The dependency of initial probability estimation may be removed at the expense of additional computational cost. Specifically, suppose that different probability estimation methods are indexed by θ, the optimal θ can be obtained by minimizing the estimated Kullback-Leibler (KL) loss between the true and estimated probabilities, over θ,

$$\hat{K}\left(p, \hat{p}(\theta)\right) = -n^{-1} \sum_{i=1}^{n} \log L\left(Y_i \mid \hat{p}_i(\theta)\right) + -n^{-1} \sum_{i=1}^{n} \mathrm{Cov}\left(\log\left(\hat{p}_i(\theta)\right) - \log\left(1 - \hat{p}_i(\theta)\right), Y_i\right),$$

where $L\left(Y_i \mid \hat{p}_i(\theta)\right)$ is the likelihood function with parameter $\hat{p}(\theta)$. In this topic, for simplicity, we use logistic regression to estimate the initial probabilities $p_i(x_i)$ and $p_i^*(x_i)$ $i = 1, \ldots, n$, which is sensible.

Multicategory Case

To treat the multicategory case, we introduce a mapping $t : \{0, \ldots, k-1\} \rightarrow \{0, 1\}^k$, which permits a treatment of the multicategory case via the result in the binary case. Precisely, $t(j)$ is defined as $\left(\underbrace{0, \ldots, 0, 1}_{j} \quad \underbrace{0, \ldots, 0}_{k-j-1} \right)$ for $j \in \{0, \ldots, k-1\}$.

With this mapping, Y and $\hat{\phi}_C(X)$ are converted to vector representations, denoted by $t(Y)$ and $t\left(\hat{\phi}_C(X)\right)$. Now let $Z = \left(Z^{(0)}, \ldots, Z^{(k-1)}\right) = t(Y)$ and the corresponding classification rule be $\hat{\phi}_C^t = \left(\hat{\phi}_C^{t(0)}, \ldots, \hat{\phi}_C^{t(k-1)}\right) = t\left(\hat{\phi}_C\right)$. By definition, $\left\{\hat{\phi}_C, (X_i, Y_i)_{i=1}^{n}\right\}$ maps one-to-one onto $\left\{\hat{\phi}_C^t, (X_i, Z_i)_{i=1}^{n}\right\}$ with $Z_i = t(Y_i)$. There fore, $GE\left(\hat{\phi}_C\right) = GE\left(\hat{\phi}_C^t\right) = P\left(Z \neq \hat{\phi}_C^t(X)\right)$. More importantly, under this new setting, $GE\left(\hat{\phi}_C\right)$ can be written as a sum of the GE's of k binary problems.

Lemma: We have

$$GE\left(\hat{\phi}_C\right) = GE\left(\hat{\phi}_C^t\right) = P\left(Z \neq \hat{\phi}_C^t(X)\right) = \frac{1}{2}\sum_{j=0}^{k-1} P\left(Z^{(j)} \neq \hat{\phi}_C^{t(j)}(X)\right).$$

In addition, $EGE\left(\hat{\phi}_C\right) = EGE\left(\hat{\phi}_C^t\right) = (1/2)\sum_{j=0}^{k-1} EGE\left(\hat{\phi}_C^{t(j)}\right).$

Note that the $\hat{\phi}_C^{t(j)}(X)$'s in Lemma are internally consistent that is, if $\hat{\phi}_C^{t(j)}(X)=1$, then $\hat{\phi}_C^{t(j)}(X)=0$, for all $j \neq j_0$. Therefore the decomposition in $GE(\hat{\phi}_C) = GE(\hat{\phi}_C^t) = P(Z \neq \hat{\phi}_C^t(X)) = \frac{1}{2}\sum_{j=0}^{k-1} P(Z^{(j)} \neq \hat{\phi}_C^{t(j)}(X))$ differs from the usual decomposition in multicategory classification with k separate components, and is applicable to classifiers with different class codings, such as one-vs-rest SVM with coding $\{1, \ldots, k\}$ and multicategory SVM with vector coding.

An application of above Lemmas yields the estimated GE of $\hat{\phi}_C$ as

$$\widehat{GE}(\hat{\phi}_C) = EGE(\hat{\phi}_C) + \sum_{j=0}^{k-1}\left(\frac{1}{n}\sum_{i=1}^{n}\widehat{Cov}\left(Z_i^{(j)}, \hat{\phi}_C^{t(j)}(X_i)\mid X^n\right) + \frac{1}{2}\hat{D}_{1n}\left(X^n, \hat{\phi}_C^{t(j)}\right)\right.$$
$$\left. + \frac{1}{2}\hat{D}_{2n}\left(X^n, Z^{n(j)}\right)\right),$$

Where $Z^{n(j)} = \left(Z_i^{(j)}\right)_{i=1}^{n}$ and $\hat{D}_{2n}\left(X^n, Z^{n(j)}\right) = E\left(Var\left(Z^{(j)}\mid X^n\right)\right) - n^{-1}\sum_i Var\left(Z_i^{(j)}\mid X_i\right)$, which leads to the corresponding comparative GE $CGE(\hat{\phi}_C)$ as well as the estimator

$$\widehat{CGE}(\hat{\phi}_C) = EGE(\hat{\phi}_C) + \sum_{j=0}^{k-1}\left(\frac{1}{n}\sum_{i=1}^{n}\widehat{Cov}\left(Z_i^{(j)}, \hat{\phi}_C^{t(j)}(X_i)\mid X^n\right) + \frac{1}{2}\hat{D}_{1n}\left(X^n, \hat{\phi}_C^{t(j)}\right)\right),$$

Where $EGE(\hat{\phi}_C)$ is the training error.

To compute $\widehat{Cov}\left(Z_i^{(j)}, \hat{\phi}_C^{t(j)}(X_i)\mid X^n\right)$ and $\hat{D}_{1n}$ in

$$\widehat{CGE}(\hat{\phi}_C) = EGE(\hat{\phi}_C) + \sum_{j=0}^{k-1}\left(\frac{1}{n}\sum_{i=1}^{n}\widehat{Cov}\left(Z_i^{(j)}, \hat{\phi}_C^{t(j)}(X_i)\mid X^n\right) + \frac{1}{2}\hat{D}_{1n}\left(X^n, \hat{\phi}_C^{t(j)}\right)\right),$$

we now modify the data perturbation technique in the binary case. Let $M(p_{i0}(X_i), \ldots, p_{i,k-1}(X_i))$ denote the conditional distribution of Y_i and X_i where $p_{ij}(X_i) = P(Y_i = j\mid X_i)$ and $\sum_j p_{ij}(X_i) = 1$. Generate X_i^*, $i = 1, \ldots, n$, as

$$X_i^* = \begin{cases} X_i & \text{with probability } 1-\tau, \\ \tilde{X}_i & \text{with probability } \tau, \end{cases}$$

Where $\tilde{X}_i$ is sampled from the empirical distribution of X^n. Generate Y_i^*, $i = 1, \ldots, n$, as

$$Y_i^* = \begin{cases} Y_i & \text{with probability } 1-\tau, \\ \tilde{Y}_i & \text{with probability } \tau, \end{cases}$$

Where $\tilde{Y}_i$ is sampled from $M\left(\hat{p}_{i0}(X_i^*), \ldots, \tilde{p}_{i,k-1}(X_i^*)\right)$, with $\hat{p}_{ij}(X_i^*)$ the estimated $P(Y_i = j\mid X_i^*)$.

Let $Z_i^* = t(Y_i^*)$ be the transformed perturbed response, and $\hat{\phi}_C^{t*}$ be the corresponding transformed classifiers based on $(X_i^*, Z_i^*)_{i=1}^n$. The MC approximations of $\widehat{\text{Cov}}$ and $\hat{D}_{1n}$ in $\widehat{CGE}(\hat{\phi}_C) = EGE(\hat{\phi}_C) + \sum_{j=0}^{k-1}\left(\frac{1}{n}\sum_{i=1}^n \widehat{\text{Cov}}\left(Z_i^{(j)}, \hat{\phi}_C^{t(j)}(X_i)|X^n\right) + \frac{1}{2}\hat{D}_{1n}\left(X^n, \hat{\phi}_C^{t(j)}\right)\right.$ are given as:

$$\widehat{\text{Cov}}\left(Z_i^{(j)}, \hat{\phi}_C^{t(j)}(X_i)|X^n\right)$$

$$\approx \frac{1}{D^2-1}\sum_{j=0}^{k-1}\sum_{l,m=1}^{D}\frac{1}{K\left(Z_i^{(j)}, \hat{p}_{ij}(X_i^{*l})\right)}\hat{\phi}_C^{t*lm(j)}\left(X_i^{*l}\right)\left(Z_i^{*lm(j)} - \bar{Z}_i^{*(j)}\right); i=1,...,n,$$

$$\hat{D}_{1n}\left(X^n, \hat{\phi}_C^{t(j)}\right)$$

$$\approx \frac{1}{n(D^2-1)}\sum_{i=1}^{n}\sum_{j=0}^{k-1}\sum_{l,m=1}^{D}\left(\left(\hat{p}_{ij}(X_i) - \hat{\phi}_C^{t*lm(j)}(X_i)\right)^2 - \left(\hat{p}_{ij}^*(X_i^{*l}) - \hat{\phi}_C^{t*lm(j)}(X_i^{*l})\right)^2\right),$$

Where $\hat{p}_{ij}(X_i)$ and $\hat{p}_{ij}^*(X_i^{*l})$ are estimates of $P(Y_i = j|X_i)$ and $P(Y_i^* = j|X_i^{*l})$, respectively. Substituting these two approximations into $\widehat{CGE}(\hat{\phi}_C) = EGE(\hat{\phi}_C) + \sum_{j=0}^{k-1}\left(\frac{1}{n}\right.$= $\sum_{i=1}^{n}\widehat{\text{Cov}}\left(Z_i^{(j)}, \hat{\phi}_C^{t(j)}(X_i)|X^n\right) + \frac{1}{2}\hat{D}_{1n}\left(X^n, \hat{\phi}_C^{t(j)}\right)$, we obtain the proposed MC approximated CGE in the multicategory case.

Semi-supervised Learning

Semi-supervised machine learning is a combination of supervised and unsupervised machine learning methods. It is a class of supervised learning tasks and techniques.

With more common supervised machine learning methods, you train a learning algorithm on a "labeled" dataset in which each record includes the outcome information. This allows the algorithm to deduce patterns and identify relationships between your target variable and the rest of the dataset based on information it already has. In contrast, unsupervised machine learning algorithms learn from a dataset without the outcome variable. In semi-supervised learning, an algorithm learns from a dataset that includes both labeled and unlabeled data, usually mostly unlabeled.

The semi-supervised learning problem belongs to the supervised category, since the goal is to minimize the classification error, and an estimate of $P(x)$ is not sought after. The difference from a standard classification setting is that along with a labeled sample $D_l = \{(x_i, y_i)|i = 1,...,n\}$ drawn i.i.d. from $P(x, y)$ we also have access to an additional unlabeled sample $D_u = \{x_{n+j} | j = 1,...,m\}$ from the marginal $P(x)$. We are especially interested in cases where $m \gg n$ which may arise in situations where obtaining an unlabeled sample is cheap and easy, while labeling the sample is expensive or difficult. We denote $X_l = (x_1,...,x_n), Y_l = (y_1,...,y_n)$ and $X_u = (x_{n+1},...,x_{n+m})$. The un-observed labels are denoted $Y_u = (y_{n+1},...,y_{n+m})$. In a straightforward generalization of SSL (not discussed here) uncertain information about Y_u is available.

There are two obvious baseline methods for SSL. We can treat it as a supervised classi-fication problem by ignoring Du, or we can treat y as a latent class variable in a mixture estimate of $P(x)$ which is fitted using an unsupervised method, then associate latent groups with observed classes using Dl. One would agree that any valid SSL technique should outperform both baseline methods significantly in a range of practically rele-vant situations. If this sounds rather vague, note that in general for a fixed SSL method it should be easy to construct data distributions for which either of the baseline meth-ods does better. In our view, SSL is much more a practical than a theoretical problem. A useful SSL technique should be configurable to the specifics of the task in a similar way as Bayesian learning, through the choice of prior and model.

Methods

Generative Models

Generative approaches to statistical learning first seek to estimate $p(x|y)$, the distri-bution of data points belonging to each class. The probability $p(y|x)$ that a given point x has label y is then proportional to $p(x|y)p(y)$ by Bayes' rule. Semi-supervised learn-ing with generative models can be viewed either as an extension of supervised learning (classification plus information about $p(x)$) or as an extension of unsupervised learn-ing (clustering plus some labels).

Generative models assume that the distributions take some particular form $p(x|y,\theta)$ parameterized by the vector θ. If these assumptions are incorrect, the unlabeled data may actually decrease the accuracy of the solution relative to what would have been obtained from labeled data alone. However, if the assumptions are correct, then the unlabeled data necessarily improves performance.

The unlabeled data are distributed according to a mixture of individual-class distri-butions. In order to learn the mixture distribution from the unlabeled data, it must be identifiable, that is, different parameters must yield different summed distributions. Gaussian mixture distributions are identifiable and commonly used for generative models.

The parameterized joint distribution can be written as $p(x,y|\theta) = p(y|\theta)p(x|y,\theta)$ by using the Chain rule. Each parameter vector θ is associated with a decision function $f_\theta(x) = \text{argmax } p(y|x,\theta)$. The parameter is then chosen based on fit to both the la-beled and unlabeled data, weighted by λ:

$$\underset{\Theta}{\text{argmax}} \left(\log p(\{x_i, y_i\}_{i=1}^l | \theta) + \lambda \log p(\{x_i\}_{i=l+1}^{l+u} | \theta) \right).$$

Low-density Separation

Another major class of methods attempts to place boundaries in regions where there are few data points (labeled or unlabeled). One of the most commonly used algorithms is the transductive support vector machine, or TSVM (which, despite its name, may be used for inductive learning as well). Whereas support vector machines for supervised learning seek a decision boundary with maximal margin over the labeled data, the goal of TSVM is a labeling of the unlabeled data such that the decision boundary has maximal margin over all of the data. In addition to the standard hinge loss $(1-yf(x))_+$ for labeled data, a loss function $(1-|f(x)|)_+$ is introduced over the unlabeled data by letting $y = \operatorname{sign} f(x)$. TSVM then selects $f^*(x) = h^*(x) + b$ from a reproducing kernel Hilbert space $\mathcal{H}$ by minimizing the regularized empirical risk:

$$f^* = \operatorname*{argmin}_f \left(\sum_{i=1}^{l} (1 - y_i f(x_i))_+ + \lambda_1 \| h \|_{\mathcal{H}}^2 + \lambda_2 \sum_{i=l+1}^{l+u} (1 - |f(x_i)|)_+ \right)$$

An exact solution is intractable due to the non-convex term $(1-|f(x)|)_+$, so research has focused on finding useful approximations.

Other approaches that implement low-density separation include Gaussian process models, information regularization, and entropy minimization (of which TSVM is a special case).

Graph-based Methods

Graph-based methods for semi-supervised learning use a graph representation of the data, with a node for each labeled and unlabeled example. The graph may be constructed using domain knowledge or similarity of examples; two common methods are to connect each data point to its k nearest neighbors or to examples within some distance ϵ. The weight W_{ij} of an edge between x_i and x_j is then set to $e^{\frac{-\|x_i - x_j\|^2}{\epsilon}}$.

Within the framework of manifold regularization, the graph serves as a proxy for the manifold. A term is added to the standard Tikhonov regularization problem to enforce smoothness of the solution relative to the manifold (in the intrinsic space of the problem) as well as relative to the ambient input space. The minimization problem becomes

$$\operatorname*{argmin}_{f \in \mathcal{H}} \left(\frac{1}{l} \sum_{i=1}^{l} V(f(x_i), y_i) + \lambda_A \| f \|_{\mathcal{H}}^2 + \lambda_I \int_{\mathcal{M}} \| \nabla_{\mathcal{M}} f(x) \|^2 dp(x) \right)$$

where $\mathcal{H}$ is a reproducing kernel Hilbert space and $\mathcal{M}$ is the manifold on which the data lie. The regularization parameters λ_A and λ_I control smoothness in the ambient and intrinsic spaces respectively. The graph is used to approximate the intrinsic regularization term. Defining the graph Laplacian $L = D - W$ where $D_{ii} = \sum_{j=1}^{l+u} W_{ij}$ and $\mathbf{f}$ the vector $[f(x_1)...f(x_{l+u})]$, we have

$$\mathbf{f}^T L \mathbf{f} = \sum_{i,j=1}^{l+u} W_{ij}(f_i - f_j)^2 \approx \int_{\mathcal{M}} \backslash \nabla_{\mathcal{M}} f(x) \backslash^2 dp(x).$$

The Laplacian can also be used to extend the supervised learning algorithms: regularized least squares and support vector machines (SVM) to semi-supervised versions Laplacian regularized least squares and Laplacian SVM.

Heuristic Approaches

Some methods for semi-supervised learning are not intrinsically geared to learning from both unlabeled and labeled data, but instead make use of unlabeled data within a supervised learning framework. For instance, the labeled and unlabeled examples $x_1,...,x_{l+u}$ may inform a choice of representation, distance metric, or kernel for the data in an unsupervised first step. Then supervised learning proceeds from only the labeled examples.

Self-training is a wrapper method for semi-supervised learning. First a supervised learning algorithm is trained based on the labeled data only. This classifier is then applied to the unlabeled data to generate more labeled examples as input for the supervised learning algorithm. Generally only the labels the classifier is most confident of are added at each step.

Co-training is an extension of self-training in which multiple classifiers are trained on different (ideally disjoint) sets of features and generate labeled examples for one another.

In Human Cognition

Human responses to formal semi-supervised learning problems have yielded varying conclusions about the degree of influence of the unlabeled data. More natural learning problems may also be viewed as instances of semi-supervised learning. Much of human concept learning involves a small amount of direct instruction (e.g. parental labeling of objects during childhood) combined with large amounts of unlabeled experience (e.g. observation of objects without naming or counting them, or at least without feedback).

Human infants are sensitive to the structure of unlabeled natural categories such as images of dogs and cats or male and female faces. More recent work has shown that infants and children take into account not only the unlabeled examples available, but the sampling process from which labeled examples arise.

Similarity Learning

Similarity measure is fundamental to many machine learning and data mining algorithms. Predefined similarity metrics are often data-dependent and sensitive to noise.

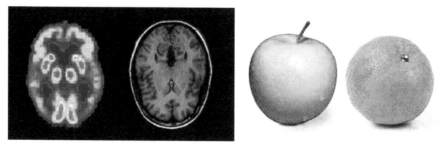

Multi-modal medical images are incomparable as apples and oranges.

Similarity is one of the most fundamental notions in many problems, especially in image sciences such as computer vision and pattern recognition. The need to quantify similarity or dissimilarity of some data is central to broad categories of problems involving comparison, search, matching, or reconstruction. For example, in content-based image or video retrieval, similarity between images and videos or their representation is used to rank the matches. In object detection and recognition, one of the classical problems in computer vision, similarity of regions in an image to some object model is used to decide whether there is an object there or not. Finally, different types of inverse problems encountered in engineering fields involve a criterion of similarity between the observed data and the data one tries to estimate.

The notion of similarity is problem-and application-dependent, and in many cases, very hard or impossible to model, since the structure of the data space is very far from being Euclidean. The data can further come from multiple modalities, such as images captured using infrared and visible spectrum imaging devices, different medical imaging modalities such as CT, MRI, and PET, or be represented using different representation or different versions of the same representation. Such data might be generated by unrelated physical processes, have distinct statistics, dimensionality, and structure. The need to compute similarity across modalities arises in many important problems such as data fusion from different sensors, medical image alignment, and comparison of different versions and representations. An attempt to directly compare objects belonging to different modalities (e.g., T1- and T2-weighted MRI images) is similar to comparing apples to oranges, as the modalities are often incommensurable.

In many cases, examples of similarity on a subset of the data are available. For instance, it is possible to acquire an image of a known object using different imaging devices and have examples of how the same object looks like in infrared and visible light. In such cases, similarity can be learned in a supervised manner, by generalizing the similarity given on a training set of examples. In particular, if the data in the problem manifest some variability or can undergo a certain class of transformation, generating examples of transformed data allows learning the invariance to such transformations. Embedding into some metric space can be used in this case to parametrize the learned data similarity. In this class of similarity-or metric-learning problems, metric geometry approaches are very intimately related to machine learning algorithms. In particular, embedding into the Hamming space can be considered as a weak binary classification problem, and constructed using boosting techniques widely used in machine learning.

Learning Setup

There are four common setups for similarity and metric distance learning.

Regression Similarity Learning

In this setup, pairs of objects are given (x_i^1, x_i^2) together with a measure of their similarity $y_i \in R$. The goal is to learn a function that approximates $f(x_i^1, x_i^2) \sim y_i$ for every new labeled triplet example (x_i^1, x_i^2, y_i). This is typically achieved by minimizing a regularized loss $\min_w \sum_i loss(w; x_i^1, x_i^2, y_i) + reg(w)$.

Classification Similarity Learning

Given are pairs of similar objects (x_i, x_i^+) and non similar objects (x_i, x_i^-). An equivalent formulation is that every pair (x_i^1, x_i^2) is given together with a binary label $y_i \in \{0,1\}$ that determines if the two objects are similar or not. The goal is again to learn a classifier that can decide if a new pair of objects is similar or not.

Ranking Similarity Learning

Given are triplets of objects (x_i, x_i^+, x_i^-) whose relative similarity obey a predefined order: x_i is known to be more similar to x_i^+ than to x_i^-. The goal is to learn a function f such that for any new triplet of objects (x, x^+, x^-), it obeys $f(x, x^+) > f(x, x^-)$. This setup assumes a weaker form of supervision than in regression, because instead of providing an exact measure of similarity, one only has to provide the relative order of similarity. For this reason, ranking-based similarity learning is easier to apply in real large-scale applications.

Locality Sensitive Hashing (LSH)

hashes input items so that similar items map to the same "buckets" in memory with high probability (the number of buckets being much smaller than the universe of possible input items). It is often applied in nearest neighbor search on large-scale high-dimensional data, e.g., image databases, document collections, time-series databases, and genome databases.

A common approach for learning similarity, is to model the similarity function as a bilinear form. For example, in the case of ranking similarity learning, one aims to learn a matrix W that parametrizes the similarity function $f_W(x,z) = x^T W z$.

Metric Learning

Similarity learning is closely related to *distance metric learning*. Metric learning is the task of learning a distance function over objects. A metric or distance function has to obey four axioms: non-negativity, Identity of indiscernibles, symmetry and subadditivity / triangle inequality. In practice, metric learning algorithms ignore the condition of identity of indiscernibles and learn a pseudo-metric.

When the objects x_i are vectors in R^d, then any matrix W in the symmetric positive semi-definite cone S_+^d defines a distance pseudo-metric of the space of x through the form $D_W(x_1,x_2)^2 = (x_1 - x_2)^T W(x_1 - x_2)$. When W is a symmetric positive definite matrix, D_W is a metric. Moreover, as any symmetric positive semi-definite matrix $W \in S_+^d$ can be decomposed as $W = L^T L$ where $L \in R^{e \times d}$ and $e \geq rank(W)$, the distance function D_W can be rewritten equivalently $D_W(x_1,x_2)^2 = (x_1 - x_2)^T L^T L(x_1 - x_2) = \|L(x_1 - x_2)\|_2^2$. The distance $D_W(x_1,x_2)^2 = \|x_1' - x_2'\|_2^2$ corresponds to the Euclidean distance between the projected feature vectors $x_1' = Lx_1$ and $x_2' = Lx_2$. Some well-known approaches for metric learning include Large margin nearest neighbor, Information theoretic metric learning (ITML).

In statistics, the covariance matrix of the data is sometimes used to define a distance metric called Mahalanobis distance.

Applications

Similarity learning is used in information retrieval for learning to rank, in face verification or face identification, and in recommendation systems. Also, many machine learning approaches rely on some metric. This includes unsupervised learning such as clustering, which groups together close or similar objects. It also includes supervised approaches like K-nearest neighbor algorithm which rely on labels of nearby objects to decide on the label of a new object. Metric learning has been proposed as a preprocessing step for many of these approaches.

Scalability

Metric and similarity learning naively scale quadratically with the dimension of the input space, as can easily see when the learned metric has a bilinear form $f_W(x,z) = x^T W z$. Scaling to higher dimensions can be achieved by enforcing a sparseness structure over the matrix model, as done with HDSL, and with COMET.

Structured Prediction

Structured prediction is a generalization of the standard paradigms of supervised learning, classification and regression. All of these can be thought of finding a function that
minimizes some loss over a training set. The differences are in the kind of functions
that are used and the losses.

In classification, the target domain are discrete class labels, and the loss is usually the
0-1 loss, i.e. counting the misclassifications. In regression, the target domain is the real
numbers, and the loss is usually mean squared error. In structured prediction, both the
target domain and the loss are more or less arbitrary. This means the goal is not to predict a label or a number, but a possibly much more complicated object like a sequence
or a graph.

In structured prediction, we often deal with finite, but large output spaces Y. This situation could be dealt with using classification with a very large number of classes. The
idea behind structured prediction is that we can do better than this, by making use of
the structure of the output space.

We will consider two types of structure. The first is the "sequence labeling" problem,
typified by the natural language processing example above, but also common in computational biology (labeling amino acids in DNA) and robotics (labeling actions in a
sequence). For this, we will develop specialized prediction algorithms that take advantage of the sequential nature of the task. We will also consider more general structures
beyond sequences, and discuss how to cast them in a generic optimization framework:
integer linear programming (or ILP).

The general framework we will explore is that of jointly scoring input/output configu-
rations. We will construct algorithms that learn a function $x, \hat{y}$ (s for "score"), where
x is an input (like an image) and y is some predicted output (like a segmentation of
that image). For any given image, there are a lot of possible segmentations (i.e., a lot of
possible), and the goal of s is to rank them in order of "how good" they are: how compatible they are with the input x. The most important thing is that the scoring function
s ranks the true segmentation y higher than any other imposter segmentation. That is,
we want to ensure that $s(x, y) > s(x, \hat{y})$ for all. The main challenge we will face is how
to do this efficiently, given that there are so many imposter $\hat{y}$s.

Structured Perceptron

Let us now consider the sequence labeling task. In sequence labeling, the outputs are
themselves variable-length vectors. An input/output pair (which must have the same
length) might look like:

x = "monsters eat tasty bunnies"

y = noun verb adj noun

To set terminology, we will refer to the entire sequence y as the "output" and a single label within as a "label". As before, our goal is to learn a scoring function that scores the true output sequence y higher than any imposter output sequence.

As before, despite the fact that y is now a vector, we can still define feature functions w over the entire input/output pair. For instance, we might want to count the number of times "monsters" has been tagged as "noun" in a given output. Or the number of times "verb" is followed by "noun" in an output. Both of these are features that are likely indicative of a correct output. We might also count the number of times "tasty" has been tagged as a verb (probably a negative feature) and the number of times two verbs are adjacent (again, probably a negative feature).

More generally, a very standard set of features would be:

- The number of times word w has been labeled with tag l, for all words w and all syntactic tags l.

- The number of times tag l is adjacent to tag l' in the output, for all tags l and l'.

The first set of features are often called unary features, because they talk only about the relationship between the input (sentence) and a single (unit) label in the output sequence. The second set of features are often called Markov features, because they talk about adjacent labels in the output sequence, which is reminiscent of Markov models which only have short term memory.

Note that for a given input of x length L (in the example, L = 4), the number of possible outputs is x, whereis the number of syntactic tags. This means that the number of possible outputs grows exponentially in the length of the input. In general, we write to mean "the set of all possible structured outputs for the input x". We have just seen that $|Y(x)| = K^{\text{len}(x)}$.

Despite the fact that the inputs and outputs have variable length, the size of the feature representation is constant. If there are V words in your vocabulary and K labels for a given word, the the number of unary features is VK and the number of Markov features is K^2, so

Algorithm 40 Structured Perceptron Train(D, MaxIter) 1:

$1: w \leftarrow 0$ // initialize weights
$2: for\ iter = 1 \ldots MaxIter\ do$
$3: \quad for\ all\ (x, y) \in D\ do$
$4: \quad \hat{y} \rightarrow argmax_{\hat{y} \in (x)}\ w \cdot \phi(x, \hat{y})$ // compute prediction

5: *if* $\hat{y} \neq y$ *then*

6:     $w \leftarrow w + \phi(x, y) - \phi(x, \hat{y})$ // update weights

7: *end if*

8: *end for*

9: *end for*

10: *return w*   // return learned weights

the total number of features is K(V + K). Of course, more complex feature representations are possible and, in general, are a good idea. For example, it is often useful to have unary features of neighboring words like "the number of times the word immediately preceding a verb was 'monsters'."

Now that we have a fixed size feature representation, we can develop a perceptron-style algorithm for sequence labeling. The core idea is the same as before. We will maintain a single weight vector. We will make predictions by choosing the (entire) output sequence that maximizes a score given by $w.\phi(x, \hat{y})$. And if this output sequence is incorrect, we will adjust the weights word the correct output sequence y and away from the incorrect output sequence. This is summarized in Algorithm.

You may have noticed that Algorithm for the structured perceptron is identical to Algorithm $s(x, y) = w.\phi(x, y)$, aside from the fact that in the multiclass perceptron the argmax is over the K possible classes, while in the structured perceptron, the argmax is over the possible output sequences.

The only difficulty in this algorithm is in line 4:

$$y \leftarrow argmax \; w.\phi(x, \hat{y})$$
$$\hat{y} \in Y(x)$$

In principle, this requires you to search over K^L possible output sequences $\hat{y}$ to find the one that maximizes the dot product. Except for very small K or very small L, this is computationally infeasible. Because of its difficulty, this is often referred to as the argmax problem in structured prediction. Below, we consider how to solve the argmax problem for sequences.

Argmax for Sequences

We now face an algorithmic question, not a machine learning question: how to compute the argmax in Eq efficiently. In general, this is not possible. However, under somewhat restrictive assumptions about the form of our features ϕ, we can solve this problem efficiently, by casting it as the problem of computing a maximum weight path through a specifically constructed lattice. This is a variant of the Viterbi algorithm for hidden Markov models, a classic example of dynamic programming.

The key observation for sequences is that—so long as we restrict our attention to unary features and Markov features—the feature function ϕ decomposes over the input. Consider the input/output sequence from before: $x =$ "monsters eat tasty bunnies" and $y =$ [noun verb adj noun]. If we want to compute the number of times "bunnies" is tagged as "noun" in this pair, we can do this by:

1. Count the number of times "bunnies" is tagged as "noun" in the first three words of the sentence

2. Add to that the number of times "bunnies" is tagged as "noun" in the final word

We can do a similar exercise for Markov features, like the number of times "adj" is followed by "noun".

However, we don't actually need these counts. All we need for computing the argmax sequence is the dot product between the weights w and these counts. In particular, we can compute $w \cdot \varphi(x, y)$ as the dot product on all-but-the-last word plus the dot product on the last word: $w \cdot \varphi_{1:3}(x, y) + w \cdot \varphi_4(x, y)$. Here, $\varphi_{1:3}$ means "features for everything up to and including position 3" and φ_4 means "features for position 4."

More generally, we can write $\phi(x, y) = \sum_{l=1}^{L} \phi_l(x, y)$ where $\phi_l(x, y)$ only includes features about position l. In particular, we're taking advantage of the associative law for addition:

$$w \cdot \phi(x, y) = w \cdot \sum_{l=1}^{L} \phi_l(x, y) \quad \textit{decomposition of structure}$$

$$= \sum_{l=1}^{L} w . \phi_l(x, y) \quad \textit{associative law}$$

What this means is that we can build a graph like that in Figure?, with one verticle slice per time step $(l\,1 \ldots L)$. Each edge in this graph will receive a weight, constructed in such a way that if you take a complete path through the lattice, and add up all the weights, this will correspond exactly to $w . \phi(x, y)$.

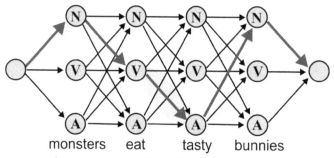

monsters　　eat　　tasty　　bunnies

Figure: A picture of a trellis sequence labeling

To complete the construction, let $\phi_l(x, \cdots \circ y \circ y')$ denote the unary features at position l together with the Markov features that end at position l. These features depend only on x, y and y', and not any of the previous parts of the output.

At each time step l the corresponding word can have any of the three possible labels. Any path through this trellis corresponds to a unique labeling of this sentence. The gold standard path is drawn with bold red arrows. The highlighted edge corresponds to the edge between and for verb/adj as described in the text. That edge has weight $w \cdot \phi_3(x, \cdots \circ verb \circ adj)$.

For example, in the running example "monsters/noun eat/verb tasty/adj bunnies/noun", consider the edge between $l = 2$ and $l = 3$ going from "verb" to "adj". (Note: this is a "correct" edge, in the sense that it belongs to the ground truth output.) The features associated with this edge will be unary features about "tasty/adj" as well as Markov features about "verb/adj". The weight of this edge will be exactly the total score (according to w) of those features.

Formally, consider an edge in the trellis that goes from time $l-1$ to l, and transitions from y to y'. Set the weight of this edge to exactly $w \cdot \phi_l(x, \cdots \circ y \circ y')$. By doing so, we guarantee that the sum of weights along any path through this lattice is exactly equal to the score of that path. Once we have constructed the graph as such, we can run any max-weight path algorithm to compute the highest scoring output. For trellises, this can be computed by the Viterbi algorithm, or by applying any of a number of path finding algorithms for more general graphs. A complete derivation of the dynamic program in this case is given in topic. for those who want to implement it directly.

The main benefit of this construction is that it is guaranteed to exactly compute the argmax output for sequences required in the structured perceptron algorithm, efficiently. In particular, it's run time is $O(LK^2)$, which is an exponential improvement on the naive) $O(K^L)$ runtime if one were to enumerate every possible output sequence. The algorithm can be naturally extended to handle "higher order" Markov assumptions, where features depend on triples or quadruples of the output. The trellis becomes larger, but the algorithm remains essentially the same. In order to handle a length M Markov features, the resulting algorithm will take $O(LK^M)$ time. In practice, it's rare that M > 3 is necessary or useful.

Support Vector Machine

A Support Vector Machine (SVM) is a supervised machine learning algorithm that can be employed for both classification and regression purposes. SVMs are more commonly used in classification problems and as such, this is what we will focus on in this post.

SVMs are based on the idea of finding a hyperplane that best divides a dataset into two classes, as shown in the image below.

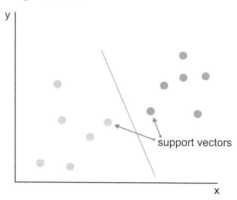

Support Vectors

Support vectors are the data points nearest to the hyperplane, the points of a data set that, if removed, would alter the position of the dividing hyperplane. Because of this, they can be considered the critical elements of a data set.

Maximal-Margin Classifier

The Maximal-Margin Classifier is a hypothetical classifier that best explains how SVM works in practice.

The numeric input variables (x) in your data (the columns) form an n-dimensional space. For example, if you had two input variables, this would form a two-dimensional space.

A hyperplane is a line that splits the input variable space. In SVM, a hyperplane is selected to best separate the points in the input variable space by their class, either class 0 or class 1. In two-dimensions you can visualize this as a line and let's assume that all of our input points can be completely separated by this line. For example:

$$B0 + (B1 * X1) + (B2 * X2) = 0$$

Where the coefficients (B1 and B2) that determine the slope of the line and the intercept (B0) are found by the learning algorithm, and X1 and X2 are the two input variables.

You can make classifications using this line. By plugging in input values into the line equation, you can calculate whether a new point is above or below the line.

- Above the line, the equation returns a value greater than 0 and the point belongs to the first class (class 0).

- Below the line, the equation returns a value less than 0 and the point belongs to the second class (class 1).

- A value close to the line returns a value close to zero and the point may be difficult to classify.

- If the magnitude of the value is large, the model may have more confidence in the prediction.

The distance between the line and the closest data points is referred to as the margin. The best or optimal line that can separate the two classes is the line that as the largest margin. This is called the Maximal-Margin hyperplane.

The margin is calculated as the perpendicular distance from the line to only the closest points. Only these points are relevant in defining the line and in the construction of the classifier. These points are called the support vectors. They support or define the hyperplane.

The hyperplane is learned from training data using an optimization procedure that maximizes the margin.

Soft Margin Classifier

In practice, real data is messy and cannot be separated perfectly with a hyperplane.

The constraint of maximizing the margin of the line that separates the classes must be relaxed. This is often called the soft margin classifier. This change allows some points in the training data to violate the separating line.

An additional set of coefficients are introduced that give the margin wiggle room in each dimension. These coefficients are sometimes called slack variables. This increases the complexity of the model as there are more parameters for the model to fit to the data to provide this complexity.

A tuning parameter is introduced called simply C that defines the magnitude of the wiggle allowed across all dimensions. The C parameters defines the amount of violation of the margin allowed. A C=0 is no violation and we are back to the inflexible Maximal-Margin Classifier described above. The larger the value of C the more violations of the hyperplane are permitted.

During the learning of the hyperplane from data, all training instances that lie within the distance of the margin will affect the placement of the hyperplane and are referred to as support vectors. And as C affects the number of instances that are allowed to fall within the margin, C influences the number of support vectors used by the model.

- The smaller the value of C, the more sensitive the algorithm is to the training data (higher variance and lower bias).

- The larger the value of C, the less sensitive the algorithm is to the training data (lower variance and higher bias).

Nonlinear Classification

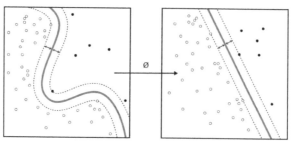

Kernel machine

The original maximum-margin hyperplane algorithm proposed by Vapnik in 1963 constructed a linear classifier. However, in 1992, Bernhard E. Boser, Isabelle M. Guyon and Vladimir N. Vapnik suggested a way to create nonlinear classifiers by applying the kernel trick (originally proposed by Aizerman) to maximum-margin hyperplanes. The resulting algorithm is formally similar, except that every dot product is replaced by a nonlinear kernel function. This allows the algorithm to fit the maximum-margin hyperplane in a transformed feature space. The transformation may be nonlinear and the transformed space high dimensional; although the classifier is a hyperplane in the transformed feature space, it may be nonlinear in the original input space.

It is noteworthy that working in a higher-dimensional feature space increases the generalization error of support vector machines, although given enough samples the algorithm still performs well.

Some common kernels include:

- Polynomial (homogeneous): $k(\overrightarrow{x_i}, \overrightarrow{x_j}) = (\overrightarrow{x_i} \cdot \overrightarrow{x_j})^d$.

- Polynomial (inhomogeneous): $k(\overrightarrow{x_i}, \overrightarrow{x_j}) = (\overrightarrow{x_i} \cdot \overrightarrow{x_j} + 1)^d$.

- Gaussian radial basis function: $k(\overrightarrow{x_i}, \overrightarrow{x_j}) = \exp(-\gamma \setminus \overrightarrow{x_i} - \overrightarrow{x_j} \setminus^2)$, for $\gamma > 0$. Sometimes parametrized using $\gamma = 1/2\sigma^2$.

- Hyperbolic tangent: $k(\overrightarrow{x_i}, \overrightarrow{x_j}) = \tanh(\kappa \overrightarrow{x_i} \cdot \overrightarrow{x_j} + c)$, for some (not every) $\kappa > 0$ and $c < 0$.

The kernel is related to the transform $\varphi(\overrightarrow{x_i})$ by the equation $k(\overrightarrow{x_i}, \overrightarrow{x_j}) = \varphi(\overrightarrow{x_i}) \cdot \varphi(\overrightarrow{x_j})$. The value w is also in the transformed space, with $\vec{w} = \sum_i \alpha_i y_i \varphi(\vec{x_i})$. Dot products with w for classification can again be computed by the kernel trick, i.e. $\vec{w} \cdot \varphi(\vec{x}) = \sum_i \alpha_i y_i k(\vec{x_i}, \vec{x})$.

Computing the SVM Classifier

Computing the (soft-margin) SVM classifier amounts to minimizing an expression of the form

$$\left[\frac{1}{n}\sum_{i=1}^{n}\max\left(0,1-y_i(w\cdot x_i-b)\right)\right]+\lambda\|w\|^2.$$

We focus on the soft-margin classifier since, as noted above, choosing a sufficiently small value for yields the hard-margin classifier for linearly classifiable input data. The classical approach, which involves reducing equation above to a quadratic programming problem.

Primal

Minimizing can be rewritten as a constrained optimization problem with a differentiable objective function in the following way.

For each $i \in \{1,\ldots,n\}$ we introduce a variable $\zeta_i = \max\left(0,1-y_i(w\cdot x_i-b)\right)$. Note that ζ_i is the smallest nonnegative number satisfying $y_i(w\cdot x_i-b)\geq 1-\zeta_i$.

Thus we can rewrite the optimization problem as follows

$$\text{minimize } \frac{1}{n}\sum_{i=1}^{n}\zeta_i+\lambda\backslash w\backslash^2$$

$$\text{subject to } y_i(w\cdot x_i-b)\geq 1-\zeta_i \text{ and } \zeta_i \geq 0, \text{for all } i.$$

This is called the *primal* problem.

Dual

By solving for the Lagrangian dual of the above problem, one obtains the simplified problem

$$\text{maximize } f(c_1\ldots c_n)=\sum_{i=1}^{n}c_i-\frac{1}{2}\sum_{i=1}^{n}\sum_{j=1}^{n}y_ic_i(x_i\cdot x_j)y_jc_j,$$

$$\text{subject to } \sum_{i=1}^{n}c_iy_i=0, \text{and } 0\leq c_i \leq \frac{1}{2n\lambda} \text{ for all } i.$$

This is called the *dual* problem. Since the dual maximization problem is a quadratic function of the c_i subject to linear constraints, it is efficiently solvable by quadratic programming algorithms.

Here, the variables c_i are defined such that

$$\vec{w}=\sum_{i=1}^{n}c_iy_i\vec{x}_i.$$

Moreover, $c_i = 0$ exactly when $\vec{x}_i$ lies on the correct side of the margin, and $0 < c_i < (2n\lambda)^{-1}$ when $\vec{x}_i$ lies on the margin's boundary. It follows that $\vec{w}$ can be written as a linear combination of the support vectors.

The offset, b can be recovered by finding an $\vec{x}_i$ on the margin's boundary and solving

$$y_i(\vec{w} \cdot \vec{x}_i - b) = 1 \Leftrightarrow b = \vec{w} \cdot \vec{x}_i - y_i.$$

(Note that $y_i^{-1} = y_i$ since $y_i = \pm 1$).

Kernel Trick

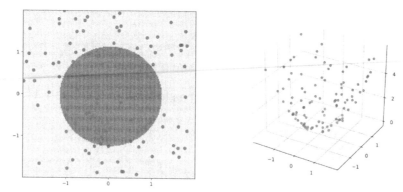

A training example of SVM with kernel given by $\varphi((a, b)) = (a, b, a^2 + b^2)$.

Suppose now that we would like to learn a nonlinear classification rule which corresponds to a linear classification rule for the transformed data points $\varphi(\vec{x}_i)$ Moreover, we are given a kernel function k which satisfies $k(\vec{x}_i, \vec{x}_j) = \varphi(\vec{x}_i) \cdot \varphi(\vec{x}_j)$.

We know the classification vector $\vec{w}$ in the transformed space satisfies

$$\vec{w} = \sum_{i=1}^{n} c_i y_i \varphi(\vec{x}_i),$$

where the c_i are obtained by solving the optimization problem

$$\text{maximize } f(c_1 \ldots c_n) = \sum_{i=1}^{n} c_i - \frac{1}{2} \sum_{i=1}^{n} \sum_{j=1}^{n} y_i c_i (\varphi(\vec{x}_i) \cdot \varphi(\vec{x}_j)) y_j c_j$$

$$= \sum_{i=1}^{n} c_i - \frac{1}{2} \sum_{i=1}^{n} \sum_{j=1}^{n} y_i c_i k(\vec{x}_i, \vec{x}_j) y_j c_j$$

$$\text{subject to } \sum_{i=1}^{n} c_i y_i = 0 \text{ and } 0 \le c_i \le \frac{1}{2n\lambda} \text{ for all } i.$$

The coefficients c_i can be solved for using quadratic programming, as before. Again, we can find some index i such that $0 < c_i < (2n\lambda)^{-1}$, so that $\varphi(\vec{x}_i)$ lies on the boundary of the margin in the transformed space, and then solve

$$b = \vec{w} \cdot \varphi(\vec{x}_i) - y_i = \left[\sum_{k=1}^{n} c_k y_k \varphi(\vec{x}_k) \cdot \varphi(\vec{x}_i) \right] - y_i$$

$$= \left[\sum_{k=1}^{n} c_k y_k k(\vec{x}_k, \vec{x}_i) \right] - y_i.$$

Finally, new points can be classified by computing

$$\vec{z} \mapsto \operatorname{sgn}(\vec{w} \cdot \varphi(\vec{z}) - b) = \operatorname{sgn}\left(\left[\sum_{i=1}^{n} c_i y_i k(\vec{x}_i, \vec{z}) \right] - b \right).$$

Modern Methods

Recent algorithms for finding the SVM classifier include sub-gradient descent and coordinate descent. Both techniques have proven to offer significant advantages over the traditional approach when dealing with large, sparse datasets—sub-gradient methods are especially efficient when there are many training examples, and coordinate descent when the dimension of the feature space is high.

Sub-gradient Descent

Sub-gradient descent algorithms for the SVM work directly with the expression

$$f(\vec{w}, b) = \left[\frac{1}{n} \sum_{i=1}^{n} \max\left(0, 1 - y_i (w \cdot x_i - b) \right) \right] + \lambda \setminus w \setminus^2 .$$

Note that f is a convex function of $\vec{w}$ and b. As such, traditional gradient descent (or SGD) methods can be adapted, where instead of taking a step in the direction of the functions gradient, a step is taken in the direction of a vector selected from the function's sub-gradient. This approach has the advantage that, for certain implementations, the number of iterations does not scale with n, the number of data points.

Coordinate Descent

Coordinate descent algorithms for the SVM work from the dual problem

$$\text{maximize } f(c_1 \ldots c_n) = \sum_{i=1}^{n} c_i - \frac{1}{2} \sum_{i=1}^{n} \sum_{j=1}^{n} y_i c_i (x_i \cdot x_j) y_j c_j,$$

$$\text{subject to } \sum_{i=1}^{n} c_i y_i = 0 \text{ and } 0 \le c_i \le \frac{1}{2n\lambda} \text{ for all } i.$$

For each $i \in \{1, \ldots, n\}$, iteratively, the coefficient c_i is adjusted in the direction of $\partial f / \partial c_i$. Then, the resulting vector of coefficients $(c_{1'}, \ldots, c_{n'})$ is projected onto the nearest vector of coefficients that satisfies the given constraints. (Typically Euclidean distances are used). The process is then repeated until a near-optimal vector of coefficients is obtained. The resulting algorithm is extremely fast in practice, although few performance guarantees have been proven.

Empirical Risk Minimization

The soft-margin support vector machine described above is an example of an empirical risk minimization (ERM) algorithm for the *hinge loss*. Seen this way, support vector machines belong to a natural class of algorithms for statistical inference, and many of its unique features are due to the behavior of the hinge loss. This perspective can provide further insight into how and why SVMs work, and allow us to better analyze their statistical properties.

Risk Minimization

In supervised learning, one is given a set of training examples $X_1 \ldots X_n$ with labels $y_1 \ldots y$, and wishes to predict y_{n+1} given X_{n+1}. To do so one forms a hypothesis, f, such that $f(X_{n+1})$ is a "good" approximation of y_{n+1}. A "good" approximation is usually defined with the help of a *loss function,* $\ell(y,z)$, which characterizes how bad z is as a prediction of y. We would then like to choose a hypothesis that minimizes the *expected risk:*

$$\varepsilon(f) = \mathbb{E}\big[\ell(y_{n+1}, f(X_{n+1}))\big].$$

In most cases, we don't know the joint distribution of X_{n+1}, y_{n+1} outright. In these cases, a common strategy is to choose the hypothesis that minimizes the *empirical risk:*

$$\hat{\varepsilon}(f) = \frac{1}{n} \sum_{k=1}^{n} \ell(y_k, f(X_k)).$$

Under certain assumptions about the sequence of random variables X_k, y_k (for example, that they are generated by a finite Markov process), if the set of hypotheses being considered is small enough, the minimizer of the empirical risk will closely approximate the minimizer of the expected risk as   grows large. This approach is called *empirical risk minimization,* or ERM.

Regularization and Stability

In order for the minimization problem to have a well-defined solution, we have to place constraints on the set $\mathcal{H}$ of hypotheses being considered. If $\mathcal{H}$ is a normed space (as is the case for SVM), a particularly effective technique is to consider only those hypotheses f for which $\|f\|_{\mathcal{H}} < k$. This is equivalent to imposing a *regularization penalty* $\mathcal{R}(f) = \lambda_k \|f\|_{\mathcal{H}}$ and solving the new optimization problem;

$$\hat{f} = \arg\min_{f \in \mathcal{H}} \hat{\varepsilon}(f) + \mathcal{R}(f)$$

This approach is called *Tikhonov regularization*.

More generally, $\mathcal{R}(f)$ can be some measure of the complexity of the hypothesis f, so that simpler hypotheses are preferred.

SVM and the Hinge Loss

Recall that the (soft-margin) SVM classifier $\hat{w}, b : x \mapsto \text{sgn}(\hat{w} \cdot x - b)$ is chosen to minimize the following expression:

$$\left[\frac{1}{n} \sum_{i=1}^{n} \max\big(0, 1 - y_i(w \cdot x_i - b)\big) \right] + \lambda \|w\|^2 .$$

In light of the above discussion, we see that the SVM technique is equivalent to empirical risk minimization with Tikhonov regularization, where in this case the loss function is the hinge loss

$$\ell(y, z) = \max\big(0, 1 - yz\big) .$$

From this perspective, SVM is closely related to other fundamental classification algorithms such as regularized least-squares and logistic regression. The difference between the three lies in the choice of loss function: regularized least-squares amounts to empirical risk minimization with the square-loss, $\ell_{sq}(y, z) = (y - z)^2$; logistic regression employs the log-loss,

$$\ell_{\log}(y, z) = \ln(1 + e^{-yz})$$

Target Functions

The difference between the hinge loss and these other loss functions is best stated in terms of *target functions* - the function that minimizes expected risk for a given pair of random variables X, y.

In particular, let y_x denote y conditional on the event that $X = x$. In the classification setting, we have:

$$y_x = \begin{cases} 1 & \text{with probability } p_x \\ -1 & \text{with probability } 1 - p_x \end{cases}$$

The optimal classifier is therefore:

$$f(x) \begin{cases} 1 & \text{if } \geq 1/2 \\ 1 & \text{otherwise} \end{cases}$$

For the square-loss, the target function is the conditional expectation function, $f_{sq}(x) = \mathbb{E}[y_x]$. For the logistic loss, it's the logit function, $f_{\log}(x) = \ln(p_x / (1 - p_x))$. While both of these target functions yield the correct classifier, as $\text{sgn}(f_{sq}) = \text{sgn}(f_{\log}) = f^*$, they give us more information than we need. In fact, they give us enough information to completely describe the distribution of y_x.

On the other hand, one can check that the target function for the hinge loss is *exactly* f^*. Thus, in a sufficiently rich hypothesis space—or equivalently, for an appropriately chosen kernel—the SVM classifier will converge to the simplest function (in terms of $\mathcal{R}$) that correctly classifies the data. This extends the geometric interpretation of SVM—for linear classification, the empirical risk is minimized by any function whose margins lie between the support vectors, and the simplest of these is the max-margin classifier.

Properties

SVMs belong to a family of generalized linear classifiers and can be interpreted as an extension of the perceptron. They can also be considered a special case of Tikhonov regularization. A special property is that they simultaneously minimize the empirical *classification error* and maximize the *geometric margin*; hence they are also known as maximum margin classifiers.

A comparison of the SVM to other classifiers has been made by Meyer, Leisch and Hornik.

Parameter Selection

The effectiveness of SVM depends on the selection of kernel, the kernel's parameters, and soft margin parameter C. A common choice is a Gaussian kernel, which has a single parameter γ. The best combination of C and γ is often selected by a grid search with exponentially growing sequences of C and γ, for example, $C \in \{2^{-5}, 2^{-3}, ..., 2^{13}, 2^{15}\}$; $\gamma \in \{2^{-15}, 2^{-13}, ..., 2^1, 2^3\}$. Typically, each combination of parameter choices is checked using cross validation, and the parameters with best cross-validation accuracy are picked. Alternatively, recent work in Bayesian optimization can be used to select C and γ, often requiring the evaluation of far fewer parameter combinations than grid search. The final model, which is used for testing and for classifying new data, is then trained on the whole training set using the selected parameters.

Issues

Potential drawbacks of the SVM include the following aspects:

- Requires full labeling of input data.

- Uncalibrated class membership probabilities - SVM stems from Vapnik's theory which avoids estimating probabilities on finite data.

- The SVM is only directly applicable for two-class tasks. Therefore, algorithms that reduce the multi-class task to several binary problems have to be applied.

- Parameters of a solved model are difficult to interpret.

Extensions

Support Vector Clustering (SVC)

SVC is a similar method that also builds on kernel functions but is appropriate for unsupervised learning. It is considered a fundamental method in data science.

Multiclass SVM

Multiclass SVM aims to assign labels to instances by using support vector machines, where the labels are drawn from a finite set of several elements.

The dominant approach for doing so is to reduce the single multiclass problem into multiple binary classification problems. Common methods for such reduction include:

- Building binary classifiers which distinguish (i) between one of the labels and the rest (*one-versus-all*) or (ii) between every pair of classes (*one-versus-one*). Classification of new instances for the one-versus-all case is done by a winner-takes-all strategy, in which the classifier with the highest output function assigns the class (it is important that the output functions be calibrated to produce comparable scores). For the one-versus-one approach, classification is done by a max-wins voting strategy, in which every classifier assigns the instance to one of the two classes, then the vote for the assigned class is increased by one vote, and finally the class with the most votes determines the instance classification.

- Directed acyclic graph SVM (DAGSVM).

- Error-correcting output codes.

Crammer and Singer proposed a multiclass SVM method which casts the multiclass classification problem into a single optimization problem, rather than decomposing it into multiple binary classification problems.

Transductive Support Vector Machines

Transductive support vector machines extend SVMs in that they could also treat partially labeled data in semi-supervised learning by following the principles of transduction. Here, in addition to the training set $\mathcal{D}$, the learner is also given a set

$$\mathcal{D}^\star = \{\vec{x}_i^\star \mid \vec{x}_i^\star \in \mathbb{R}^p\}_{i=1}^k$$

of test examples to be classified. Formally, a transductive support vector machine is defined by the following primal optimization problem:

Minimize (in $\vec{w}, b, \vec{y^*}$)

$$\frac{1}{2} \backslash \vec{w} \backslash^2$$

subject to (for any $i = 1, \ldots, n$ and any $j = 1, \ldots, k$)

$$y_i(\vec{w} \cdot \vec{x_i} - b) \geq 1,$$

$$y_j^*(\vec{w} \cdot \vec{x_j^*} - b) \geq 1$$

and

$$y_j^* \in \{-1, 1\}$$

Transductive support vector machines were introduced by Vladimir N. Vapnik.

Structured SVM

SVMs have been generalized to structured SVMs, where the label space is structured and of possibly infinite size.

Regression

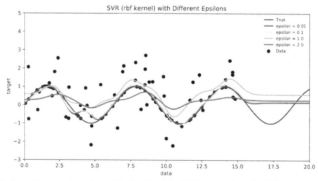

Support Vector Regression (prediction) with different thresholds ε. As ε increases, the prediction becomes less sensitive to errors.

A version of SVM for regression was proposed in 1996 by Vladimir N. Vapnik, Harris Drucker, Christopher J. C. Burges, Linda Kaufman and Alexander J. Smola. This method is called support vector regression (SVR). The model produced by support vector classification (as described above) depends only on a subset of the training data, because the cost function for building the model does not care about training points that lie beyond the margin. Analogously, the model produced by SVR depends only on a subset of the training data, because the cost function for building the model ignores any training data close to the model prediction. Another SVM version known as least squares support vector machine (LS-SVM) has been proposed by Suykens and Vandewalle.

Training the original SVR means solving

$$\text{minimize } \frac{1}{2}\backslash w\backslash^2$$

$$\text{subject to } \begin{cases} y_i - \langle w, x_i \rangle - b \le \varepsilon \\ \langle w, x_i \rangle + b - y_i \le \varepsilon \end{cases}$$

where x_i is a training sample with target value y_i. The inner product plus intercept $\langle w, x_i \rangle + b$ is the prediction for that sample, and ε is a free parameter that serves as a threshold: all predictions have to be within an ε range of the true predictions. Slack variables are usually added into the above to allow for errors and to allow approximation in the case the above problem is infeasible.

Bayesian SVM

In 2011 it was shown by Polson and Scott that the SVM admits a Bayesian interpretation through the technique of data augmentation. In this approach the SVM is viewed as a graphical model (where the parameters are connected via probability distributions). This extended view allows for the application of Bayesian techniques to SVMs, such as flexible feature modeling, automatic hyperparameter tuning, and predictive uncertainty quantification. Recently, a scalable version of the Bayesian SVM was developed by Wenzel et al. enabling the application of Bayesian SVMs to big data.

Advantages and Disadvantages of SVMs

As a classification technique, the SVM has many advantages, many of which are due to its computational efficiency on large datasets.

Advantages

- High-Dimensionality - The SVM is an effective tool in high-dimensional spaces, which is particularly applicable to document classification and sentiment analysis where the dimensionality can be extremely large ($\ge 106 \ge 106$).

- Memory Efficiency - Since only a subset of the training points are used in the actual decision process of assigning new members, only these points need to be stored in memory (and calculated upon) when making decisions.

- Versatility - Class separation is often highly non-linear. The ability to apply new kernels allows substantial flexibility for the decision boundaries, leading to greater classification performance.

Disadvantages

- p>np>n - In situations where the number of features for each object (pp) exceeds the number of training data samples (nn), SVMs can perform poorly. This can be seen intuitively, as if the high-dimensional feature space is much larger than the samples, then there are less effective support vectors on which to support the optimal linear hyperplanes, leading to poorer classification performance as new unseen samples are added.

- Non-Probabilistic - Since the classifier works by placing objects above and below a classifying hyperplane, there is no direct probabilistic interpretation for group membership. However, one potential metric to determine "effectiveness" of the classification is how far from the decision boundary the new point is.

References

- Belsley, David (1991). Conditioning diagnostics : collinearity and weak data in regression. New York: Wiley. ISBN 978-0471528890

- Regression-classification-supervised-machine-learning: geeksforgeeks.org, Retrieved 15 May 2018

- M. Belkin; P. Niyogi (2004). "Semi-supervised Learning on Riemannian Manifolds". Machine Learning. 56 (Special Issue on Clustering): 209–239. doi:10.1023/b:mach.0000033120.25363.1e

- Supervised-learning-machine-learning-workflow-and-algorithms: mathworks.com, Retrieved 19 July 2018

- Shakhnarovich, Greg (2011). "Notes on derivation of bias-variance decomposition in linear regression" (PDF). Archived from the original (PDF) on 21 August 2014. Retrieved 20 August 2014

- Support-vector-machines-simple-explanation: kdnuggets.com, Retrieved 15 April 2018

- Chechik, G.; Sharma, V.; Shalit, U.; Bengio, S. (2010). "Large Scale Online Learning of Image Similarity Through Ranking" (PDF). Journal of Machine Learning research. 11: 1109–1135

- Support-Vector-Machines-A-Guide-for-Beginners: quantstart.com, Retrieved 19 March 2018

- Chapelle, Olivier; Schölkopf, Bernhard; Zien, Alexander (2006). Semi-supervised learning. Cambridge, Mass.: MIT Press. ISBN 978-0-262-03358-9

Dimensionality Reduction

In machine learning, any reduction in the number of random variables through obtaining a set of principal variables is known as dimensionality reduction. The aim of this chapter is to explore the fundamentals of dimensionality reduction, such as feature extraction, independent component analysis, feature selection, principal component analysis, etc.

Dimensionality reduction is a series of techniques in machine learning and statistics to reduce the number of random variables to consider. It involves feature selection and feature extraction. Dimensionality reduction makes analyzing data much easier and faster for machine learning algorithms without extraneous variables to process, making machine learning algorithms faster and simpler in turn.

Feature selection techniques find a smaller subset of a many-dimensional data set to create a data model. The major strategies for feature set are filter, wrapper (using a predictive model) and embedded, which perform feature selection while building a model.

Feature extraction involves transforming high-dimensional data into spaces of fewer dimensions. Methods include principal component analysis, kernel PCA, graph-based kernel PCA, and linear discriminant analysis and generalized discriminant analysis.

Importance of Dimensionality Reduction in Machine Learning and Predictive Modeling

An intuitive example of dimensionality reduction can be discussed through a simple e-mail classification problem, where we need to classify whether the e-mail is spam or not. This can involve a large number of features, such as whether or not the e-mail has a generic title, the content of the e-mail, whether the e-mail uses a template, etc. However, some of these features may overlap. In another condition, a classification problem that relies on both humidity and rainfall can be collapsed into just one underlying feature, since both of the aforementioned are correlated to a high degree. Hence, we can reduce the number of features in such problems. A 3-D classification problem can be hard to visualize, whereas a 2-D one can be mapped to a simple 2 dimensional space, and a 1-D problem to a simple line. The below figure illustrates this concept, where a 3-D feature space is split into two 1-D feature spaces, and later, if found to be correlated, the number of features can be reduced even further.

Dimensionality Reduction

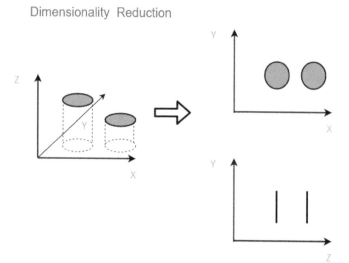

Components of Dimensionality Reduction

There are two components of dimensionality reduction:

- Feature selection: In this, we try to find a subset of the original set of variables, or features, to get a smaller subset, which can be used to model the problem. It usually involves three ways:

    1. Filter

    2. Wrapper

    3. Embedded

- Feature extraction: This reduces the data in a high dimensional space to a lower dimension space, i.e. a space with lesser no. of dimensions.

Methods of Dimensionality Reduction

The various methods used for dimensionality reduction include:

- Principal Component Analysis (PCA).

- Linear Discriminant Analysis (LDA).

- Generalized Discriminant Analysis (GDA).

Dimensionality reduction may be both linear and non-linear, depending upon the method used. The prime linear method called Principal Component Analysis, or PCA.

Principal Component Analysis

This method was introduced by Karl Pearson. It works on a condition that while the data in a higher dimensional space is mapped to data in a lower dimension space, the variance of the data in the lower dimensional space should be maximum.

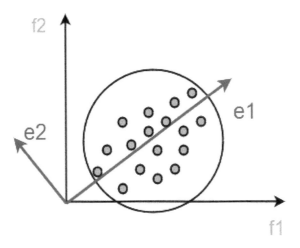

It involves the following steps:

- Construct the covariance matrix of the data.
- Compute the eigenvectors of this matrix.
- Eigenvectors corresponding to the largest eigenvalues are used to reconstruct a large fraction of variance of the original data.

Hence, we are left with a lesser number of eigenvectors, and there might have been some data loss in the process. But, the most important variances should be retained by the remaining eigenvectors.

Advantages of Dimensionality Reduction

- It helps in data compression, and hence reduced storage space.
- It reduces computation time.
- It also helps remove redundant features, if any.

Disadvantages of Dimensionality Reduction

- It may lead to some amount of data loss.
- PCA tends to find linear correlations between variables, which is sometimes undesirable.
- PCA fails in cases where mean and covariance are not enough to define datasets.
- We may not know how many principal components to keep in practice, some thumb rules are applied.

Feature Extraction

Feature extraction a type of dimensionality reduction that efficiently represents interesting parts of an image as a compact feature vector. This approach is useful when image sizes are large and a reduced feature representation is required to quickly complete tasks such as image matching and retrieval.

Examples of Feature Extraction Techniques

Image processing basics

A linear filter has the property that any pixel of the filtered image can be expressed as a weighted sum of the original image's pixels. A subclass of these filters (that is easily enough for our purposes) uses a weighted sum to map from only neighboring pixels to a new filtered pixel. Let $I : \mathbb{Z}^2 \to \mathbb{R}, I(x,y) \mapsto c_{x,y} \in \mathbb{R}$ be a gray scale image. Then F as in

$$(F(I))(x,y) = \sum_{-1 \le i \le 1} \sum_{-1 \le i \le 1} \omega_{i,j} \cdot I(x+i, y=j) =$$

$$\omega_{-1,1} \cdot I(x-1, y+1) + \omega_{0,1} \cdot I(x, y+1) + \omega_{-1,-1} \cdot I(x+1, y+1) + \omega_{-1,0} \cdot I(x-1, y) + \omega_{-1,0} \cdot I(x,y) +$$

$$+ \omega_{1,0} \cdot I(x+1, y) + \omega_{-1,-1} \cdot I(x-1, y-1) + \omega_{0,-1} \cdot I(x, y-1) + \omega_{1,-1} \cdot I(x, y-1)$$

describes a linear filter that takes into consideration only a 3 × 3 neighborhood of any pixel (x, y). It is obvious that this type of filter is fully described by a 3 × 3 matrix A of the weights $\omega_{i,j}$:

$$A = \begin{pmatrix} \omega_{-1,1} & \omega_{0,1} & \omega_{1,1} \\ \omega_{-1,0} & \omega_{0,0} & \omega_{1,0} \\ \omega_{-1,-1} & \omega_{0,-1} & \omega_{1,-1} \end{pmatrix}$$

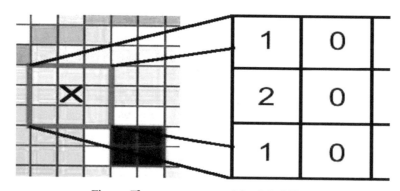

Figure: The x-component of the Sobel filter

From for an $n \times m$ image x and y would have to be in a range of $\{0, 1...n - 1\}$ and $\{0, 1...m - 1\}$ respectively. Thus for border pixels the kernel could not be applied as

$(-1, y)$ and $(x, -1)$ as well was (n, y) and (x, m) are out of range. The solution is to either drop the border pixels, clamp x and y to image dimensions or "wrap" the image (eg. Define $I(-1, y) := I(n - 1, y)$ y accordingly).

As you can see the nine neighboring pixels are convoluted to form the "new" filtered pixel. This type of filter is called convolution (or kernel) filter and A it's convolution kernel. Filters that do not change the "brightness" of the image are subject to $\sum_{-1\le i\le 1} \sum_{-1\le j\le 1} \omega_{i,j} = 1$. The filter shown in figure is an edge filter. In figure you can see the result of applying this filter to the Lena image. For better visibility the image is added to a 50% gray image. Analogously, of course, one can use 5×5 or 7×7 kernels.

Figure: Application of the convolution filter

Sobel Edge Detection

A pixel is at an edge when intensity sharply changes to its neighbors. The edge itself is a linear shape along which that change is maximal. Looking at images as functions of intensity, we can rephrase this property to "a maximum of the first derivative". On the level of pixels we have a discrete input $t (x, y) \in \mathbb{Z}$ and we can use the discrete differential operator to approximate the first derivative in either direction. For x that is

$$(\delta_x(I)) (x, y) = I(x, y) - I(x + 1, y)$$

thus the kernel filter

$$E'_x = \begin{pmatrix} 0 & 0 & 0 \\ -1 & 1 & 0 \\ 0 & 0 & 0 \end{pmatrix}$$

This is already the simplest edge detector, as the minima and maxima in the filtered image ("darkest and brightest spots") are edges. In Practice this Image filter is extremely sensitive to noise, though. Starting with E'_x we will now derive the Sobel operator, which cannnot be written as a convolution filter but is a nonlinear combination of such linear filters.

Firstly, to reduce noise we can blur the image using another linear filter 1. In order not to degrade the edges, we only blur the y-direction when we wish to find edges in x-direction (and vise versa). This can be done with the kernel.

$$BY = \frac{1}{4}\begin{pmatrix} 0 & 1 & 0 \\ 0 & 2 & 0 \\ 0 & 1 & 0 \end{pmatrix}$$. Now, the only difference of the Sobel edge detection along x to the concatenation of our two kernels is the slight change from E'_X to $E_X\begin{pmatrix} 0 & 0 & 0 \\ 1 & 0 & -1 \\ 0 & 0 & 0 \end{pmatrix}$. Obviously the concatenation of BY and E_X canbe written as a single kernel $S_X\begin{pmatrix} 1 & 0 & -1 \\ 2 & 0 & -1 \\ 1 & 0 & -2 \end{pmatrix}$.

Now let G_X and G_Y refer to images filtered using the kernels S and $S_X = S_X^T$ Usually, one is equally interested in edges of any direction. That's why the Sobel edge detector for any pixel (x, y) returns the euclidean norm of the vector of the intensities of G_X and G_Y sampled at (x, y). This is the magnitude of the gradient.

$$\left\| \left(G_X(x, y) \; G_Y(x, y) \right)^T \right\|^2 = \sqrt{G_X(x, y)^2 G_Y(x, y)^2}$$

For an edge point (x, y) the edge's direction Θ can be extracted by

$$\Theta = arctan\left(\frac{G_y}{G_x}\right)$$

Canny Edge Detection

Canny's intention was to create a perfect edge detector. Unlike Sobel, Canny extracts thin, clear edges. It works by a two step algorithm in which firstly an edge filter just like Sobel is applied and secondly a non-maxima suppression is applied to get thin lines that represent the edges. Be aware that Sobel considers 3 × 3 kernels and thus detects edges of that scale best. For Canny in a more general scheme, scale (or smoothing) is one parameter that critically influences the results. For a basic understanding it is enough to think of the first step as a simple Sobel filter though.

The second step is essential to obtain thin lines as edges. Starting from a point of greater gradient magnitude than a threshold value T_1, the algorithm follows a ridge, that's to say a path of local maxima perpendicular to the edge direction. Points that are not along that ridge are suppressed, the path itself is the final edge. The path stops as soon as the gradient magnitude falls below a second threshold T_2. The introduction of a second threshold was to avoid "dashed" edges where the edge's gradient magnitude is close to one threshold, noise would make it pass the threshold frequently. An Issue with the method as explained here, by the way, is that Y-junctions of edges are impossible, as only linear paths are followed. Where three edges meet in a point, two would connect and the third one would stop just before the actual junction because it is suppressed as the first two edges are tracked.

Figure: Canny applied to skyline scene

Of course feature extraction is not all about edges. There exits a manifold of different techniques. For instance, it is possible to find corners by a local analysis of small regions with two different dominant edges. Blob detectors

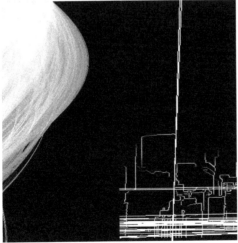

Figure: Hough transform of scene from figue and the 40% most prominent lines

look for local extrema in intensity rather than gradient. Another particularly different approach will be discussed in the next subsection.

Hough Transformation

The Idea of the hough transformation is to convert image space into a parameter space. This conversion is a mapping that analyses the image looking for a special sort of parameterized features usually lines or circles. It's beauty lies in the many different shapes that can be detected together with their parameters. In this seminar we are going to deal only with the special case of lines. Assuming the reader is familiar with the parametric representation $d = cos(\Theta) \cdot x + sin(\Theta) \cdot y$ of a line, where Θ is the angle between the line and the x-axis, d the distance to the origin and any $(x, y)^T$ which verifies the equation a point on that line, the Hough transformation for lines is a relatively simple construct.

The concept is to create a number of bins for lines of a certain range of their parameters s (d, Θ) to (d', Θ'). A bin is an accumulator cell for that range of parameters. For each edge point in image space we can assign a bin by taking the pixel position and gradient direction into account. Pixels along a straight edge all contribute to the same bin, because lines through these pixels of thier gradient direction all have about the same distance to the origin. The fullest bins represent the most prominent or "best" lines. Fot a better fit the parameters used for that line can for instance be computed as the mean parameters of all edge pixels that contributed to that bin.

Be aware that the number of bins used influence the minimum "difference" of two lines that are to be differed. Using too many bins "blurs" the maxima. Noise influences gradient information and pixels from the same original linear edge may fall into two neighboring bins when the bins are too small.

Feature Selection

Feature selection is also called variable selection or attribute selection. It is the automatic selection of attributes in your data (such as columns in tabular data) that are most relevant to the predictive modeling problem you are working on.

Feature selection is different from dimensionality reduction. Both methods seek to reduce the number of attributes in the dataset, but a dimensionality reduction method do so by creating new combinations of attributes, where as feature selection methods include and exclude attributes present in the data without changing them.

Examples of dimensionality reduction methods include Principal Component Analysis, Singular Value Decomposition and Sammon's Mapping.

The Problem Solved by Feature Selection

Feature selection methods aid you in your mission to create an accurate predictive model. They help you by choosing features that will give you as good or better accuracy whilst requiring less data.

Feature selection methods can be used to identify and remove unneeded, irrelevant and redundant attributes from data that do not contribute to the accuracy of a predictive model or may in fact decrease the accuracy of the model.

Fewer attributes is desirable because it reduces the complexity of the model, and a simpler model is simpler to understand and explain.

> The objective of variable selection is three-fold: improving the prediction performance of the predictors, providing faster and more cost-effective predictors, and providing a better understanding of the underlying process that generated the data.
>
> — Guyon and Elisseeff

Feature Selection Algorithms

There are three general classes of feature selection algorithms: filter methods, wrapper methods and embedded methods.

Filter Methods

Filter feature selection methods apply a statistical measure to assign a scoring to each feature. The features are ranked by the score and either selected to be kept or removed from the dataset. The methods are often univariate and consider the feature independently, or with regard to the dependent variable.

Some examples of some filter methods include the Chi squared test, information gain and correlation coefficient scores.

Wrapper Methods

Wrapper methods consider the selection of a set of features as a search problem, where different combinations are prepared, evaluated and compared to other combinations. A predictive model us used to evaluate a combination of features and assign a score based on model accuracy.

The search process may be methodical such as a best-first search, it may stochastic such as a random hill-climbing algorithm, or it may use heuristics, like forward and backward passes to add and remove features.

An example if a wrapper method is the recursive feature elimination algorithm.

Embedded Methods

Embedded methods learn which features best contribute to the accuracy of the model while the model is being created. The most common type of embedded feature selection methods are regularization methods.

Regularization methods are also called penalization methods that introduce additional constraints into the optimization of a predictive algorithm (such as a regression algorithm) that bias the model toward lower complexity (fewer coefficients).

Examples of regularization algorithms are the LASSO, Elastic Net and Ridge Regression.

Optimality Criteria

The choice of optimality criteria is difficult as there are multiple objectives in a feature selection task. Many common ones incorporate a measure of accuracy, penalised by the number of features selected (e.g. the Bayesian information criterion). The oldest are Mallows's C_p statistic and Akaike information criterion (AIC). These add variables if the t-statistic is bigger than $\sqrt{2}$.

Other criteria are Bayesian information criterion (BIC) which uses $\sqrt{\log n}$, minimum description length (MDL) which asymptotically uses $\sqrt{\log n}$, Bonferroni / RIC which use $\sqrt{2 \log p}$, maximum dependency feature selection, and a variety of new criteria that are motivated by false discovery rate (FDR) which use something close to $\sqrt{2 \log \frac{p}{q}}$. A maximum entropy rate criterion may also be used to select the most relevant subset of features.

Structure Learning

Filter feature selection is a specific case of a more general paradigm called Structure Learning. Feature selection finds the relevant feature set for a specific target variable whereas structure learning finds the relationships between all the variables, usually by expressing these relationships as a graph. The most common structure learning algorithms assume the data is generated by a Bayesian Network, and so the structure is a directed graphical model. The optimal solution to the filter feature selection problem is the Markov blanket of the target node, and in a Bayesian Network, there is a unique Markov Blanket for each node.

Minimum-redundancy-maximum-relevance (mRMR) Feature Selection

Peng *et al.* proposed a feature selection method that can use either mutual information, correlation, or distance/similarity scores to select features. The aim is to penalise a feature's relevancy by its redundancy in the presence of the other selected features. The relevance of a feature set S for the class c is defined by the average value of all mutual information values between the individual feature f_i and the class c as follows:

$$D(S,c) = \frac{1}{|S|} \sum_{f_i \in S} I(f_i; c).$$

The redundancy of all features in the set S is the average value of all mutual information values between the feature f_i and the feature f_j:

$$R(S) = \frac{1}{|S|^2} \sum_{f_i, f_j \in S} I(f_i; f_j)$$

The mRMR criterion is a combination of two measures given above and is defined as follows:

$$\text{mRMR} = \max_S \left[\frac{1}{|S|} \sum_{f_i \in S} I(f_i; c) - \frac{1}{|S|^2} \sum_{f_i, f_j \in S} I(f_i; f_j) \right].$$

Suppose that there are n full-set features. Let x_i be the set membership indicator function for feature f_i, so that $x_i = 1$ indicates presence and $x_i = 0$ indicates absence of the feature f_i in the globally optimal feature set. Let $c_i = I(f_i; c)$ and $a_{ij} = I(f_i; f_j)$. The above may then be written as an optimization problem:

$$\text{mRMR} = \max_{x \in \{0,1\}^n} \left[\frac{\sum_{i=1}^{n} c_i x_i}{\sum_{i=1}^{n} x_i} - \frac{\sum_{i,j=1}^{n} a_{ij} x_i x_j}{\left(\sum_{i=1}^{n} x_i \right)^2} \right].$$

The mRMR algorithm is an approximation of the theoretically optimal maximum-dependency feature selection algorithm that maximizes the mutual information between the joint distribution of the selected features and the classification variable. As mRMR approximates the combinatorial estimation problem with a series of much smaller problems, each of which only involves two variables, it thus uses pairwise joint probabilities which are more robust. In certain situations the algorithm may underestimate the usefulness of features as it has no way to measure interactions between features which can increase relevancy. This can lead to poor performance when the features are individually useless, but are useful when combined (a pathological case is found when the class is a parity function of the features). Overall the algorithm is more efficient (in terms of the amount of data required) than the theoretically optimal max-dependency selection, yet produces a feature set with little pairwise redundancy.

mRMR is an instance of a large class of filter methods which trade off between relevancy and redundancy in different ways.

Global Optimization Formulations

mRMR is a typical example of an incremental greedy strategy for feature selection: once a feature has been selected, it cannot be deselected at a later stage. While mRMR could be optimized using floating search to reduce some features, it might also be reformulated as a global quadratic programming optimization problem as follows:

$$\text{QPFS} : \min_{\mathbf{x}} \left\{ \alpha \mathbf{x}^T H \mathbf{x} - \mathbf{x}^T F \right\} \quad \text{s.t.} \sum_{i=1}^{n} x_i = 1, x_i \geq 0$$

where $F_{n \times 1} = [I(f_1;c),\dots,I(f_n;c)]^T$ is the vector of feature relevancy assuming there are n features in total, $H_{n \times n} = [I(f_i;f_j)]_{i,j=1\dots n}$ is the matrix of feature pairwise redundancy, and $\mathbf{x}_{n \times 1}$ represents relative feature weights. QPFS is solved via quadratic programming. It is recently shown that QFPS is biased towards features with smaller entropy, due to its placement of the feature self-redundancy term $I(f_i;f_i)$ on the diagonal of H.

Another global formulation for the mutual information based feature selection problem is based on the conditional relevancy:

$$\text{SPEC}_{\text{CMI}} : \max_{\mathbf{x}} \left\{ \mathbf{x}^T Q \mathbf{x} \right\} \quad \text{s.t.} \|\mathbf{x}\| = 1, x_i \geq 0$$

where

$$Q_{ii} = I(f_i;c) \text{ and } Q_{ij} = I(f_i;c \mid f_j), i \neq j.$$

An advantage of SPEC_{CMI} is that it can be solved simply via finding the dominant eigenvector of Q, thus is very scalable. SPEC_{CMI} also handles second-order feature interaction.

For high-dimensional and small sample data (e.g., dimensionality $> 10^5$ and the number of samples $< 10^3$), the Hilbert-Schmidt Independence Criterion Lasso (HSIC Lasso) is useful. HSIC Lasso optimization problem is given as:

$$\text{HSIC}_{\text{Lasso}} : \min_{\mathbf{x}} \frac{1}{2} \sum_{k,l=1}^{n} x_k x_l \text{HSIC}(f_k, f_l) - \sum_{k=1}^{n} x_k \text{HSIC}(f_k, c) + \lambda \|\mathbf{x}\|_1, \quad \text{s.t.} \ x_1,\dots,x_n \geq 0,$$

where $\text{HSIC}(f_k, c) = \text{tr}(\overline{\mathbf{K}}^{(k)} \overline{\mathbf{L}})$ is a kernel-based independence measure called the (empirical) Hilbert-Schmidt independence criterion (HSIC), $\text{tr}(\cdot)$ denotes the trace, λ is the regularization parameter, $\overline{\mathbf{K}}^{(k)} = \Gamma K^{(k)} \Gamma$ and $\overline{\mathbf{L}} = \Gamma L \Gamma$ are input and output centered Gram matrices, $K_{i,j}^{(k)} = K(u_{k,i}, u_{k,j})$ and $L_{i,j} = L(c_i, c_j)$ are Gram matrices, $K(u,u')$ and $L(c,c')$ are kernel functions, $\Gamma = I_m - \frac{1}{m} 1_m 1_m^T$ is the centering matrix, $\mathbf{I}_m$ is the m-dimensional identity matrix (m: the number of samples), $\mathbf{1}_m$ is the m-dimensional vector with all ones, and $\|\cdot\|_1$ is the ℓ_1-norm. HSIC always takes a non-negative value, and is zero if and only if two random variables are statistically independent when a universal reproducing kernel such as the Gaussian kernel is used.

The HSIC Lasso can be written as:

$$\text{HSIC}_{\text{Lasso}} : \min_{\mathbf{x}} \frac{1}{2} \left\| \overline{\mathbf{L}} - \sum_{k=1}^{n} x_k \overline{\mathbf{K}}^{(k)} \right\|_F^2 + \lambda \| \mathbf{x} \|_1, \quad \text{s.t. } x_1, \ldots, x_n \geq 0,$$

where $\| \cdot \|_F$ is the Frobenius norm. The optimization problem is a Lasso problem, and thus it can be efficiently solved with a state-of-the-art Lasso solver such as the dual augmented Lagrangian method.

Correlation Feature Selection

The Correlation Feature Selection (CFS) measure evaluates subsets of features on the basis of the following hypothesis: "Good feature subsets contain features highly correlated with the classification, yet uncorrelated to each other". The following equation gives the merit of a feature subset S consisting of k features:

$$\text{Merit}_{S_k} = \frac{k \overline{r_{cf}}}{\sqrt{k + k(k-1)\overline{r_{ff}}}}.$$

Here, $\overline{r_{cf}}$ is the average value of all feature-classification correlations, and $\overline{r_{ff}}$ is the average value of all feature-feature correlations. The CFS criterion is defined as follows:

$$\text{CFS} = \max_{S_k} \left[\frac{r_{cf_1} + r_{cf_2} + \cdots + r_{cf_k}}{\sqrt{k + 2(r_{f_1 f_2} + \cdots + r_{f_i f_j} + \cdots + r_{f_k f_1})}} \right].$$

The r_{cf_i} and $r_{f_i f_j}$ variables are referred to as correlations, but are not necessarily Pearson's correlation coefficient or Spearman's ρ. Dr. Mark Hall's dissertation uses neither of these, but uses three different measures of relatedness, minimum description length (MDL), symmetrical uncertainty, and relief.

Let x_i be the set membership indicator function for feature f_i; then the above can be rewritten as an optimization problem:

$$\text{CFS} = \max_{x \in \{0,1\}^n} \left[\frac{\left(\sum_{i=1}^{n} a_i x_i \right)^2}{\sum_{i=1}^{n} x_i + \sum_{i \neq j} 2 b_{ij} x_i x_j} \right].$$

The combinatorial problems above are, in fact, mixed 0–1 linear programming problems that can be solved by using branch-and-bound algorithms.

Regularized Trees

The features from a decision tree or a tree ensemble are shown to be redundant. A recent method called regularized tree can be used for feature subset selection. Regularized trees penalize using a variable similar to the variables selected at previous tree nodes for splitting the current node. Regularized trees only need build one tree model (or one tree ensemble model) and thus are computationally efficient.

Regularized trees naturally handle numerical and categorical features, interactions and nonlinearities. They are invariant to attribute scales (units) and insensitive to outliers, and thus, require little data preprocessing such as normalization. Regularized random forest (RRF) is one type of regularized trees. The guided RRF is an enhanced RRF which is guided by the importance scores from an ordinary random forest.

Linear Discriminant Analysis

Linear Discriminant Analysis (LDA) is most commonly used as dimensionality reduction technique in the pre-processing step for pattern-classification and machine learning applications. The goal is to project a dataset onto a lower-dimensional space with good class-separability in order avoid overfitting ("curse of dimensionality") and also reduce computational costs.

Ronald A. Fisher formulated the *Linear Discriminant* in 1936 and it also has some practical uses as classifier. The original linear discriminant was described for a 2-class problem, and it was then later generalized as "multi-class Linear Discriminant Analysis" or "Multiple Discriminant Analysis" by C. R. Rao in 1948.

The general LDA approach is very similar to a Principal Component Analysis but in addition to finding the component axes that maximize the variance of our data (PCA), we are additionally interested in the axes that maximize the separation between multiple classes (LDA).

So, in a nutshell, often the goal of an LDA is to project a feature space (a dataset n-dimensional samples) onto a smaller subspace kk (where k≤n−1k≤n−1) while maintaining the class-discriminatory information.

In general, dimensionality reduction does not only help reducing computational costs for a given classification task, but it can also be helpful to avoid overfitting by minimizing the error in parameter estimation ("curse of dimensionality").

LDA in 5 Steps

After we went through several preparation steps, our data is finally ready for the actual

LDA. In practice, LDA for dimensionality reduction would be just another preprocessing step for a typical machine learning or pattern classification task.

Step 1: Computing the d-dimensional mean vectors

In this first step, we will start off with a simple computation of the mean vectors $m_i, (i = 1,2,3)$ of the 3 different flower classes:

$$m_i \begin{bmatrix} \mu_{\omega i}(\text{sepal length}) \\ \mu_{\omega i}(\text{sepal width}) \\ \mu_{\omega i}(\text{petal length}) \\ \mu_{\omega i}(\text{petal width}) \end{bmatrix}, \text{with } i = 1,2,3$$

```
np.set_printoptions(precision=4)


mean_vectors = []
for cl in range(1,4):
    mean_vectors.append(np.mean(X[y==cl], axis=0))
    print('Mean Vector class %s: %s\n' %(cl, mean_vectors[cl-1]))
Mean Vector class 1: [ 5.006  3.418  1.464  0.244]


Mean Vector class 2: [ 5.936  2.77   4.26   1.326]


Mean Vector class 3: [ 6.588  2.974  5.552  2.026]
```

Step 2: Computing the Scatter Matrices

Now, we will compute the two 4x4-dimensional matrices: The within-class and the between-class scatter matrix.

Within-class Scatter Matrix SW:

The within-class scatter matrix SW is computed by the following equation:

$$S_W = \sum_{i=1}^{c} Si$$

Where,

$$Si = \sum_{x \in Di}^{n} (x - m_i)(x - m_i)^T$$

(scatter matrix for every class)

and m_i is the mean vector

$$m_i = \frac{1}{n_i} \sum_{x \in Di}^{n} x_k$$

```
S_W = np.zeros((4,4))
for cl,mv in zip(range(1,4), mean_vectors):
    class_sc_mat = np.zeros((4,4))                          # scatter ma-
trix for every class
    for row in X[y == cl]:
        row, mv = row.reshape(4,1), mv.reshape(4,1) # make column
vectors
        class_sc_mat += (row-mv).dot((row-mv).T)
    S_W += class_sc_mat                                     # sum class
scatter matrices
print('within-class Scatter Matrix:\n', S_W)
within-class Scatter Matrix:
 [[ 38.9562   13.683    24.614      5.6556]
 [ 13.683    17.035     8.12       4.9132]
 [ 24.614     8.12     27.22       6.2536]
 [  5.6556    4.9132    6.2536     6.1756]]
```

Alternatively, we could also compute the class-covariance matrices by adding the scaling factor $\frac{1}{N-1}$ to the within-class scatter matrix, so that our equation becomes

$$\sum_i \frac{1}{N-1} \sum_{x \in Di}^{n} (x - m_i)(x - m_i)^T$$

and $S_W = \sum_{i=1}^{c} (N_i - 1) \sum_i$

where N_i is the sample size of the respective class (here: 50), and in this particular case, we can drop the term (N_{i-1}) since all classes have the same sample size.

However, the resulting eigenspaces will be identical (identical eigenvectors, only the eigenvalues are scaled differently by a constant factor).

Between-class scatter matrix S_B

The between-class scatter matrix S_B is computed by the following equation:

$$S_B = \sum_{i=1}^{c} N_i (m_i - m)(m_i - m)^T$$

where

m is the overall mean, and m_i and N_i are the sample mean and sizes of the respective classes.

```
overall_mean = np.mean(X, axis=0)


S_B = np.zeros((4,4))
for i,mean_vec in enumerate(mean_vectors):
    n = X[y==i+1,:].shape
    mean_vec = mean_vec.reshape(4,1) # make column vector
    overall_mean = overall_mean.reshape(4,1) # make column vector
    S_B += n * (mean_vec - overall_mean).dot((mean_vec - overall_
mean).T)


print('between-class Scatter Matrix:\n', S_B)
between-class Scatter Matrix:
 [[   63.2121   -19.534     165.1647     71.3631]
 [  -19.534      10.9776    -56.0552    -22.4924]
 [  165.1647    -56.0552    436.6437    186.9081]
 [   71.3631    -22.4924    186.9081     80.6041]]
```

Step 3: Solving the generalized eigenvalue problem for the matrix $S^{-1}_W SB$

Next, we will solve the generalized eigenvalue problem for the matrix $S{-1}_W S_B$ to obtain the linear discriminants.

```
eig_vals, eig_vecs = np.linalg.eig(np.linalg.inv(S_W).dot(S_B))
```

```
for i in range(len(eig_vals)):
    eigvec_sc = eig_vecs[:,i].reshape(4,1)
    print('\nEigenvector {}: \n{}'.format(i+1, eigvec_sc.real))
    print('Eigenvalue {:}: {:.2e}'.format(i+1, eig_vals[i].real))
Eigenvector 1:
[[-0.2049]
 [-0.3871]
 [ 0.5465]
 [ 0.7138]]
Eigenvalue 1: 3.23e+01


Eigenvector 2:
[[-0.009 ]
 [-0.589 ]
 [ 0.2543]
 [-0.767 ]]
Eigenvalue 2: 2.78e-01


Eigenvector 3:
[[ 0.179 ]
 [-0.3178]
 [-0.3658]
 [ 0.6011]]
Eigenvalue 3: -4.02e-17
```

```
Eigenvector 4:
[[ 0.179 ]
 [-0.3178]
 [-0.3658]
 [ 0.6011]]
Eigenvalue 4: -4.02e-17
```

Depending on which version of NumPy and LAPACK we are using, we may obtain the matrix W with its signs flipped. Please note that this is not an issue; if v is an eigenvector of a matrix Σ, we have

$$\sum v = \lambda \, v.$$

Here, λ is the eigenvalue, and v is also an eigenvector that the same eigenvalue, since $Sigma(-v) = -- v\Sigma = -\lambda v = \lambda(-v)$.

After this decomposition of our square matrix into eigenvectors and eigenvalues, let us briefly recapitulate how we can interpret those results. As we remember from our first linear algebra class in high school or college, both eigenvectors and eigenvalues are providing us with information about the distortion of a linear transformation: The eigenvectors are basically the direction of this distortion, and the eigenvalues are the scaling factor for the eigenvectors that describing the magnitude of the distortion.

If we are performing the LDA for dimensionality reduction, the eigenvectors are important since they will form the new axes of our new feature subspace; the associated eigenvalues are of particular interest since they will tell us how "informative" the new "axes" are.

Eigenvector-eigenvalue calculation

A quick check that the eigenvector-eigenvalue calculation is correct and satisfy the equation:

$$Av = \lambda v$$

Where

$$A = S_W^{-1} S_B$$

$$v = \text{Eigenvector}$$

λ = Eigenvalue

```
for i in range(len(eig_vals)):
    eigv = eig_vecs[:,i].reshape(4,1)
        np.testing.assert_array_almost_equal(np.linalg.inv(S_W).
dot(S_B).dot(eigv),
                                            eig_vals[i] * eigv,
                                            decimal=6, err_msg='',
verbose=True)
print('ok')
ok
```

Step 4: Selecting linear discriminants for the new feature subspace

Sorting the eigenvectors by decreasing eigenvalues

Remember from the introduction that we are not only interested in merely projecting the data into a subspace that improves the class separability, but also reduces the dimensionality of our feature space, (where the eigenvectors will form the axes of this new feature subspace).

However, the eigenvectors only define the directions of the new axis, since they have all the same unit length 1.

So, in order to decide which eigenvectors we want to drop for our lower-dimensional subspace, we have to take a look at the corresponding eigenvalues of the eigenvectors. Roughly speaking, the eigenvectors with the lowest eigenvalues bear the least information about the distribution of the data, and those are the ones we want to drop.

The common approach is to rank the eigenvectors from highest to lowest corresponding eigenvalue and choose the top k eigenvectors.

```
# Make a list of (eigenvalue, eigenvector) tuples

eig_pairs = [(np.abs(eig_vals[i]), eig_vecs[:,i]) for i in
range(len(eig_vals))]


# Sort the (eigenvalue, eigenvector) tuples from high to low

eig_pairs = sorted(eig_pairs, key=lambda k: k, reverse=True)
```

```
# Visually confirm that the list is correctly sorted by decreasing
eigenvalues
```

```
print('Eigenvalues in decreasing order:\n')
```

```
for i in eig_pairs:
```

```
    print(i)
```

```
Eigenvalues in decreasing order:
```

```
32.2719577997
```

```
0.27756686384
```

```
5.71450476746e-15
```

```
5.71450476746e-15
```

If we take a look at the eigenvalues, we can already see that 2 eigenvalues are close to 0. The reason why these are close to 0 is not that they are not informative but it's due to floating-point imprecision. In fact, these two last eigenvalues should be exactly zero: In LDA, the number of linear discriminants is at most $c-1$ where cc is the number of class labels, since the in-between scatter matrix S is the sum of c matrices with rank 1 or less. Note that in the rare case of perfect collinearity (all aligned sample points fall on a straight line), the covariance matrix would have rank one, which would result in only one eigenvector with a nonzero eigenvalue.

Now, let's express the "explained variance" as percentage:

```
print('Variance explained:\n')
```

```
eigv_sum = sum(eig_vals)
```

```
for i,j in enumerate(eig_pairs):
```

```
        print('eigenvalue {0:}: {1:.2%}'.format(i+1, (j/eigv_sum).
real))
```

```
Variance explained:
```

```
eigenvalue 1: 99.15%
```

```
eigenvalue 2: 0.85%
```

```
eigenvalue 3: 0.00%
```

```
eigenvalue 4: 0.00%
```

The first eigenpair is by far the most informative one, and we won't loose much information if we would form a 1D-feature spaced based on this eigenpair.

Choosing k eigenvectors with the largest eigenvalues

After sorting the eigenpairs by decreasing eigenvalues, it is now time to construct our $k \times d$-dimensional eigenvector matrix W (here 4×2: based on the 2 most informative eigenpairs) and thereby reducing the initial 4-dimensional feature space into a 2-dimensional feature subspace.

```
W = np.hstack((eig_pairs.reshape(4,1), eig_pairs.reshape(4,1)))

print('Matrix W:\n', W.real)

Matrix W:

 [[-0.2049 -0.009 ]

 [-0.3871 -0.589 ]

 [ 0.5465  0.2543]

 [ 0.7138 -0.767 ]]
```

Step 5: Transforming the samples onto the new subspace

In the last step, we use the 4×2-dimensional matrix W that we just computed to transform our samples onto the new subspace via the equation

$$Y = X \times W$$

(where X is a n×d-dimensional matrix representing the n samples, and Y are the transformed n×k-dimensional samples in the new subspace).

```
X_lda = X.dot(W)

assert X_lda.shape == (150,2), "The matrix is not 150x2 dimensional."

from matplotlib import pyplot as plt


def plot_step_lda():


    ax = plt.subplot(111)

    for label,marker,color in zip(

        range(1,4),('^', 's', 'o'),('blue', 'red', 'green')):
```

```
        plt.scatter(x=X_lda[:,0].real[y == label],

            y=X_lda[:,1].real[y == label],

            marker=marker,

            color=color,

            alpha=0.5,

            label=label_dict[label]

            )


    plt.xlabel('LD1')

    plt.ylabel('LD2')


    leg = plt.legend(loc='upper right', fancybox=True)

    leg.get_frame().set_alpha(0.5)

     plt.title('LDA: Iris projection onto the first 2 linear dis-
criminants')


    # hide axis ticks

        plt.tick_params(axis="both", which="both", bottom="off",
top="off",

        labelbottom="on", left="off", right="off", labelleft="on")


    # remove axis spines

    ax.spines["top"].set_visible(False)

    ax.spines["right"].set_visible(False)

    ax.spines["bottom"].set_visible(False)

    ax.spines["left"].set_visible(False)


    plt.grid()
```

```
plt.tight_layout

plt.show()
```

```
plot_step_lda()
```

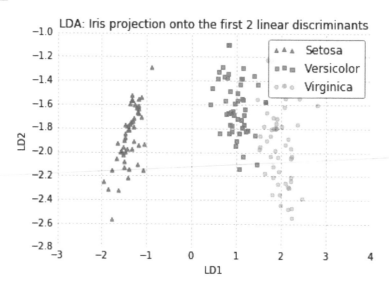

The scatter plot above represents our new feature subspace that we constructed via LDA. We can see that the first linear discriminant "LD1" separates the classes quite nicely. However, the second discriminant, "LD2", does not add much valuable information, which we've already concluded when we looked at the ranked eigenvalues is step 4.

Applications

In addition to the examples given below, LDA is applied in positioning and product management.

Bankruptcy Prediction

In bankruptcy prediction based on accounting ratios and other financial variables, linear discriminant analysis was the first statistical method applied to systematically explain which firms entered bankruptcy vs. survived. Despite limitations including known nonconformance of accounting ratios to the normal distribution assumptions of LDA, Edward Altman's 1968 model is still a leading model in practical applications.

Face Recognition

In computerised face recognition, each face is represented by a large number of pixel values. Linear discriminant analysis is primarily used here to reduce the number of features to a more manageable number before classification. Each of the new dimensions is a linear combination of pixel values, which form a template. The linear combinations obtained using Fisher's linear discriminant are called *Fisher faces*, while those obtained using the related principal component analysis are called *eigenfaces*.

Marketing

In marketing, discriminant analysis was once often used to determine the factors which distinguish different types of customers and/or products on the basis of surveys or other forms of collected data. Logistic regression or other methods are now more commonly used. The use of discriminant analysis in marketing can be described by the following steps:

1. Formulate the problem and gather data—Identify the salient attributes consumers use to evaluate products in this category—Use quantitative marketing research techniques (such as surveys) to collect data from a sample of potential customers concerning their ratings of all the product attributes. The data collection stage is usually done by marketing research professionals. Survey questions ask the respondent to rate a product from one to five (or 1 to 7, or 1 to 10) on a range of attributes chosen by the researcher. Anywhere from five to twenty attributes are chosen. They could include things like: ease of use, weight, accuracy, durability, colourfulness, price, or size. The attributes chosen will vary depending on the product being studied. The same question is asked about all the products in the study. The data for multiple products is codified and input into a statistical program such as R, SPSS or SAS.

2. Estimate the Discriminant Function Coefficients and determine the statistical significance and validity—Choose the appropriate discriminant analysis method. The direct method involves estimating the discriminant function so that all the predictors are assessed simultaneously. The stepwise method enters the predictors sequentially. The two-group method should be used when the dependent variable has two categories or states. The multiple discriminant method is used when the dependent variable has three or more categorical states. Use Wilks's Lambda to test for significance in SPSS or F stat in SAS. The most common method used to test validity is to split the sample into an estimation or analysis sample, and a validation or holdout sample. The estimation sample is used in constructing the discriminant function. The validation sample is used to construct a classification matrix which contains the number of correctly classified and incorrectly classified cases. The percentage of correctly classified cases is called the *hit ratio*.

3. Plot the results on a two dimensional map, define the dimensions, and interpret the results. The statistical program (or a related module) will map the results. The map will plot each product (usually in two-dimensional space). The

distance of products to each other indicate either how different they are. The dimensions must be labelled by the researcher. This requires subjective judgement and is often very challenging.

Biomedical Studies

The main application of discriminant analysis in medicine is the assessment of severity state of a patient and prognosis of disease outcome. For example, during retrospective analysis, patients are divided into groups according to severity of disease – mild, moderate and severe form. Then results of clinical and laboratory analyses are studied in order to reveal variables which are statistically different in studied groups. Using these variables, discriminant functions are built which help to objectively classify disease in a future patient into mild, moderate or severe form.

In biology, similar principles are used in order to classify and define groups of different biological objects, for example, to define phage types of Salmonella enteritidis based on Fourier transform infrared spectra, to detect animal source of Escherichia coli studying its virulence factors etc.

Earth Science

This method can be used to separate the alteration zones. For example, when different data from various zones are available, discriminant analysis can find the pattern within the data and classify it effectively.

Comparison to Logistic Regression

Discriminant function analysis is very similar to logistic regression, and both can be used to answer the same research questions. Logistic regression does not have as many assumptions and restrictions as discriminant analysis. However, when discriminant analysis' assumptions are met, it is more powerful than logistic regression. Unlike logistic regression, discriminant analysis can be used with small sample sizes. It has been shown that when sample sizes are equal, and homogeneity of variance/covariance holds, discriminant analysis is more accurate. With all this being considered, logistic regression has become the common choice, since the assumptions of discriminant analysis are rarely met.

Principal Component Analysis

Principal component analysis is a method of extracting important variables (in form of components) from a large set of variables available in a data set. It extracts low dimensional set of features from a high dimensional data set with a motive to capture as much information as possible. With fewer variables, visualization also becomes much more meaningful. PCA is more useful when dealing with 3 or higher dimensional data.

It is always performed on a symmetric correlation or covariance matrix. This means the matrix should be numeric and have standardized data.

For Example

Let's say we have a data set of dimension 300 (*n*) × 50 (*p*). *n* represents the number of observations and *p* represents number of predictors. Since we have a large p = 50, there can be p(p-1)/2 scatter plots i.e more than 1000 plots possible to analyze the variable relationship. Wouldn't is be a tedious job to perform exploratory analysis on this data ?

In this case, it would be a lucid approach to select a subset of *p (p << 50)* predictor which captures as much information. Followed by plotting the observation in the resultant low dimensional space.

The image below shows the transformation of a high dimensional data (3 dimension) to low dimensional data (2 dimension) using PCA. Not to forget, each resultant dimension is a linear combination of *p* features

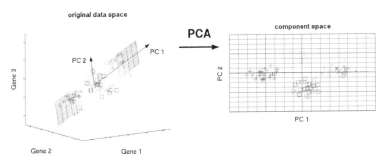

Principal Components

A principal component is a normalized linear combination of the original predictors in a data set. In image above, *PC1* and *PC2* are the principal components. Let's say we have a set of predictors as X^1, X^2...,X^p

The principal component can be written as:

$$Z^1 = \Phi^{11}X^1 + \Phi^{21}X^2 + \Phi^{31}X^3 + ... + \Phi^{p1}X^p$$

where,

- Z^1 is first principal component.

- Φ^{p1} is the loading vector comprising of loadings (Φ^1, Φ^2..) of first principal component. The loadings are constrained to a sum of square equals to 1. This is because large magnitude of loadings may lead to large variance. It also defines the direction of the principal component (Z¹) along which data varies the most. It results in a line in p dimensional space which is closest to the n observations. Closeness is measured using average squared euclidean distance.

- X¹..Xᵖ are normalized predictors. Normalized predictors have mean equals to zero and standard deviation equals to one.

Therefore,

First principal component is a linear combination of original predictor variables which captures the maximum variance in the data set. It determines the direction of highest variability in the data. Larger the variability captured in first component, larger the information captured by component. No other component can have variability higher than first principal component.

The first principal component results in a line which is closest to the data i.e. it minimizes the sum of squared distance between a data point and the line.

Similarly, we can compute the second principal component also.

Second principal component (Z²) is also a linear combination of original predictors, which captures the remaining variance in the data set and is uncorrelated with Z¹. In other words, the correlation between first and second component should is zero. It can be represented as:

$$Z^2 = \Phi^{12}X^1 + \Phi^{22}X^2 + \Phi^{32}X^3 + ... + \Phi^{p2}X^p$$

If the two components are uncorrelated, their directions should be orthogonal. This image is based on a simulated data with 2 predictors. Notice the direction of the components, as expected they are orthogonal. This suggests the correlation b/w these components in zero.

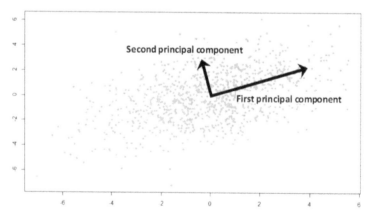

All succeeding principal component follows a similar concept i.e. they capture the remaining variation without being correlated with the previous component. In general, for $n \times p$ dimensional data, min(n-1, p) principal component can be constructed.

The directions of these components are identified in an unsupervised way i.e. the response variable(Y) is not used to determine the component direction. Therefore, it is an unsupervised approach.

Properties and Limitations of PCA

Properties

Some properties of PCA include:

Property 1: For any integer q, $1 \leq q \leq p$, consider the orthogonal linear transformation

$$y = \mathbf{B}'x$$

where y is a q-*element* vector and $\mathbf{B}'$ is a $(q \times p)$ matrix, and let $\Sigma_y = \mathbf{B}'\Sigma\mathbf{B}$ be the variance-covariance matrix for y. Then the trace of Σ_y, denoted $\mathrm{tr}(\Sigma_y)$, is maximized by taking $\mathbf{B} = \mathbf{A}_q$, where $\mathbf{A}_q$ consists of the first q columns of $\mathbf{A}$ ($\mathbf{B}'$ is the transposition of $\mathbf{B}$).

Property 2: Consider again the orthonormal transformation

$$y = \mathbf{B}'x$$

with $x, \mathbf{B}, \mathbf{A}$ and Σ_y defined as before. Then $\mathrm{tr}(\Sigma_y)$ is minimized by taking $\mathbf{B} = \mathbf{A}_q^*$ where $\mathbf{A}_q^*$ consists of the last q columns of A.

The statistical implication of this property is that the last few PCs are not simply unstructured left-overs after removing the important PCs. Because these last PCs have variances as small as possible they are useful in their own right. They can help to detect unsuspected near-constant linear relationships between the elements of x, and they may also be useful in regression, in selecting a subset of variables from x, and in outlier detection.

Property 3: (Spectral Decomposition of Σ)

$$\Sigma = \lambda_1 \alpha_1 \alpha_1' + \cdots + \lambda_p \alpha_p \alpha_p'$$

Before we look at its usage, we first look at diagonal elements,

$$\mathrm{Var}(x_j) = \sum_{k=1}^{P} \lambda_k \alpha_{kj}^2$$

Then, perhaps the main statistical implication of the result is that not only can we decompose the combined variances of all the elements of x into decreasing contributions due to each PC, but we can also decompose the whole covariance matrix into contributions $\lambda_k \alpha_k \alpha_{k'}$ from each PC. Although not strictly decreasing, the elements of $\lambda_k \alpha_k \alpha_{k'}$

will tend to become smaller as k, increases, as $\lambda_k \alpha_k \alpha_{k'}$ is nonincreasing for increasing k, whereas the elements of α_k tend to stay about the same size because of the normalization constraints: $\alpha_{k'} \alpha_k = 1, k = 1, \cdots, p$.

Limitations

As noted above, the results of PCA depend on the scaling of the variables. A scale-invariant form of PCA has been developed.

The applicability of PCA is limited by certain assumptions made in its derivation.

The other limitation is the mean-removal process before constructing the covariance matrix for PCA. In fields such as astronomy, all the signals are non-negative, and the mean-removal process will force the mean of some astrophysical exposures to be zero, which consequently creates unphysical negative fluxes, and forward modeling has to be performed to recover the true magnitude of the signals. As an alternative method, non-negative matrix factorization focusing only on the non-negative elements in the matrices, which is well-suited for astrophysical observations. Relation between PCA and Non-negative Matrix Factorization.

PCA and Information Theory

Dimensionality reduction loses information, in general. PCA-based dimensionality reduction tends to minimize that information loss, under certain signal and noise models.

Under the assumption that

$$\mathbf{x} = \mathbf{s} + \mathbf{n}$$

i.e., that the data vector $\mathbf{x}$ is the sum of the desired information-bearing signal $\mathbf{s}$ and a noise signal $\mathbf{n}$ one can show that PCA can be optimal for dimensionality reduction, from an information-theoretic point-of-view.

In particular, Linsker showed that if $\mathbf{s}$ is Gaussian and $\mathbf{n}$ is Gaussian noise with a covariance matrix proportional to the identity matrix, the PCA maximizes the mutual information $I(\mathbf{y};\mathbf{s})$ between the desired information $\mathbf{s}$ and the dimensionality-reduced output $\mathbf{y} = \mathbf{W}_L^T \mathbf{x}$.

If the noise is still Gaussian and has a covariance matrix proportional to the identity matrix (i.e., the components of the vector $\mathbf{n}$ are iid), but the information-bearing signal $\mathbf{s}$ is non-Gaussian (which is a common scenario), PCA at least minimizes an upper bound on the *information loss*, which is defined as

$$I(\mathbf{x};\mathbf{s}) - I(\mathbf{y};\mathbf{s}).$$

The optimality of PCA is also preserved if the noise $\mathbf{n}$ is iid and at least more Gaussian (in terms of the Kullback–Leibler divergence) than the information-bearing signal s. In general, even if the above signal model holds, PCA loses its information-theoretic optimality as soon as the noise n becomes dependent.

Computing PCA using the Covariance Method

The following is a detailed description of PCA using the covariance method as opposed to the correlation method.

The goal is to transform a given data set X of dimension p to an alternative data set Y of smaller dimension L. Equivalently, we are seeking to find the matrix Y, where Y is the Karhunen–Loève transform (KLT) of matrix X:

$$\mathbf{Y} = \mathbb{KLT}\{\mathbf{X}\}$$

Organize the Data Set

Suppose you have data comprising a set of observations of p variables, and you want to reduce the data so that each observation can be described with only L variables, $L < p$. Suppose further, that the data are arranged as a set of n data vectors $\mathbf{x}_1 \ldots \mathbf{x}_n$ with each $\mathbf{x}_i$ representing a single grouped observation of the p variables.

- Write $\mathbf{x}_1 \ldots \mathbf{x}_n$ as row vectors, each of which has p columns.

- Place the row vectors into a single matrix X of dimensions $n \times p$.

Calculate the Empirical Mean

- Find the empirical mean along each column $j = 1, \ldots, p$.

- Place the calculated mean values into an empirical mean vector u of dimensions $p \times 1$.

$$u_j = \frac{1}{n}\sum_{i=1}^{n} X_{ij}$$

Calculate the Deviations from the mean

Mean subtraction is an integral part of the solution towards finding a principal component basis that minimizes the mean square error of approximating the data. Hence we proceed by centering the data as follows:

- Subtract the empirical mean vector $\mathbf{u}^T$ from each row of the data matrix X.

- Store mean-subtracted data in the $n \times p$ matrix B.

$$\mathbf{B} = \mathbf{X} - \mathbf{h}\mathbf{u}^T$$

where h is an $n \times 1$ column vector of all 1s:

$$h_i = 1 \qquad \text{for } i = 1,\ldots,n$$

Find the Covariance Matrix

- Find the $p \times p$ empirical covariance matrix C from the outer product of matrix B with itself:

$$C = \frac{1}{n-1} B^* \otimes B$$

  where * is the conjugate transpose operator. Note that if B consists entirely of real numbers, which is the case in many applications, the "conjugate transpose" is the same as the regular transpose.

- The reasoning behind using $N - 1$ instead of N to calculate the covariance is Bessel's correction.

Find the Eigenvectors and Eigenvalues of the Covariance Matrix

- Compute the matrix V of eigenvectors which diagonalizes the covariance matrix C:

$$V^{-1}CV = D$$

  where D is the diagonal matrix of eigenvalues of C. This step will typically involve the use of a computer-based algorithm for computing eigenvectors and eigenvalues. These algorithms are readily available as sub-components of most matrix algebra systems, such as SAS, R, MATLAB, Mathematica, SciPy, IDL (Interactive Data Language), or GNU Octave as well as OpenCV.

- Matrix D will take the form of an $p \times p$ diagonal matrix, where

$$D_{kl} = \lambda_k \qquad \text{for } k = l$$

  is the jth eigenvalue of the covariance matrix C, and

$$D_{kl} = 0 \qquad \text{for } k \neq l.$$

- Matrix V, also of dimension $p \times p$, contains p column vectors, each of length p, which represent the p eigenvectors of the covariance matrix C.

- The eigenvalues and eigenvectors are ordered and paired. The jth eigenvalue corresponds to the jth eigenvector.

- Matrix V denotes the matrix of *right* eigenvectors (as opposed to *left* eigenvectors). In general, the matrix of right eigenvectors need *not* be the (conjugate) transpose of the matrix of left eigenvectors.

Rearrange the Eigenvectors and Eigenvalues

- Sort the columns of the eigenvector matrix V and eigenvalue matrix D in order of *decreasing* eigenvalue.

- Make sure to maintain the correct pairings between the columns in each matrix.

Compute the Cumulative Energy Content for Each Eigenvector

- The eigenvalues represent the distribution of the source data's energy among each of the eigenvectors, where the eigenvectors form a basis for the data. The cumulative energy content g for the jth eigenvector is the sum of the energy content across all of the eigenvalues from 1 through j:

$$g_j = \sum_{k=1}^{j} D_{kk} \qquad \text{for} \qquad j = 1, \ldots, p$$

Select a Subset of the Eigenvectors as Basis Vectors

- Save the first L columns of V as the $p \times L$ matrix W:

$$W_{kl} = V_{kl} \qquad \text{for} \qquad k = 1, \ldots, p \qquad l = 1, \ldots, L$$

  where
  $1 \le L \le p.$

- Use the vector g as a guide in choosing an appropriate value for L. The goal is to choose a value of L as small as possible while achieving a reasonably high value of g on a percentage basis. For example, you may want to choose L so that the cumulative energy g is above a certain threshold, like 90 percent. In this case, choose the smallest value of L such that

$$\frac{g_L}{g_p} \ge 0.9$$

Project the z-scores of the Data Onto the New Basis

- The projected vectors are the columns of the matrix

$$\mathbf{T} = \mathbf{Z} \cdot \mathbf{W} = \mathbb{KLT}\{\mathbf{X}\}.$$

- The rows of matrix T represent the Kosambi-Karhunen–Loève transforms (KLT) of the data vectors in the rows of matrix X.

Derivation of PCA using the Covariance Method

Let X be a d-dimensional random vector expressed as column vector. Without loss of generality, assume X has zero mean.

We want to find (∗) a $d \times d$ orthonormal transformation matrix P so that PX has a diagonal covariance matrix (*i.e.* PX is a random vector with all its distinct components pairwise uncorrelated).

A quick computation assuming P were unitary yields:

$$\begin{aligned}
\text{cov}(PX) &= \mathbb{E}[PX \ (PX)^*] \\
&= \mathbb{E}[PX \ X^* P^*] \\
&= P\mathbb{E}[XX^*]P^* \\
&= P \ \text{cov}(X)P^{-1}
\end{aligned}$$

Hence (∗) holds if and only if $\text{cov}(X)$ were diagonalisable by P.

This is very constructive, as cov(X) is guaranteed to be a non-negative definite matrix and thus is guaranteed to be diagonalisable by some unitary matrix.

Iterative Computation

In practical implementations especially with high dimensional data (large p), the covariance method is rarely used because it is not efficient. One way to compute the first principal component efficiently is shown in the following pseudo-code, for a data matrix X with zero mean, without ever computing its covariance matrix.

r = a random vector of length p

$$\mathbf{r} = \frac{\mathbf{r}}{|\mathbf{r}|}$$

do c times:

  s = 0 (a vector of length p)

  for each row $\mathbf{x} \in \mathbf{X}$

    $\mathbf{s} = \mathbf{s} + (\mathbf{x} \cdot \mathbf{r})\mathbf{x}$

    eigenvalue $= \mathbf{r}^T \mathbf{s}$

    error $= |\ eigenvalue \cdot \mathbf{r} - \mathbf{s}\ |$

    $\mathbf{r} = \dfrac{\mathbf{s}}{|\mathbf{s}|}$

  exit if *error* < *tolerance*

return *eigenvalue*, $\mathbf{r}$

This power iteration algorithm simply calculates the vector $X^T(X\ r)$, normalizes, and places the result back in r. The eigenvalue is approximated by $r^T\ (X^TX)\ r$, which is the Rayleigh quotient on the unit vector r for the covariance matrix X^TX. The algorithm avoids the np^2 operations of explicitly calculating and storing the covariance matrix X^TX, i.e. is one of matrix-free methods based on the function evaluating the product $X^T(X\ r)$ at the cost of $2np$ operations. If the largest singular value is well separated from the next largest one, the vector r gets close to the first principal component of X within the number of iterations c, which is small relative to p, at the total cost $2cnp$. The power iteration convergence can be accelerated without noticeably sacrificing the small cost per iteration using more advanced matrix-free methods, such as the Lanczos algorithm or the Locally Optimal Block Preconditioned Conjugate Gradient (LOBPCG) method.

Subsequent principal components can be computed one-by-one via deflation or simultaneously as a block. In the former approach, imprecisions in already computed approximate principal components additively affect the accuracy of the subsequently computed principal components, thus increasing the error with every new computation. The latter approach in the block power method replaces single-vectors r and s with block-vectors, matrices R and S. Every column of R approximates one of the leading principal components, while all columns are iterated simultaneously. The main calculation is evaluation of the product $X^T(X\ R)$. Implemented, e.g., in LOBPCG, efficient blocking eliminates the accumulation of the errors, allows using high-level BLAS matrix-matrix product functions, and typically leads to faster convergence, compared to the single-vector one-by-one technique.

The NIPALS Method

Non-linear iterative partial least squares (NIPALS) is an algorithm for computing the first few components in a principal component or partial least squares analysis. For very-high-dimensional datasets, such as those generated in the *omics sciences (e.g., genomics, metabolomics) it is usually only necessary to compute the first few PCs. The non-linear iterative partial least squares (NIPALS) algorithm calculates t_1 and w_1^T from X. The outer product, $t_1w_1^T$ can then be subtracted from X leaving the residual matrix E_1. This can be then used to calculate subsequent PCs. This results in a dramatic reduction in computational time since calculation of the covariance matrix is avoided.

However, for large data matrices, or matrices that have a high degree of column collinearity, NIPALS suffers from loss of orthogonality due to machine precision limitations accumulated in each iteration step. A Gram–Schmidt (GS) re-orthogonalization algorithm is applied to both the scores and the loadings at each iteration step to eliminate this loss of orthogonality.

Online/sequential Estimation

In an "online" or "streaming" situation with data arriving piece by piece rather than being stored in a single batch, it is useful to make an estimate of the PCA projection that can be updated sequentially. This can be done efficiently, but requires different algorithms.

PCA and Qualitative Variables

In PCA, it is common that we want to introduce qualitative variables as supplementary elements. For example, many quantitative variables have been measured on plants. For these plants, some qualitative variables are available as, for example, the species to which the plant belongs. These data were subjected to PCA for quantitative variables. When analyzing the results, it is natural to connect the principal components to the qualitative variable *species*. For this, the following results are produced.

- Identification, on the factorial planes, of the different species e.g. using different colors.

- Representation, on the factorial planes, of the centers of gravity of plants belonging to the same species.

- For each center of gravity and each axis, p-value to judge the significance of the difference between the center of gravity and origin.

These results are what is called *introducing a qualitative variable as supplementary element*. This procedure is detailed in and Husson. Few software offer this option in an "automatic" way. This is the case of SPAD that historically, following the work of Ludovic Lebart, was the first to propose this option, and the R package FactoMineR.

Applications

Quantitative Finance

In quantitative finance, principal component analysis can be directly applied to the risk management of interest rate derivatives portfolios. Trading multiple swap instruments which are usually a function of 30-500 other market quotable swap instruments is sought to be reduced to usually 3 or 4 principal components, representing the path of interest rates on a macro basis. Converting risks to be represented as those to factor loadings (or multipliers) provides assessments and understanding beyond that available to simply collectively viewing risks to individual 30-500 buckets.

PCA has also been applied to share portfolios in a similar fashion. One application is to reduce portfolio risk, where allocation strategies are applied to the "principal portfolios" instead of the underlying stocks. A second is to enhance portfolio return, using the principal components to select stocks with upside potential.

Neuroscience

A variant of principal components analysis is used in neuroscience to identify the specific properties of a stimulus that increase a neuron's probability of generating an action potential. This technique is known as spike-triggered covariance analysis. In a typical application an experimenter presents a white noise process as a stimulus (usually either as a sensory input to a test subject, or as a current injected directly into the neuron) and records a train of action potentials, or spikes, produced by the neuron as a result. Presumably, certain features of the stimulus make the neuron more likely to spike. In order to extract these features, the experimenter calculates the covariance matrix of the *spike-triggered ensemble*, the set of all stimuli (defined and discretized over a finite time window, typically on the order of 100 ms) that immediately preceded a spike. The eigenvectors of the difference between the spike-triggered covariance matrix and the covariance matrix of the *prior stimulus ensemble* (the set of all stimuli, defined over the same length time window) then indicate the directions in the space of stimuli along which the variance of the spike-triggered ensemble differed the most from that of the prior stimulus ensemble. Specifically, the eigenvectors with the largest positive eigenvalues correspond to the directions along which the variance of the spike-triggered ensemble showed the largest positive change compared to the variance of the prior. Since these were the directions in which varying the stimulus led to a spike, they are often good approximations of the sought after relevant stimulus features.

In neuroscience, PCA is also used to discern the identity of a neuron from the shape of its action potential. Spike sorting is an important procedure because extracellular recording techniques often pick up signals from more than one neuron. In spike sorting, one first uses PCA to reduce the dimensionality of the space of action potential waveforms, and then performs clustering analysis to associate specific action potentials with individual neurons.

PCA as a dimension reduction technique is particularly suited to detect coordinated activities of large neuronal ensembles. It has been used in determining collective variables, i.e. order parameters, during phase transitions in the brain.

Relation with other Methods

Correspondence Analysis

Correspondence analysis (CA) was developed by Jean-Paul Benzécri and is conceptually similar to PCA, but scales the data (which should be non-negative) so that rows and columns are treated equivalently. It is traditionally applied to contingency tables. CA decomposes the chi-squared statistic associated to this table into orthogonal factors. Because CA is a descriptive technique, it can be applied to tables for which the chi-squared statistic is appropriate or not. Several variants of CA are available including detrended correspondence analysis and canonical correspondence analysis. One special extension is multiple correspondence analysis, which may be seen as the counterpart of principal component analysis for categorical data.

Factor Analysis

Principal component analysis creates variables that are linear combinations of the original variables. The new variables have the property that the variables are all orthogonal. The PCA transformation can be helpful as a pre-processing step before clustering. PCA is a variance-focused approach seeking to reproduce the total variable variance, in which components reflect both common and unique variance of the variable. PCA is generally preferred for purposes of data reduction (i.e., translating variable space into optimal factor space) but not when the goal is to detect the latent construct or factors.

Factor analysis is similar to principal component analysis, in that factor analysis also involves linear combinations of variables. Different from PCA, factor analysis is a correlation-focused approach seeking to reproduce the inter-correlations among variables, in which the factors "represent the common variance of variables, excluding unique variance". In terms of the correlation matrix, this corresponds with focusing on explaining the off-diagonal terms (i.e. shared co-variance), while PCA focuses on explaining the terms that sit on the diagonal. However, as a side result, when trying to reproduce the on-diagonal terms, PCA also tends to fit relatively well the off-diagonal correlations. Results given by PCA and factor analysis are very similar in most situations, but this is not always the case, and there are some problems where the results are significantly different. Factor analysis is generally used when the research purpose is detecting data structure (i.e., latent constructs or factors) or causal modeling.

K-means Clustering

It was asserted in that the relaxed solution of k-means clustering, specified by the cluster indicators, is given by the principal components, and the PCA subspace spanned by the principal directions is identical to the cluster centroid subspace. However, that PCA is a useful relaxation of k-means clustering was not a new result, and it is straightforward to uncover counterexamples to the statement that the cluster centroid subspace is spanned by the principal directions.

Non-negative Matrix Factorization

Non-negative matrix factorization (NMF) is a dimension reduction method where only non-negative elements in the matrices are used, which is therefore a promising method in astronomy, in the sense that astrophysical signals are non-negative. The PCA components are orthogonal to each other, while the NMF components are all non-negative and therefore constructs a non-orthogonal basis.

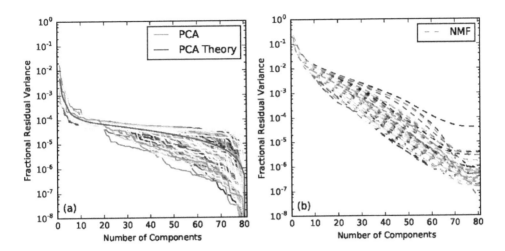

Fractional residual variance (FRV) plots for PCA and NMF; for PCA, the theoretical values are the contribution from the residual eigenvalues. In comparison, the FRV curves for PCA reaches a flat plateau where no signal are captured effectively; while the NMF FRV curves are declining continuously, indicating a better ability to capture signal. The FRV curves for NMF also converges to higher levels than PCA, indicating the less-over-fitting property of NMF.

In PCA, the contribution of each component is ranked based on the magnitude of its corresponding eigenvalue, which is equivalent to the fractional residual variance (FRV) in analyzing empirical data. For NMF, its components are ranked based only on the empirical FRV curves. The residual fractional eigenvalue plots, i.e., $1 - \sum_{i=1}^{k} \lambda_i / \sum_{k=1}^{n} \lambda_k$ as a function of component number k given a total of n components, for PCA has a flat plateau, where no data is captured to remove the quasi-static noise, then the curves dropped quickly as an indication of over-fitting and captures random noise. The FRV curves for NMF is decreasing continuously when the NMF components are constructed sequentially, indicating the continuous capturing of quasi-static noise; then converge to higher levels than PCA, indicating the less over-fitting property of NMF.

Generalizations

Nonlinear Generalizations

Linear PCA versus nonlinear Principal Manifolds for visualization of breast cancer microarray data: a) Configuration of nodes and 2D Principal Surface in the 3D PCA linear manifold. The dataset is curved and cannot be mapped adequately on a 2D principal plane; b) The distribution in the internal 2D non-linear principal surface coordinates (ELMap2D) together with an estimation of the density of points; c) The same as b), but for the linear 2D PCA manifold (PCA2D).

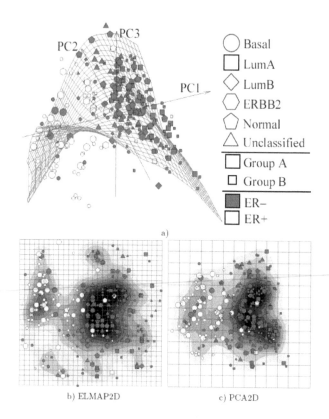

b) ELMAP2D   c) PCA2D

The "basal" breast cancer subtype is visualized more adequately with ELMap2D and some features of the distribution become better resolved in comparison to PCA2D. Principal manifolds are produced by the elastic maps algorithm. Data are available for public competition. Software is available for free non-commercial use.

Most of the modern methods for nonlinear dimensionality reduction find their theoretical and algorithmic roots in PCA or K-means. Pearson's original idea was to take a straight line (or plane) which will be "the best fit" to a set of data points. Principal curves and manifolds give the natural geometric framework for PCA generalization and extend the geometric interpretation of PCA by explicitly constructing an embedded manifold for data approximation, and by encoding using standard geometric projection onto the manifold, as it is illustrated by Fig. Another popular generalization is kernel PCA, which corresponds to PCA performed in a reproducing kernel Hilbert space associated with a positive definite kernel.

Multilinear Generalizations

In multilinear subspace learning, PCA is generalized to multilinear PCA (MPCA) that extracts features directly from tensor representations. MPCA is solved by performing PCA in each mode of the tensor iteratively. MPCA has been applied to face recognition, gait recognition, etc. MPCA is further extended to uncorrelated MPCA, non-negative MPCA and robust MPCA.

Higher Order

N-way principal component analysis may be performed with models such as Tucker decomposition, PARAFAC, multiple factor analysis, co-inertia analysis, STATIS, and DISTATIS.

Robustness – weighted PCA

While PCA finds the mathematically optimal method (as in minimizing the squared error), it is sensitive to outliers in the data that produce large errors PCA tries to avoid. It therefore is common practice to remove outliers before computing PCA. However, in some contexts, outliers can be difficult to identify. For example, in data mining algorithms like correlation clustering, the assignment of points to clusters and outliers is not known beforehand. A recently proposed generalization of PCA based on a weighted PCA increases robustness by assigning different weights to data objects based on their estimated relevancy.

Robust PCA via Decomposition in Low-rank and Sparse Matrices

Robust principal component analysis (RPCA) via decomposition in low-rank and sparse matrices is a modification of PCA that works well with respect to grossly corrupted observations.

Robustness – L1 Weighting

Outlier-resistant versions of PCA have also been proposed on L1-norm formulations (L1-PCA).

Sparse PCA

A particular disadvantage of PCA is that the principal components are usually linear combinations of all input variables. Sparse PCA overcomes this disadvantage by finding linear combinations that contain just a few input variables.

Similar Techniques

Independent Component Analysis

Independent component analysis (ICA) is directed to similar problems as principal component analysis, but finds additively separable components rather than successive approximations.

Network Component Analysis

Given a matrix E, it tries to decompose it into two matrices such that $E = AP$. A key difference from techniques such as PCA and ICA is that some of the entries of A are constrained to be 0. Here P is termed the regulatory layer. While in general such a decomposition can have multiple solutions, they prove that if the following conditions are satisfied :-

1. A has full column rank

2. Each column of A must have at least $L-1$ zeroes where L is the number of columns of A (or alternatively the number of rows of P). The justification for this criterion is that if a node is removed from the regulatory layer along with all the output nodes connected to it, the result must still be characterized by a connectivity matrix with full column rank.

3. P must have full row rank.

then the decomposition is unique up to multiplication by a scalar.

Kernel Principal Component Analysis

Kernel PCA is the nonlinear form of PCA, which better exploits the complicated spatial structure of high-dimensional features.

Constructing the Kernel Matrix

Assume we have a nonlinear transformation $\phi(x)$ from the original D-dimensional feature space to an Mdimensional feature space, where usually $M \gg D$. Then each data point x_i i is projected to a point $\phi(x_i)$. We can perform standard PCA in the new feature space, but this can be extremely costly and inefficient. Fortunately, we can use kernel methods to simplify the computation.

First, we assume that the projected new features have zero mean:

$$\frac{1}{N} \sum_{i=1}^{N} \phi(x_i) = 0.$$

The covariance matrix of the projected features is M × M, calculated by

$$C = \frac{1}{N} \sum_{i=1}^{N} \phi(x_i) \phi(x_i)^{\mathrm{T}}.$$

Its eigenvalues and eigenvectors are given by

$$C v_k = \lambda_k v_k,$$

where $k = 1, 2, \cdots, M$. From Equation $C = \dfrac{1}{N} \sum_{i=1}^{N} \phi(\mathbf{x}_i)\phi(\mathbf{x}_i)^{\mathrm{T}}$. and equation $C\mathbf{v}_k = \lambda_k \mathbf{v}_k$, we have

$$\frac{1}{N} \sum_{i=1}^{N} \phi(\mathbf{x}_i)\left\{\phi(\mathbf{x}_i)^{\mathrm{T}} \mathbf{v}_k\right\} = \lambda_k \mathbf{v}_k,$$

which can be rewritten as

$$\mathbf{v}_k = \sum_{i=1}^{N} a_{ki}\phi(x_i).$$

Now by substituting $\mathbf{v}_k$ in $\dfrac{1}{N} \sum_{i=1}^{N} \phi(\mathbf{x}_i)\left\{\phi(\mathbf{x}_i)^{\mathrm{T}} \mathbf{v}_k\right\} = \lambda_k \mathbf{v}_k$, with $\mathbf{v}_k = \sum_{i=1}^{N} a_{ki}\phi(x_i)$, we have

$$\frac{1}{N} \sum_{i=1}^{N} \phi(\mathbf{x}_i)\phi(\mathbf{x}_i)^{\mathrm{T}} \sum_{j=1}^{N} a_{ki}\phi(x_j) = \lambda_k \sum_{i=1}^{N} a_{ki}\phi(x_i).$$

If we define the kernel function

$$\kappa(\mathbf{x}_i, \mathbf{x}_j) = \phi(x_i)^{\mathrm{T}} \phi(x_j),$$

and multiply both sides of equation $\dfrac{1}{N} \sum_{i=1}^{N} \phi(\mathbf{x}_i)\phi(\mathbf{x}_i)^{\mathrm{T}} \sum_{j=1}^{N} a_{ki}\phi(x_j) = \lambda_k \sum_{i=1}^{N} a_{ki}\phi(x_i)$. by $\phi(\mathbf{x}_l)^{T}$, we have

$$\frac{1}{N} \sum_{i=1}^{N} k(\mathbf{x}_l, \mathbf{x}_i) \sum_{j=1}^{N} a_{kj} k(\mathbf{x}_i, \mathbf{x}_j) = \lambda_k \sum_{i=1}^{N} a_{ki} k(\mathbf{x}_l, \mathbf{x}_i).$$

We can use the matrix notation

$$\mathbf{K}^2 \mathbf{a}_k = \lambda_k N \mathbf{K} \mathbf{a}_k,$$

Where

$$\mathbf{K}_{i,j} = \kappa(x_i, x_j),$$

and $\mathbf{a}_k$ is the N-dimensional column vector of a_{ki}:

$$\mathbf{a}_k = \begin{bmatrix} a_{k1} & a_{k2} & \cdots & a_{kN} \end{bmatrix}^{T}$$

$\mathbf{a}_k$ can be solved by

$$\mathbf{K} \mathbf{a}_k = \lambda_k N \mathbf{a}_k,$$

and the resulting kernel principal components can be calculated using

$$y_k(x) = \phi(x)^T v_k = \sum_{i=1}^{N} a_{ki} k(x, x_i).$$

If the projected dataset $\{\varphi(x_i)\}$ does not have zero mean, we can use the Gram matrix $\tilde{K}$ to substitute the kernel matrix K The Gram matrix is given by.

$$\tilde{K} = K - 1_N K - K1_N + 1_N K1_N,$$

where 1_N is the N × N matrix with all elements equal to 1/N.

The power of kernel methods is that we do not have to compute $\phi(x_i)$ explicitly. We can directly construct the kernel matrix from the training data set $\{x_i\}$. Two commonly used kernels are the polynomial kernel.

$$\kappa(x, y) = (x^T y)^d$$

or

$$\kappa(x, y) = (x^T y + c)^d,$$

Where $c > 0$ is a constant, and the Gaussian kernel

$$\kappa(x, y) = \exp\left(\|-x - y\|^2 / 2\sigma^2\right)$$

with parameter σ.

The standard steps of kernel PCA dimensionality reduction can be summarized as:

1. Construct the kernel matrix K from the training data set {x} using equation $K_{i,j} = \kappa(x_i, x_j)$.

2. Compute the Gram matrix $\tilde{K}$ using equation $\tilde{K} = K - 1_N K - K1_N + 1_N K1_N$.

3. Use equation $Ka_k = \lambda_k N a_k$, to solve for the vectors a_i (substitute K with $\tilde{K}$).

4. Compute the kernel principal components $y_k(x)$ using equation $\tilde{K} = K - 1_N K - K1_N + 1_N K1_N$.

Reconstructing Pre-image

So far, we have discussed how to generate new features $y_k(x)$ using kernel PCA. This is enough for applications such as feature extraction and data classification. However, for some other applications, we need to approximately reconstruct the pre-images $\{x_i\}$

from the kernel PCA feature $\{y_i\}$. This is the case in active shape models, where we not only need to use PCA features to describe the deformation patterns, but also have to reconstruct the shapes from the PCA features.

In standard PCA, the pre-image x_i can simply be approximated by equation $\tilde{x}_i = \sum_{k=1}^{M} (x_i^T u_k) u_k$. However, equation $\tilde{x}_i = \sum_{k=1}^{M} (x_i^T u_k) u_k$, cannot be used for kernel PCA. For kernel PCA, we define a projection operator P_m which project $\phi(x)$ to its approximation

$$P_m \phi(x) = \sum_{k=1}^{m} y_k(x) v_k,$$

where v_k is the eigenvector of the C matrix, which is define by equation $C = \frac{1}{N} \sum_{i=1}^{N} \phi(x_i) \phi(x_i)^T$. If m is large enough, we have $P_m \phi(x) \approx \phi(x)$. Since finding the exact pre-image x is difficult, we turn to find an approximation z such that

$$\phi(z) \approx P_m \phi(x).$$

This can be approximated by minimizing

$$\rho(z) = \left\| \phi(z) - P_m \phi(x) \right\|^2.$$

Pre-Images for Gaussian Kernel

There are some existing techniques to compute z for specific kernels. For a Gaussian kernel $\kappa(x,y) = \exp\left(\|-x-y\|^2 / 2\sigma^2\right)$, z should satisfy":

$$z = \frac{\sum_{i=1}^{N} \gamma_i \exp\left(-\|z-x_i\|^2 / 2\sigma^2\right) x_i}{\sum_{i=1}^{N} \gamma_i \exp\left(-\|z-x_i\|^2 / 2\sigma^2\right)},$$

Where,

$$\gamma_i = \sum_{k=1}^{m} y_k a_{ki}.$$

We can compute z iteratively:

$$\mathbf{z}_{t+1} = \frac{\sum\limits_{i=1}^{N} \gamma_i \exp\left(-\|\mathbf{z}_t - \mathbf{x}_i\|^2 / 2\sigma^2\right)\mathbf{x}_i}{\sum\limits_{i=1}^{N} \gamma_i \exp\left(-\|\mathbf{z}_t - \mathbf{x}_i\|^2 / 2\sigma^2\right)}.$$

Non-negative Matrix Factorization

Nonnegative matrix factorization (NMF) has become a widely used tool for the analysis of high-dimensional data as it automatically extracts sparse and meaningful features from a set of nonnegative data vectors.

Given a non-negative matrix V, find non-negative matrix factors W and H such that:

$$V \approx WH$$

NMF can be applied to the statistical analysis of multivariate data in the following manner. Given a set of of multivariate n-dimensional data vectors, the vectors are placed in the columns of an $n \times m$ matrix V where m is the number of examples in the data set. This matrix is then approximately factorized into an n x r matrix W and an r x m matrix H. Usually r is chosen to be smaller than n or m, so that W and H are smaller than the original matrix V. This results in a compressed version of the original data matrix.

What is the significance of the approximation in equation $V \approx WH$? It can be rewritten column by column as $V \approx Wh$ where v and h are the corresponding columns of V and H. In other words, each data vector v is approximated by a linear combination of the columns of W, weighted by the components of h. Therefore W can be regarded as containing a basis that is optimized for the linear approximation of the data in V. Since relatively few basis vectors are used to represent many data vectors, good approximation can only be achieved if the basis vectors discover structure that is latent in the data.

The present submission is not about applications of NMF, but focuses instead on the technical aspects of finding non-negative matrix factorizations. Of course, other types of matrix factorizations have been extensively studied in numerical linear algebra, but the nonnegativity constraint makes much of this previous work inapplicable to the present case.

Here we discuss two algorithms for NMF based on iterative updates of W and H. Because these algorithms are easy to implement and their convergence properties are guaranteed, we have found them very useful in practical applications. Other algorithms may possibly be more efficient in overall computation time, but are more difficult to implement and may not generalize to different cost functions. Algorithms similar to ours where only one of the factors is adapted have previously been used for the deconvolution of emission tomography and astronomical images .

At each iteration of our algorithms, the new value of W or H is found by multiplying the current value by some factor that depends on the quality of the approximation in equation $V \approx WH$. We prove that the quality of the approximation improves monotonically with the application of these multiplicative update rules. In practice, this means that repeated iteration of the update rules is guaranteed to converge to a locally optimal matrix factorization.

Clustering Property

NMF has an inherent clustering property, i.e., it automatically clusters the columns of input data $\mathbf{V} = (v_1, \cdots, v_n)$. It is this property that drives most applications of NMF.

More specifically, the approximation of $\mathbf{V}$ by $\mathbf{V} \simeq \mathbf{WH}$ is achieved by minimizing the error function

$$\min_{W,H} ||V - WH||_F \text{ subject to } W \geq 0, H \geq 0.$$

Furthermore, the computed $\mathbf{H}$ gives the cluster indicator, i.e., if $\mathbf{H}_{kj} > 0$, that fact indicates input data v_j belongs to k^{th} cluster. And the computed W gives the cluster centroids, i.e., the kth column gives the cluster centroid of kth cluster. This centroid's representation can be significantly enhanced by convex NMF.

When the orthogonality $HH^T = I$ is not explicitly imposed, the orthogonality holds to a large extent, and the clustering property holds too. Clustering is the main objective of most data mining applications of NMF.

When the error function to be used is Kullback–Leibler divergence, NMF is identical to the Probabilistic latent semantic analysis, a popular document clustering method.

Types

Approximate non-negative matrix factorization

Usually the number of columns of W and the number of rows of H in NMF are selected so the product WH will become an approximation to V. The full decomposition of V then amounts to the two non-negative matrices W and H as well as a residual U, such that: V = WH + U. The elements of the residual matrix can either be negative or positive.

When W and H are smaller than V they become easier to store and manipulate. Another reason for factorizing V into smaller matrices W and H, is that if one is able to approximately represent the elements of V by significantly less data, then one has to infer some latent structure in the data.

Convex Non-negative Matrix Factorization

In standard NMF, matrix factor $W \in \mathbb{R}_+^{m \times k}$, i.e., W can be anything in that space. Convex NMF restricts the columns of W to convex combinations of the input data vectors $(v_1, \cdots, v_n)$. This greatly improves the quality of data representation of W. Furthermore, the resulting matrix factor H becomes more sparse and orthogonal.

Non-negative Rank Factorization

In case the nonnegative rank of V is equal to its actual rank, V = WH is called a non-negative rank factorization. The problem of finding the NRF of V, if it exists, is known to be NP-hard.

Different Cost Functions and Regularizations

There are different types of non-negative matrix factorizations. The different types arise from using different cost functions for measuring the divergence between V and WH and possibly by regularization of the W and/or H matrices.

Two simple divergence functions studied by Lee and Seung are the squared error (or Frobenius norm) and an extension of the Kullback–Leibler divergence to positive matrices (the original Kullback–Leibler divergence is defined on probability distributions). Each divergence leads to a different NMF algorithm, usually minimizing the divergence using iterative update rules.

The factorization problem in the squared error version of NMF may be stated as: Given a matrix **V** find nonnegative matrices W and H that minimize the function

$$F(W,H) = \| V - WH \|_F^2$$

Another type of NMF for images is based on the total variation norm.

When L1 regularization (akin to Lasso) is added to NMF with the mean squared error cost function, the resulting problem may be called non-negative sparse coding due to the similarity to the sparse coding problem, although it may also still be referred to as NMF.

Online NMF

Many standard NMF algorithms analyze all the data together; i.e., the whole matrix is available from the start. This may be unsatisfactory in applications where there are too many data to fit into memory or where the data are provided in streaming fashion. One such use is for collaborative filtering in recommendation systems, where there may be many users and many items to recommend, and it would be inefficient to recalculate everything when one user or one item is added to the system. The cost function for optimization in these cases may or may not be the same as for standard NMF, but the algorithms need to be rather different.

Algorithms

There are several ways in which the W and H may be found: Lee and Seung's multiplicative update rule has been a popular method due to the simplicity of implementation. This algorithm is:

initialize: W and H non negative.

Then update the values in W and H by computing the following, with n as an index of the iteration.

$$H_{[i,j]}^{n+1} \leftarrow H_{[i,j]}^{n} \frac{((W^n)^T V)_{[i,j]}}{((W^n)^T W^n H^n)_{[i,j]}}$$

and

$$W_{[i,j]}^{n+1} \leftarrow W_{[i,j]}^{n} \frac{(V(H^{n+1})^T)_{[i,j]}}{(W^n H^{n+1}(H^{n+1})^T)_{[i,j]}}$$

Until W and H are stable.

The updates are done on an element by element basis not matrix multiplication. We note that W and H multiplicative factor is identity matrix when V = W H.

More recently other algorithms have been developed. Some approaches are based on alternating non-negative least squares: in each step of such an algorithm, first H is fixed and W found by a non-negative least squares solver, then W is fixed and H is found analogously. The procedures used to solve for W and H may be the same or different, as some NMF variants regularize one of W and H. Specific approaches include the projected gradient descent methods, the active set method, the optimal gradient method, and the block principal pivoting method among several others.

Current algorithms are sub-optimal in that they only guarantee finding a local minimum, rather than a global minimum of the cost function. A provably optimal algorithm is unlikely in the near future as the problem has been shown to generalize the k-means clustering problem which is known to be NP-complete. However, as in many other data mining applications, a local minimum may still prove to be useful.

Fractional residual variance (FRV) plots for PCA and sequential NMF; for PCA, the theoretical values are the contribution from the residual eigenvalues. In comparison, the FRV curves for PCA reaches a flat plateau where no signal are captured effectively; while the NMF FRV curves are declining continuously, indicating a better ability to capture signal. The FRV curves for NMF also converges to higher levels than PCA, indicating the less-overfitting property of NMF.

Sequential NMF

The sequential construction of NMF components (W and H) was firstly used to relate NMF with Principal Component Analysis (PCA) in astronomy. The contribution from the PCA components are ranked by the magnitude of their corresponding eigenvalues; for NMF, its components can be ranked empirically when they are constructed one by one (sequentially), i.e., learn the $(n+1)$-th component with the first n components constructed.

The contribution of the sequential NMF components can be compared with the Karhunen–Loève theorem, an application of PCA, using the plot of eigenvalues. A typical choice of the number of components with PCA is based on the "elbow" point, then the existence of the flat plateau is indicating that PCA is not capturing the data efficiently, and at last there exists a sudden drop reflecting the capture of random noise and falls into the regime of overfitting. For sequential NMF, the plot of eigenvalues is approximated by the plot of the fractional residual variance curves, where the curves decreases continuously, and converge to a higher level than PCA, which is the indication of less over-fitting of sequential NMF.

Exact NMF

Exact solutions for the variants of NMF can be expected (in polynomial time) when additional constraints hold for matrix V. A polynomial time algorithm for solving nonnegative rank factorization if V contains a monomial sub matrix of rank equal to its rank was given by Campbell and Poole in 1981. Kalofolias and Gallopoulos (2012) solved the symmetric counterpart of this problem, where V is symmetric and contains a diagonal principal sub matrix of rank r. Their algorithm runs in $O(rm^2)$ time in the dense case. Arora, Ge, Halpern, Mimno, Moitra, Sontag, Wu, & Zhu (2013) give a polynomial time algorithm for exact NMF that works for the case where one of the factors W satisfies the separability condition.

Relation to other Techniques

In *Learning the parts of objects by non-negative matrix factorization* Lee and Seung proposed NMF mainly for parts-based decomposition of images. It compares NMF to vector quantization and principal component analysis, and shows that although the three techniques may be written as factorizations, they implement different constraints and therefore produce different results.

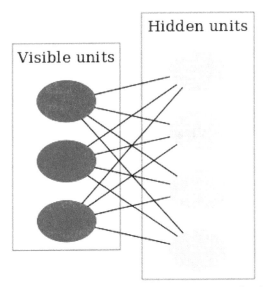

NMF as a probabilistic graphical model: visible units (V) are connected to hidden units (H) through weights W, so that V is generated from a probability distribution with mean $\sum_a W_{ia} h_a$.

It was later shown that some types of NMF are an instance of a more general probabilistic model called "multinomial PCA". When NMF is obtained by minimizing the Kullback–Leibler divergence, it is in fact equivalent to another instance of multinomial PCA, probabilistic latent semantic analysis, trained by maximum likelihood estimation. That method is commonly used for analyzing and clustering textual data and is also related to the latent class model.

NMF with the least-squares objective is equivalent to a relaxed form of K-means clustering: the matrix factor W contains cluster centroids and H contains cluster membership indicators. This provides a theoretical foundation for using NMF for data clustering. However, k-means does not enforce non-negativity on its centroids, so the closest analogy is in fact with "semi-NMF".

NMF can be seen as a two-layer directed graphical model with one layer of observed random variables and one layer of hidden random variables.

NMF extends beyond matrices to tensors of arbitrary order. This extension may be viewed as a non-negative counterpart to, e.g., the PARAFAC model.

Other extensions of NMF include joint factorisation of several data matrices and tensors where some factors are shared. Such models are useful for sensor fusion and relational learning.

NMF is an instance of nonnegative quadratic programming (NQP), just like the support vector machine (SVM). However, SVM and NMF are related at a more intimate level than that of NQP, which allows direct application of the solution algorithms developed for either of the two methods to problems in both domains.

Uniqueness

The factorization is not unique: A matrix and its inverse can be used to transform the two factorization matrices by, e.g.,

$$\mathbf{WH} = \mathbf{WBB}^{-1}\mathbf{H}$$

If the two new matrices $\tilde{\mathbf{W}} = \mathbf{WB}$ and $\tilde{\mathbf{H}} = \mathbf{B}^{-1}\mathbf{H}$ are non-negative they form another parametrization of the factorization.

The non-negativity of $\tilde{\mathbf{W}}$ and $\tilde{\mathbf{H}}$ applies at least if B is a non-negative monomial matrix. In this simple case it will just correspond to a scaling and a permutation.

More control over the non-uniqueness of NMF is obtained with sparsity constraints.

Applications

Astronomy

In astronomy, NMF is a promising method for dimension reduction in the sense that astrophysical signals are non-negative. NMF has been applied to the spectroscopic observations and the direct imaging observations as a method to study the common properties of astronomical objects and post-process the astronomical observations. The advances in the spectroscopic observations by Blanton & Roweis takes into account of the uncertainties of astronomical observations, which is later improved by where missing data are also considered and parallel computing is enabled. Their method is then adopted by Ren. to the direct imaging field as one of the methods of detecting exoplanets, especially for the direct imaging of circumstellar disks.

Ren are able to prove the stability of NMF components when they are constructed sequentially (i.e., one by one), which enables the linearity of the NMF modeling process; the linearity property is used to separate the stellar light and the light scattered from the exoplanets and circumstellar disks.

In direct imaging, to reveal the faint exoplanets and circumstellar disks from bright the surrounding stellar lights, which has a typical contrast from 10^5 to 10^{10}, various statistical methods have been adopted, however the light from the exoplanets or circumstellar disks are usually over-fitted, where forward modeling have to be adopted to recover the true flux. Forward modeling is currently optimized for point sources, however not for extended sources, especially for irregularly shaped structures such as circumstellar disks. In this situation, NMF has been an excellent method, being less over-fitting in the sense of the non-negativity and sparsity of the NMF modeling coefficients, therefore forward modeling can be performed with a few scaling factors, rather than a computationally intensive data re-reduction on generated models.

Text Mining

NMF can be used for text mining applications. In this process, a *document-term* matrix is constructed with the weights of various terms (typically weighted word frequency information) from a set of documents. This matrix is factored into a term-feature and a feature-document matrix. The features are derived from the contents of the documents, and the feature-document matrix describes data clusters of related documents.

One specific application used hierarchical NMF on a small subset of scientific abstracts from PubMed. Another research group clustered parts of the Enron email dataset with 65,033 messages and 91,133 terms into 50 clusters. NMF has also been applied to citations data, with one example clustering and scientific journals based on the outbound scientific citations.

Arora, Ge, Halpern, Mimno, Moitra, Sontag, Wu, & Zhu have given polynomial-time algorithms to learn topic models using NMF. The algorithm assumes that the topic matrix satisfies a separability condition that is often found to hold in these settings.

Spectral Data Analysis

NMF is also used to analyze spectral data; one such use is in the classification of space objects and debris.

Scalable Internet Distance Prediction

NMF is applied in scalable Internet distance (round-trip time) prediction. For a network with N hosts, with the help of NMF, the distances of all the N^2 end-to-end links can be predicted after conducting only $O(N)$ measurements. This kind of method was firstly introduced in Internet Distance Estimation Service (IDES). Afterwards, as a fully decentralized approach, Phoenix network coordinate system is proposed. It achieves better overall prediction accuracy by introducing the concept of weight.

Non-stationary Speech Denoising

Speech denoising has been a long lasting problem in audio signal processing. There are lots of algorithms for denoising if the noise is stationary. For example, the Wiener filter is suitable for additive Gaussian noise. However, if the noise is non-stationary, the classical denoising algorithms usually have poor performance because the statistical information of the non-stationary noise is difficult to estimate. Schmidt et al. use NMF to do speech denoising under non-stationary noise, which is completely different from classical statistical approaches. The key idea is that clean speech signal can be sparsely represented by a speech dictionary, but non-stationary noise cannot. Similarly, non-stationary noise can also be sparsely represented by a noise dictionary, but speech cannot.

The algorithm for NMF denoising goes as follows. Two dictionaries, one for speech and one for noise, need to be trained offline. Once a noisy speech is given, we first calculate the magnitude of the Short-Time-Fourier-Transform. Second, separate it into two parts via NMF, one can be sparsely represented by the speech dictionary, and the other part can be sparsely represented by the noise dictionary. Third, the part that is represented by the speech dictionary will be the estimated clean speech.

Bioinformatics

NMF has been successfully applied in bioinformatics for clustering gene expression and DNA methylation data and finding the genes most representative of the clusters. In the analysis of cancer mutations it has been used to identify common patterns of mutations that occur in many cancers and that probably have distinct causes.

Nuclear Imaging

NMF, also referred in this field as factor analysis, has been used since the 1980s to analyze sequences of images in SPECT and PET dynamic medical imaging. Non-uniqueness of NMF was addressed using sparsity constraints.

Independent Component Analysis

Independent component analysis (ICA) is a statistical and computational technique for revealing hidden factors that underlie sets of random variables, measurements, or signals.

ICA defines a generative model for the observed multivariate data, which is typically given as a large database of samples. In the model, the data variables are assumed to be linear mixtures of some unknown latent variables, and the mixing system is also unknown. The latent variables are assumed nongaussian and mutually independent, and they are called the independent components of the observed data. These independent components, also called sources or factors, can be found by ICA.

ICA is superficially related to principal component analysis and factor analysis. ICA is a much more powerful technique, however, capable of finding the underlying factors or sources when these classic methods fail completely.

The data analyzed by ICA could originate from many different kinds of application fields, including digital images, document databases, economic indicators and psychometric measurements. In many cases, the measurements are given as a set of parallel signals or time series; the term blind source separation is used to characterize this problem. Typical examples are mixtures of simultaneous speech signals that have been picked up by several microphones, brain waves recorded by multiple sensors, interfering radio signals arriving at a mobile phone, or parallel time series obtained from some industrial process.

We can use a statistical "latent variables" model. Assume that we observe n linear mixtures $x_1,...,x_n$ of n independent components $x_j = a_j 1s1 + a_j 2s2 + ... + a_{jn} s_n$, for all j.

We have now dropped the time index t; in the ICA model, we assume that each mixture x_j as well as each independent component s_k is a random variable, instead of a proper time signal. The observed values $x_i(t)$, e.g., the microphone signals in the cocktail party problem, are then a sample of this random variable. Without loss of generality, we can assume that both the mixture variables and the independent components have zero mean: If this is not true, then the observable variables x_i can always be centered by subtracting the sample mean, which makes the model zero-mean.

It is convenient to use vector-matrix notation instead of the sums like in the previous equation. Let us denote by x the random vector whose elements are the mixtures x ,...,x , and likewise by s the random vector with elements $s_1,...,s_n$. Let us denote by A the matrix with elements a_{ij} Generally, bold lower case letters indicate vectors and bold upper-case letters denote matrices. All vectors are understood as column vectors; thus x^T , or the transpose of x, is a row vector. Using this vector-matrix notation, the above mixing model is written as:

$$x = As.$$

Sometimes we need the columns of matrix A; denoting them by a_j the model can also be written as:

$$x = \sum_i^n a_i s_i.$$

The statistical model in equation $x = As$. is called independent component analysis, or ICA model. The ICA model is a generative model, which means that it describes how the observed data are generated by a process of mixing the components s_i. The independent components are latent variables, meaning that they cannot be directly observed. Also the mixing matrix is assumed to be unknown. All we observe is the random vector x, and we must estimate both A and s using it. This must be done under as general assumptions as possible.

The starting point for ICA is the very simple assumption that the components s_i are statistically independent. We must also assume that the independent component must have nongaussian distributions. However, in the basic model we do not assume these distributions known (if they are known, the problem is considerably simplified.) For simplicity, we are also assuming that the unknown mixing matrix is square, but this assumption can be sometimes relaxed. Then, after estimating the matrix A, we can compute its inverse, say W, and obtain the independent component simply by:

$$s = Wx.$$

ICA is very closely related to the method called blind source separation (BSS) or blind signal separation. A "source" means here an original signal, i.e. independent component, like the speaker in a cocktail party problem. "Blind" means that we no very little, if anything, on the mixing matrix, and make little assumptions on the source signals. ICA is one method, perhaps the most widely used, for performing blind source separation.

In many applications, it would be more realistic to assume that there is some noise in the measurements, which would mean adding a noise term in the model. For simplicity, we omit any noise terms, since the estimation of the noise-free model is difficult enough in itself, and seems to be sufficient for many applications.

Ambiguities of ICA

In the ICA model in equation $x = As.$, it is easy to see that the following ambiguities will hold:

1. We cannot determine the variances (energies) of the independent components.

The reason is that, both s and A being unknown, any scalar multiplier in one of the sources s_i could always be cancelled by dividing the corresponding column a_i of A by the same scalar. As a consequence, we may quite as well fix the magnitudes of the independent components; as they are random variables, the most natural way to do this is to assume that each has unit variance: $E\{s_i^2\} = 1$. Then the matrix A will be adapted in the ICA solution methods to take into account this restriction. This still leaves the ambiguity of the sign: we could multiply the an independent component by −1 without affecting the model. This ambiguity is, fortunately, insignificant in most applications.

2. We cannot determine the order of the independent components.

The reason is that, again both s and A being unknown, we can freely change the order of the terms in the sum in (5), and call any of the independent components the first one. Formally, a permutation matrix P and its inverse can be substituted in the model to give $x = AP^{-1}Ps$. The elements of Ps are the original independent variables s_j, but in another order. The matrix AP−1 is just a new unknown mixing matrix, to be solved by the ICA algorithms.

Illustration of ICA

To illustrate the ICA model in statistical terms, consider two independent components that have the following uniform distributions:

$$p(si) = \begin{cases} \dfrac{1}{2\sqrt{3}} & \text{if } |si| \le \sqrt{3} \\ 0 & \text{otherwise} \end{cases}$$

The range of values for this uniform distribution were chosen so as to make the mean zero and the variance equal to one, as was agreed in the Section. The joint density of s_1 and s_2 is then uniform on a square. This follows from the basic definition that the joint density of two independent variables is just the product of their marginal densities.

Now let as mix these two independent components. Let us take the following mixing matrix:

$$\begin{pmatrix} 2 & 3 \\ 2 & 1 \end{pmatrix}$$

This gives us two mixed variables, x_1 and x_2. It is easily computed that the mixed data has a uniform distribution on a parallelogram. The random variables x_1 and x_2 are not independent any more; an easy way to see this is to consider, whether it is possible to predict the value of one of them, say x_2, from the value of the other. Clearly if x_1 attains one of its maximum or minimum values, then this completely determines the value of x_2. They are therefore not independent.

The problem of estimating the data model of ICA is now to estimate the mixing matrix A_0 using only information contained in the mixtures x_1 and x_2. Actually, an intuitive way of estimating A: The edges of the parallelogram are in the directions of the columns of A. This means that we could, in principle, estimate the ICA model by first estimating the joint density of x_1 and x_2, and then locating the edges.

Binary Independent Component Analysis

A special variant of ICA is Binary ICA in which both signal sources and monitors are in binary form and observations from monitors are disjunctive mixtures of binary independent sources. The problem was shown to have applications in many domains including medical diagnosis, multi-cluster assignment, network tomography and internet resource management.

Let $x_1, x_2, \ldots, x_m$ be the set of binary variables from m monitors and $y_1, y_2, \ldots, y_n$ be the set of binary variables from n sources. Source-monitor connections are represented by the (unknown) mixing matrix $\mathbf{G}$, where $g_{ij} = 1$ indicates that signal from the i-th source can be observed by the j-th monitor. The system works as follows: at any time, if a source i is active ($y_i = 1$) and it is connected to the monitor j ($g_{ij} = 1$) then the monitor j will observe some activity ($x_j = 1$). Formally we have:

$$x_i = \bigvee_{j=1}^{n} (g_{ij} \wedge y_j), i = 1, 2, \ldots, m,$$

where $\wedge$ is Boolean AND and $\vee$ is Boolean OR. Noise is not explicitly modelled, rather, can be treated as independent sources.

The above problem can be heuristically solved by assuming variables are continuous and running FastICA on binary observation data to get the mixing matrix $\mathbf{G}$ (real values), then apply round number techniques on G to obtain the binary values. This approach has been shown to produce a highly inaccurate result.

Another method is to use dynamic programming: recursively breaking the observation matrix $\mathbf{X}$ into its sub-matrices and run the inference algorithm on these sub-matrices. The key observation, which leads to this algorithm is the sub-matrix $\mathbf{X}^o$ of $\mathbf{X}$ where $x_{ij} = 0, \forall j$ corresponds to the unbiased observation matrix of hidden components that do not have connection to the i-th monitor. Experimental results from show that this approach is accurate under moderate noise levels.

The Generalized Binary ICA framework introduces a broader problem formulation which does not necessitate any knowledge on the generative model. In other words, this method attempts to decompose a source into its independent components (as much as possible, and without losing any information) with no prior assumption on the way it was generated. Although this problem appears quite complex, it can be accurately solved with a branch and bound search tree algorithm or tightly upper bounded with a single multiplication of a matrix with a vector.

Methods for Blind Source Separation

Projection Pursuit

Signal mixtures tend to have Gaussian probability density functions, and source signals tend to have non-Gaussian probability density functions. Each source signal can be extracted from a set of signal mixtures by taking the inner product of a weight vector and those signal mixtures where this inner product provides an orthogonal projection of the signal mixtures. The remaining challenge is finding such a weight vector. One type of method for doing so is projection pursuit.

Projection pursuit seeks one projection at a time such that the extracted signal is as non-Gaussian as possible. This contrasts with ICA, which typically extracts M signals simultaneously from M signal mixtures, which requires estimating a $M \times M$ unmixing matrix. One practical advantage of projection pursuit over ICA is that fewer than M signals can be extracted if required, where each source signal is extracted from M signal mixtures using an M-element weight vector.

We can use kurtosis to recover the multiple source signal by finding the correct weight vectors with the use of projection pursuit.

The kurtosis of the probability density function of a signal, for a finite sample, is computed as

$$K = \frac{E[(\mathbf{y}-\bar{\mathbf{y}})^4]}{(E[(\mathbf{y}-\bar{\mathbf{y}})^2])^2} - 3$$

where $\bar{\mathbf{y}}$ is the sample mean of $\mathbf{y}$, the extracted signals. The constant 3 ensures that Gaussian signals have zero kurtosis, Super-Gaussian signals have positive kurtosis, and Sub-Gaussian signals have negative kurtosis. The denominator is the variance of $\mathbf{y}$, and ensures that the measured kurtosis takes account of signal variance. The goal of projection pursuit is to maximize the kurtosis, and make the extracted signal as non-normal as possible.

Using kurtosis as a measure of non-normality, we can now examine how the kurtosis of a signal $\mathbf{y} = \mathbf{w}^T\mathbf{x}$ extracted from a set of M mixtures $\mathbf{x} = (x_1, x_2, \ldots, x_M)^T$ varies as the weight vector $\mathbf{w}$ is rotated around the origin. Given our assumption that each source signal $\mathbf{s}$ is super-gaussian we would expect:

1. The kurtosis of the extracted signal $\mathbf{y}$ to be maximal precisely when $\mathbf{y} = \mathbf{s}$,

2. The kurtosis of the extracted signal $\mathbf{y}$ to be maximal when $\mathbf{w}$ is orthogonal to the projected axes S_1 or S_2, because we know the optimal weight vector should be orthogonal to a transformed axis S_1 or S_2.

For multiple source mixture signals, we can use kurtosis and Gram-Schmidt Orthogonalization (GSO) to recover the signals. Given M signal mixtures in an M-dimensional space, GSO project these data points onto an $(M-1)$-dimensional space by using the weight vector. We can guarantee the independence of the extracted signals with the use of GSO.

In order to find the correct value of $\mathbf{w}$, we can use gradient descent method. We first of all whiten the data, and transform $\mathbf{x}$ into a new mixture $\mathbf{z}$, which has unit variance, and $\mathbf{z} = (z_1, z_2, \ldots, z_M)^T$. This process can be achieved by applying Singular value decomposition to $\mathbf{x}$,

$$\mathbf{x} = \mathbf{UDV}^T.$$

Rescaling each vector $U_i = U_i / E(U_i^2)$, and let $\mathbf{z} = \mathbf{U}$. The signal extracted by a weighted vector $\mathbf{w}$ is $\mathbf{y} = \mathbf{w}^T\mathbf{z}$. If the weight vector w has unit length, that is $E[(\mathbf{w}^T\mathbf{z})^2] = 1$, then the kurtosis can be written as:

$$K = \frac{E[\mathbf{y}^4]}{(E[\mathbf{y}^2])^2} - 3 = E[(\mathbf{w}^T\mathbf{z})^4] - 3.$$

The updating process for $\mathbf{w}$ is:

$$\mathbf{w}_{new} = \mathbf{w}_{old} - \eta\, E[\mathbf{z}(\mathbf{w}_{old}^T\mathbf{z})^3].$$

where η is a small constant to guarantee that $\mathbf{w}$ converge to the optimal solution. After each update, we normalized $\mathbf{w}_{new} = \dfrac{\mathbf{w}_{new}}{|\mathbf{w}_{new}|}$, and set $\mathbf{w}_{old} = \mathbf{w}_{new}$, and repeat the updating process till it converges. We can also use another algorithm to update the weight vector $\mathbf{w}$.

Another approach is using negentropy instead of kurtosis. Negentropy is a robust method for kurtosis, as kurtosis is very sensitive to outliers. The negentropy method are based on an important property of Gaussian distribution: a Gaussian variable has the largest entropy among all continuous random variables of equal variance. This is also the reason why we want to find the most nongaussian variables. A simple proof can be found in Differential entropy.

$$J(x) = S(y) - S(x)$$

y is a Gaussian random variable of the same covariance matrix as x

$$S(x) = -\int p_x(u) \log p_x(u) du$$

An approximation for negentropy is

$$J(x) = \frac{1}{12}(E(x^3))^2 + \frac{1}{48}(kurt(x))^2$$

This approximation also suffers the same problem as kurtosis (sensitive to outliers). Other approaches were developed.

$$J(y) = k_1(E(G_1(y)))^2 + k_2(E(G_2(y)) - E(G_2(v))^2$$

A choice of G_1 and G_2 are

$$G_1 = \frac{1}{a_1}\log(\cosh(a_1 u)) \text{ and } G_2 = -\exp(-\frac{u^2}{2})$$

Based on Infomax

ICA is essentially a multivariate, parallel version of projection pursuit. Whereas projection pursuit extracts a series of signals one at a time from a set of M signal mixtures, ICA extracts M signals in parallel. This tends to make ICA more robust than projection pursuit.

The projection pursuit method uses Gram-Schmidt orthogonalization to ensure the independence of the extracted signal, while ICA use infomax and maximum likelihood estimate to ensure the independence of the extracted signal. The Non-Normality of the extracted signal is achieved by assigning an appropriate model, or prior, for the signal.

The process of ICA based on infomax in short is: given a set of signal mixtures x and a set of identical independent model cumulative distribution functions(cdfs) g, we seek the unmixing matrix W which maximizes the joint entropy of the signals $Y = g(y)$, where y = Wx are the signals extracted by W. Given the optimal W, the signals Y have maximum entropy and are therefore independent, which ensures that the extracted signals $y = g^{-1}(Y)$ are also independent. g is an invertible function, and is the signal model. If the source signal model probability density function p_s matches the probability density function of the extracted signal p_y, then maximizing the joint entropy of Y also maximizes the amount of mutual information between x and Y. For this reason, using entropy to extract independent signals is known as infomax.

Consider the entropy of the vector variable $Y = g(y)$, where $Y = Wx$ is the set of signals extracted by the unmixing matrix. For a finite set of values sampled from a distribution with pdf p_y, the entropy of Y can be estimated as:

$$H(\mathbf{Y}) = -\frac{1}{N}\sum_{t=1}^{N}\ln p_Y(\mathbf{Y}^t)$$

The joint pdf p_Y can be shown to be related to the joint pdf p_y of the extracted signals by the multivariate form:

$$p_Y(Y) = \frac{p_y(\mathbf{y})}{\left|\dfrac{\partial \mathbf{Y}}{\partial \mathbf{y}}\right|}$$

where $\mathbf{J} = \dfrac{\partial \mathbf{Y}}{\partial \mathbf{y}}$ is the Jacobian matrix. We have $|\mathbf{J}| = g'(\mathbf{y})$, and g' is the pdf assumed for source signals $g' = p_s$, therefore,

$$p_Y(Y) = \frac{p_y(\mathbf{y})}{\left|\dfrac{\partial \mathbf{Y}}{\partial \mathbf{y}}\right|} = \frac{p_y(\mathbf{y})}{p_s(\mathbf{y})}$$

therefore,

$$H(\mathbf{Y}) = -\frac{1}{N}\sum_{t=1}^{N}\ln\frac{p_y(\mathbf{y})}{p_s(\mathbf{y})}$$

We know that when $p_y = p_s$, p_Y is of uniform distribution, and $H(\mathbf{Y})$ is maximized. Since

$$p_y(\mathbf{y}) = \frac{p_x(\mathbf{x})}{\left|\dfrac{\partial \mathbf{y}}{\partial \mathbf{x}}\right|} = \frac{p_x(\mathbf{x})}{|\mathbf{W}|}$$

where $|\mathbf{W}|$ is the absolute value of the determinant of the unmixing matix W. Therefore,

$$H(\mathbf{Y}) = -\frac{1}{N}\sum_{t=1}^{N}\ln\frac{p_x(\mathbf{x}^t)}{|\mathbf{W}|p_s(\mathbf{y}^t)}$$

so,

$$H(\mathbf{Y}) = \frac{1}{N}\sum_{t=1}^{N}\ln p_s(\mathbf{y}^t) + \ln|\mathbf{W}| + H(\mathbf{x})$$

since $H(\mathbf{x}) = -\frac{1}{N}\sum_{t=1}^{N}\ln p_x(\mathbf{x}^t)$, and maximizing W does not affect H_x, so we can maximize the function

$$h(\mathbf{Y}) = \frac{1}{N}\sum_{t=1}^{N}\ln p_s(\mathbf{y}^t) + \ln|\mathbf{W}|$$

to achieve the independence of extracted signal.

If there are M marginal pdfs of the model joint pdf p_s are independent and use the commonly super-gaussian model pdf for the source signals $p_s = (1 - \tanh(\mathbf{s})^2)$, then we have

$$(\mathbf{Y}) = -\sum_{i=1}^{M}\sum_{t=1}^{N}\ln(1 - \tanh(\mathbf{w}^T\mathbf{x}^t)\,) + \ln|\mathbf{W}|.$$

In the sum, given an observed signal mixture $\mathbf{x}$, the corresponding set of extracted signals $\mathbf{y}$ and source signal model $p_s = g'$, we can find the optimal unmixing matrix $\mathbf{W}$, and make the extracted signals independent and non-gaussian. Like the projection pursuit situation, we can use gradient descent method to find the optimal solution of the unmixing matrix.

Based on Maximum Likelihood Estimation

Maximum likelihood estimation (MLE) is a standard statistical tool for finding parameter values (e.g. the unmixing matrix W) that provide the best fit of some data (e.g., the extracted signals y) to a given a model (e.g., the assumed joint probability density function (pdf) p_s of source signals).

The ML "model" includes a specification of a pdf, which in this case is the pdf p_s of the unknown source signals s. Using ML ICA, the objective is to find an unmixing matrix that yields extracted signals $y = \mathbf{W}x$ with a joint pdf as similar as possible to the joint pdf p_s of the unknown source signals s.

MLE is thus based on the assumption that if the model pdf p_s and the model parameters

A are correct then a high probability should be obtained for the data x that were actually observed. Conversely, if A is far from the correct parameter values then a low probability of the observed data would be expected.

Using MLE, we call the probability of the observed data for a given set of model parameter values (e.g., a pdf p_s and a matrix A) the *likelihood* of the model parameter values given the observed data.

We define a likelihood function L(W) of W:

$$\mathbf{L}(\mathbf{W}) = p_s(\mathbf{W}x) | \det \mathbf{W} |$$

This equals to the probability density at x, since $s = Wx$.

Thus, if we wish to find a W that is most likely to have generated the observed mixtures x from the unknown source signals s with pdf p_s then we need only find that Wwhich maximizes the *likelihood* L(W). The unmixing matrix that maximizes equation is known as the MLE of the optimal unmixing matrix.

It is common practice to use the log *likelihood*, because this is easier to evaluate. As the logarithm is a monotonic function, the W that maximizes the function L(W) also maximizes its logarithm ln L(W). This allows us to take the logarithm of equation above, which yields the log likelihood function.

$$\ln \mathbf{L}(\mathbf{W}) = \sum_i \sum_t \ln p_s(w_i^T x_t) + N \ln | \det \mathbf{W} |$$

If we substitute a commonly used high-Kurtosis model pdf for the source signals $p_s = (1 - \tanh(s)^2)$ then we have

$$\ln \mathbf{L}(\mathbf{W}) = \frac{1}{N} \sum_i^M \sum_t^N \ln(1 - \tanh(w_i^T x_t)^2) + \ln | \det \mathbf{W} |$$

This matrix W that maximizes this function is the maximum likelihood estimation.

Applications of ICA

In this topic we review some applications of ICA. The most classical application of ICA, the cocktail-party problem, was already explained in the opening section of this paper.

Separation of Artifacts in MEG Data

Magnetoencephalography (MEG) is a noninvasive technique by which the activity or the cortical neurons can be measured with very good temporal resolution and moderate spatial resolution. When using a MEG record, as a research or clinical tool, the investigator may face a problem of extracting the essential features of the neuromagnetic signals in the presence of artifacts. The amplitude of the disturbances may be higher than that of the brain signals, and the artifacts may resemble pathological signals in shape.

In the authors introduced a new method to separate brain activity from artifacts using ICA. The approach is based on the assumption that the brain activity and the artifacts, e.g. eye movements or blinks, or sensor malfunctions, are anatomically and physiologically separate processes, and this separation is reflected in the statistical independence between the magnetic signals generated by those processes. The approach follows the earlier experiments with EEG signals.

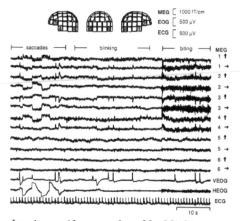

Fig.: Samples of MEG signals, showing artifacts produced by blinking, saccades bitting and cardiac cycle. For each of the 6 positions shown, the two orthogonal directons of the sensors are plotted.

The MEG signals were recorded in a magnetically shielded room with a 122-channel whole-scalp Neuromag-122 neuromagnetometer. This device collects data at 61 locations over the scalp, using orthogonal double-loop pick-up coils that couple strongly to a local source just underneath. The test person was asked to blink and make horizontal saccades, in order to produce typical ocular (eye) artifacts. Moreover, to produce myographic (muscle) artifacts, the subject was asked to bite his teeth for as long as 20 seconds. Yet another artifact was created by placing a digital watch one meter away from the helmet into the shielded room.

Figure presents a subset of 12 spontaneous MEG signals xi(t) from the frontal, temporal, and occipital areas. The figure also shows the positions of the corresponding sensors on the helmet. Due to the dimension of the data (122 magnetic signals were recorded), it is impractical to plot all the MEG signals $x_i(t)$, $i = 1,...,122$. Also two electro-oculogram channels and the electrocardiogram are presented, but they were not used in computing the ICA.

The signal vector x in the ICA model consists now of the amplitudes $x_i(t)$ of the 122 signals at a certain time point, so the dimensionality is n = 122. In the theoretical model, x is regarded as a random vector, and the measurements x(t) give a set of realizations of x as time proceeds. Note that in the basic ICA model that we are using, the temporal correlations in the signals are not utilized at all.

The x(t) vectors were whitened using PCA and the dimensionality was decreased at the same time. Then, using the FastICA algorithm, a subset of the rows of the separating matrix W of equation $s = Wx$. were computed. Once a vector wi has become available, an ICA signal $s_i(t)$ can be computed from $s_i(t) = w_i^T x'(t)$ with $x'(t)$ now denoting the whitened and lower dimensional signal vector.

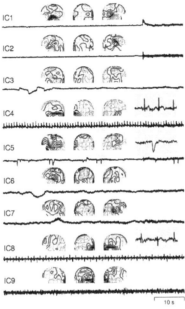

Fig.: Nine independent components found from the MEG data. For each component the left, back and right views of the field patterns generated by these components are shown-full line stands for magnetic flux coming out from the head, and dotted line the flux inwards.

Figure shows independent components (IC's) $s_i(t), i = 1,...,9$ found from the recorded data together with the corresponding field patterns. The first two IC's are clearly due to the musclular activity originated from the biting. Their separation into two components seems to correspond, on the basis of the field patterns, to two different sets of muscles that were activated during the process. IC3 and IC5 are showing the horizontal eye movements and the eye blinks, respectively. IC4 represents the cardiac artifact that is very clearly extracted.

To find the remaining artifacts, the data were high-pass filtered, with cutoff frequency at 1 Hz. Next, the independent component IC8 was found. It shows clearly the artifact originated at the digital watch, located to the right side of the magnetometer. The last independent component IC9 is related to a sensor presenting higher RMS (root mean squared) noise than the others.

The results of figure clearly show that using the ICA technique and the FastICA algorithm, it is possible to isolate both eye movement and eye blinking artifacts, as well as cardiac, myographic, and other artifacts from MEG signals. The FastICA algorithm is an especially suitable tool, because artifact removal is an interactive technique and the investigator may freely choose how many of the IC's he or she wants.

In addition to reducing artifacts, ICA can be used to decompose evoked fields, which enables direct access to the underlying brain functioning, which is likely to be of great significance in neuroscientific research.

Finding Hidden Factors in Financial Data

It is a tempting alternative to try ICA on financial data. There are many situations in that application domain in which parallel time series are available, such as currency exchange rates or daily returns of stocks, that may have some common underlying factors. ICA might reveal some driving mechanisms that otherwise remain hidden. In a recent study of a stock portfolio, it was found that ICA is a complementary tool to PCA, allowing the underlying structure of the data to be more readily observed.

In we applied ICA on a different problem: the cashflow of several stores belonging to the same retail chain, trying to find the fundamental factors common to all stores that affect the cashflow data. Thus, the cashflow effect of the factors specific to any particular store, i.e., the effect of the actions taken at the individual stores and in its local environment could be analyzed.

The assumption of having some underlying independent components in this specific application may not be unrealistic. For example, factors like seasonal variations due to holidays and annual variations, and factors having a sudden effect on the purchasing power of the customers like prize changes of various commodities, can be expected to have an effect on all the retail stores, and such factors can be assumed to be roughly independent of each other. Yet, depending on the policy and skills of the individual manager like e.g. advertising efforts, the effect of the factors on the cash flow of specific retail outlets are slightly different. By ICA, it is possible to isolate both the underlying factors and the effect weights, thus also making it possible to group the stores on the basis of their managerial policies using only the cash flow time series data.

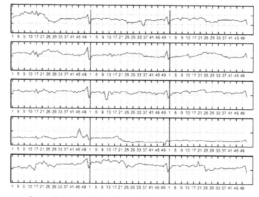

Fig.: Five samples of the original cashflow time series (mean removed, normalized to unit standard deviation). Horizontal axis: time in weeks.

The data consisted of the weekly cash flow in 40 stores that belong to the same retail chain; the cash flow measurements cover 140 weeks. Some examples of the original data $x_i(t)$ are shown in figure.

The prewhitening was performed so that the original signal vectors were projected to the subspace spanned by their first five principal components and the variances were normalized to 1. Thus the dimension of the signal space was decreased from 40 to 5. Using the FastICA algorithm, four IC's $s_i(t)$, $i = 1,...,5$ were estimated. As depicted in figure, the FastICA algorithm has found several clearly different fundamental factors hidden in the original data.

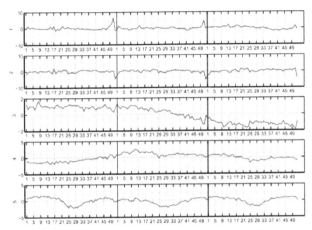

Fig.: Four independent components or fundamental factors found from the cashflow data.

The factors have clearly different interpretations. The upmost two factors follow the sudden changes that are caused by holidays etc.; the most prominent example is the Christmas time. The factor on the bottom row, on the other hand, reflects the slower seasonal variation, with the effect of the summer holidays clearly visible. The factor on the third row could represent a still slower variation, something resembling a trend. The last factor, on the fourth row, is different from the others; it might be that this factor follows mostly the relative competitive position of the retail chain with respect to its competitors, but other interpretations are also possible.

Reducing Noise in Natural Images

The third example deals with finding ICA filters for natural images and, based on the ICA decomposition, removing noise from images corrupted with additive Gaussian noise.

A set of digitized natural images were used to denote the vector of pixel gray levels in an image window by x. We are not this time considering multivalued time series or images changing with time; instead the elements of x are indexed by the location in the image window or patch. The sample windows were taken at random locations. The 2-D structure of the windows is of no significance here: row by row scanning was used to turn a square image window into a vector of pixel values. The independent components of such image windows are represented in figure. Each window in this figure corresponds to one of the columns ai of the mixing matrix A. Thus an observed image window is a superposition of these windows, with independent coefficients. Now, suppose a noisy image model holds:

$$z = x + n$$

where n is uncorrelated noise, with elements indexed in the image window in the same way as x, and z is the measured image window corrupted with noise. Let us further assume that n is Gaussian and x is non-Gaussian. There are many ways to clean the noise; one example is to make a transformation to spatial frequency space by DFT, do low-pass filtering, and return to the image space by IDFT. This is not very efficient, however. A better method is the recently introduced Wavelet Shrinkage method in which a transform based on wavelets is used, or methods based on median filtering. None of these methods is explicitly taking advantage of the image statistics.

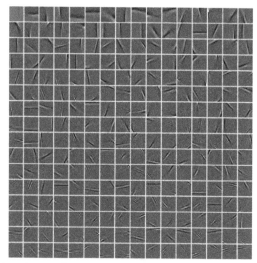

Fig.: Basis functions in ICA of natural images. The input window size was 16 x 16 Pixels. These basis functions can be considered as the independent features of images.

We have recently introduced another, statistically principled method called Sparse Code Shrinkage. It is very closely related to independent component analysis. Briefly, if we model the density of x by ICA, and assume n Gaussian, then the Maximum Likelihood (ML) solution for x given the measurement z can be developed in the signal model.

The ML solution can be simply computed, albeit approximately, by using a decomposition that is an orthogonalized version of ICA. The transform is given by

$$Wz = Wx + Wn = s + Wn,$$

where W is here an orthogonal matrix that is the best orthognal approximation of the inverse of the ICA mixing matrix. The noise term Wn is still Gaussian and white. With a suitably chosen orthogonal transform W, however, the density of Wx = s becomes highly non-Gaussian, e.g., super-Gaussian with a high positive kurtosis. This depends of course on the original x signals, as we are assuming in fact that there exists a model x = W^{T}s for the signal, such that the "source signals" or elements of s have a positive kurtotic density, in which case the ICA transform gives highly supergaussian components. This seems to hold at least for image windows of natural scenes.

It was shown that, assuming a Laplacian density for s_i, the ML solution for si is given by a "shrinkage function" $\hat{s}_i = g([Wz]i)$, or in vector form, $\hat{s} = g(Wz)$. Function g(.) has a characteristic shape: it is zero close to the origin and then linear after a cutting value depending on the parameters of the Laplacian density and the Gaussian noise density. Assuming other forms for the densities, other optimal shrinkage functions can be derived.

In the Sparse Code Shrinkage method, the shrinkage operation is performed in the rotated space, after which the estimate for the signal in the original space is given by rotating back:

$$\hat{x} = W^T \hat{s} = W^T g(Wz).$$

Thus we get the Maximum Likelihood estimate for the image window x in which much of the noise has been removed.

The rotation operator W is such that the sparsity of the components s = Wx is maximized. This operator can be learned with a modification of the FastICA algorithm.

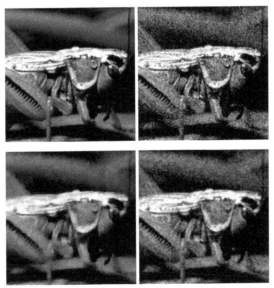

Fig.: An experiment in denoising. Upper left: original image. Upper right: Original image corrupted with noise; the noise level is 50%. Lower left: the recovered image after applying sparse code shrinkage. Lower right: for comparison, a wiener filtered image.

A noise cleaning result is shown in figure. A noiseless image and a noisy version, in which the noise level is 50 % of the signal level, are shown. The results of the Sparse Code Shrinkage method and classic wiener filtering are given, indicating that Sparse Code Shrinkage may be a promising approach. The noise is reduced without blurring edges or other sharp features as much as in wiener filtering. This is largely due to the strongly nonlinear nature of the shrinkage operator, that is optimally adapted to the inherent statistics of natural images.

Telecommunications

Finally, we mention another emerging application area of great potential: telecommunications. An example of a real-world communications application where blind separation techniques are useful is the separation of the user's own signal from the interfering other users' signals in CDMA (Code-Division Multiple Access) mobile communications. This problem is semi-blind in the sense that certain additional prior information is available on the CDMA data model. But the number of parameters to be estimated is often so high that suitable blind source separation techniques taking into account the available prior knowledge provide a clear performance improvement over more traditional estimation techniques.

References

- Roffo, G.; Melzi, S.; Cristani, M. (2015-12-01). "Infinite Feature Selection". 2015 IEEE International Conference on Computer Vision (ICCV): 4202–4210. doi:10.1109/ICCV.2015.478. ISBN 978-1-4673-8391-2

- Fisher, R. A. (1936). "The Use of Multiple Measurements in Taxonomic Problems". Annals of Eugenics. 7 (2): 179–188. doi:10.1111/j.1469-1809.1936.tb02137.x. hdl:2440/15227

- Dimensionality-reduction: geeksforgeeks.org, Retrieved 19 April 2018

- Roffo, Giorgio; Melzi, Simone (September 2016). "Features Selection via Eigenvector Centrality" (PDF). NFmcp2016. Retrieved 12 November 2016

- Rao, R. C. (1948). "The utilization of multiple measurements in problems of biological classification". Journal of the Royal Statistical Society, Series B. 10 (2): 159–203. JSTOR 2983775

- An-introduction-to-feature-selection: machinelearningmastery.com, Retrieved 23 April 2018

- McLachlan, G. J. (2004). Discriminant Analysis and Statistical Pattern Recognition. Wiley Interscience. ISBN 0-471-69115-1. MR 1190469

- Perriere, G.; Thioulouse, J. (2003). "Use of Correspondence Discriminant Analysis to predict the subcellular location of bacterial proteins". Computer Methods and Programs in Biomedicine. 70: 99–105. doi:10.1016/s0169-2607(02)00011-1

- Practical-guide-principal-component-analysis-python: analyticsvidhya.com, Retrieved 30 May 2018

- Garson, G. D. (2008). Discriminant function analysis. "Archived copy". Archived from the original on 2008-03-12. Retrieved 2008-03-04

Reinforcement Learning

Reinforcement learning is concerned with the way a software agent takes an action to maximize some result. All the diverse principles of reinforcement learning have been carefully analyzed in this chapter. It includes vital topics such as Q-learning, state-action-reward-state-action and temporal difference learning, among others.

Reinforcement learning is an area of machine learning reinforcement. It is about taking suitable action to maximize reward in a particular situation. It is employed by various software and machines to find the best possible behavior or path it should take in a specific situation. Reinforcement learning differs from the supervised learning in a way that in supervised learning the training data has the answer key with it so the model is trained with the correct answer itself whereas in reinforcement learning, there is no answer but the reinforcement agent decides what to do to perform the given task. In the absence of training dataset, it is bound to learn from its experience.

Example: The problem is as follows: We have an agent and a reward, with many hurdles in between. The agent is supposed to find the best possible path to reach the reward. The following problem explains the problem more easily.

The above image shows robot, diamond and fire. The goal of the robot is to get the reward that is the diamond and avoid the hurdles that are fire. The robot learns by trying all the possible paths and then choosing the path which gives him the reward with the least hurdles. Each right step will give the robot a reward and each wrong step will subtract the reward of the robot. The total reward will be calculated when it reaches the final reward that is the diamond.

Main points in Reinforcement learning –

- Input: The input should be an initial state from which the model will start.

- Output: There are many possible output as there are variety of solution to a particular problem.

- Training: The training is based upon the input, The model will return a state and the user will decide to reward or punish the model based on its output.

- The model keeps continues to learn.

- The best solution is decided based on the maximum reward.

Types of Reinforcement

There are two types of reinforcement:

1. Positive

Positive Reinforcement is defined as when an event, occurs due to a particular behavior, increases the strength and the frequency of the behavior. In other words it has a positive effect on the behavior.

Advantages of reinforcement learning are:

- Maximizes performance

- Sustain change for a long period of time

Disadvantages of reinforcement learning:

- Too much Reinforcement can lead to overload of states which can diminish the results

2. Negative

Negative Reinforcement is defined as strengthening of a behavior because a negative condition is stopped or avoided.

Advantages of reinforcement learning:

- Increases behavior

- Provide defiance to minimum standard of performance

Disadvantages of reinforcement learning:

- It only provides enough to meet up the minimum behavior

Reinforcement Learning Applications

Robotics and Industrial Automation

Reinforcement Learning (RL) enables a robot to autonomously discover an optimal behavior through trial-and-error interactions with its environment. In Reinforcement Learning, the agent (i.e., the designer of a control task) provides constructive feedback in terms of a scalar objective function that measures the one-step performance of the robot. This serves as a guideline for deciding the next action.

Industrial automation is another major area where Reinforcement Learning has contributed significantly. A classic example would be of Google, which has reduced energy consumption (HVAC) in its own data centers through RL technologies from DeepMind. Startups like Bonsai use RL for industrial applications.

Data Science and Machine Learning

With machine learning libraries becoming more accessible, deep learning techniques are widely being used by data scientists and machine learning engineers, to help people identify and tune neural network architectures are active areas of research. Several research groups have used RL to make the process of designing neural network architectures easier. AutoML from Google, for example, uses RL to produce state-of-the-art machine-generated neural network architectures for computer vision and language modeling.

Education and Training

Reinforcement Learning is already showing ripples in online tutorials and virtual classrooms. Deep Learning researchers are looking for new ways use RL and other machine learning methods in online tutoring systems and personalized learning. Reinforcement Learning tutorials will be instrumental in providing custom instruction and materials to serve the needs of individual students. RL algorithms and statistical methods may also be developed in such a way that requires less data for use in future tutoring systems.

Healthcare

Healthcare is another area where Reinforcement Learning is fast creating impressions. The RL setup of an agent may interact with an environment receiving feedback based on actions taken. Several RL applications in health care mostly pertain to finding optimal treatment policies. Deep learning scientists are researching on RL applications that serve the purpose of medical equipment, medication dosing, and two-stage clinical trials.

Some of the other applications of Reinforcement Learning include cross-channel marketing optimization and real-time bidding systems for online display advertising.

Approaches to Reinforcement Theory of Learning

Reinforcement Learning has a number of approaches. Here, discussed three most well-known approaches: Value-based Learning, Policy-based Learning, and Model-Based Learning Approaches.

Value Based Learning Approach

Value-based Learning estimates the optimal value function, which is the maximum value achievable under any policy. Storing the value function (or) policy might not be possible especially if the state-action pairs are high dimensional. Thus, function approximators like linear regression, Neural networks are used. In value-based RL, the goal is to optimize the value function $V(s)$. The value function is a function that tells us the maximum expected future reward the agent will get in each state.

The value of each state is the total amount of the reward an agent can expect to accumulate over the future, starting in that state. Then the agent uses this value function to select which state to choose at each step. The agent decides to take up the state with the biggest value.

Policy-based Learning Approach

Policy-based Learning searches directly for the optimal policy, which achieves the maximum future reward. In policy-based approach, we want to directly optimize the policy function $\pi(s)$ without using a value function. The policy is what defines the agent behavior at a given time. We learn a policy function. This lets us map each state to the best corresponding action.

This approach has two types of policy

- Deterministic: a policy at a given state will always return the same action.
- Stochastic: output a distribution probability over actions.
- Model-Based Learning Approach:

Model Based Learning Approach

In Model-based RL, the environment is treated as a model for learning. This means a model of the environmental behavior is created. This is a great approach until you discover that each environment will need a different model representation.

Q-learning

Q-learning is a form of model-free reinforcement learning. It can also be viewed as a method of asynchronous dynamic programming (DP). It provides agents with the capability of learning to act optimally in Markovian domains by experiencing the consequences of actions, without requiring them to build maps of the domains. Q-learning is a primitive form of learning, but, as such, it can operate as the basis of far more sophisticated devices.

Consider a computational agent moving around some discrete, finite world, choosing one from a finite collection of actions at every time step. The world constitutes a controlled Markov process with the agent as a controller. At step n the agent is equipped to register the state x_n ($\in X$) of the world, and can choose its action a_n ($\in \alpha$)[1] accordingly. The agent receives a probabilistic reward r_n, whose mean value $\Re_{x_n}(a_n)$ depends only on the state and action, and the state of the world changes probabilistically to y_n according to the law:

$$\text{Prob}\left[y_n = y \middle| x_n, a_n\right] = P_{x_n y}\left[a_n\right].$$

The task facing the agent is that of determining an optimal policy, one that maximizes total discounted expected reward. By discounted reward, we mean that rewards received s steps hence are worth less than rewards received now, by a factor of γ^s $(0 < \gamma < 1)$. Under a policy π, the value of state x is:

$$V^\pi(x) = \Re_x\left(\pi(x)\right) + \gamma \sum_y P_{xy}\left[\pi(x)\right] V^\pi(y \text{ bracket close in eq.}$$

because the agent expects to receive $\Re_x\left(\pi(x)\right)$ immediately for performing the action π, recommends, and then moves to a state that is 'worth' $V^\pi(y)$ to it, with probability $P_{xy}\left[\pi(x)\right]$. The theory of DP assures us that there is at least one optimal stationary policy π^* which is such that

$$V^*(x) \equiv V^{\pi^*}(x) = \max_a \left\{ \Re_x(a) + \gamma \sum_y P_{xy}[a] V^{\pi^*}(y) \right\}$$

is as well as an agent can do from state x. Although this might look circular, it is actually well defined, and DP provides a number of methods for calculating V^* and one π^*, assuming that $\Re_x(a)$ and $P_{xy}[a]$ are known. The task facing a Q learner is that of determining a π^* without initially knowing these values. There are traditional methods for learning $\Re_x(a)$ and $P_{xy}[a]$ while concurrently performing DP, but any assumption of certainty equivalence, i.e., calculating actions as if the current model were accurate, costs dearly in the early stages of learning. Classes Q-learning as incremental dynamic programming, because of the step-by-step manner in which it determines the optimal policy.

For a policy π, define Q values (or action-values) as:

$$Q^\pi(x,a) = \Re_x(a) + \gamma \sum_y P_{xy}\left[\pi(x)a\right] V^\pi(y).$$

In other words, the Q value is the expected discounted reward for executing action a at state x and following policy π hereafter. The object in Q-learning is to estimate the Q values for an optimal policy. For convenience, define these as $Q^*(x,a) \equiv Q^{\pi^*}(x,a), \forall x,a$. It is straightforward to show that $V^*(x) = max_a\ Q^*(x, a)$ and that if a* is an action at which the maximum is attained, then an optimal policy can be formed as $\pi^*(x) \equiv a^*$. Herein lies the utility of the Q, values—if an agent can learn them, it can easily decide what it is optimal to do. Although there may be more than one optimal policy or a*, the Q^* values are unique.

In Q-learning, the agent's experience consists of a sequence of distinct stages or episodes. In the nth episode, the agent:

- Observes its current state x_n,

- Selects and performs an action a_n,

- Observes the subsequent state y_n,

- Receives an immediate payoff r_n, and

- Adjusts its Q_{n-1} values using a learning factor a_n, according to:

$$Q_n(x,a) = \begin{cases} (1-\alpha_n) \quad Q_{n-1}(x,a) + \alpha_n \left[r_n + \gamma V_{n-1}(y_n) \right] & \text{if } x = x_n \text{ and } a = a_n, \\ Q_{n-1}(x,a) & \text{otherwise,} \end{cases}$$

where

$$V_{n-1}(y) \equiv \max_b \{ Q_{n-1}(y,b) \}.$$

is the best the agent thinks it can do from state y. Of course, in the early stages of learning, the Q, values may not accurately reflect the policy they implicitly define (the maximizing actions in equation). The initial Q, values, Q, o (X, a), for all states and actions are assumed given.

Theorem

Given bounded rewards $|r_n| \le \Re,$, learning rates $0 \le \alpha_n < 1$, and

$$\sum_{i=1}^{\infty} \alpha_n^i(x,a) = \infty, \sum_{i=1}^{\infty} \left[\alpha_n^i(x,a) \right]^2 < \infty, \forall x, a,$$

then $Q_n(x, a) \to Q^*(x, a)$ as $n \to \infty$, $\forall x, a$, with probability 1.

The Convergence Proof

The key to the convergence proof is an artificial controlled Markov process called the action replay process ARP, which is constructed from the episode sequence and the learning rate sequence α_n.

A formal description of the ARP is given in the appendix, but the easiest way to think of it is in terms of a card game. Imagine each episode $\langle x_t, a_t, y_t, r_t, a_t, \rangle$ written on a card.

All the cards together form an infinite deck, with the first episode-card next-to-bottom and stretching infinitely upwards, in order. The bottom card (numbered 0) has written on it the agent's initial values $Q_0\langle x, a\rangle$ for all pairs of x and a. A state of the ARP, $\langle x, n\rangle$ consists of a card number (or level) n, together with a state x from the real process. The actions permitted in the ARP are the same as those permitted in the real process.

The next state of the ARP, given current state (x, n) and action a, is determined as follows. First, all the cards for episodes later than n are eliminated, leaving just a finite deck. Cards are then removed one at a time from top of this deck and examined until one is found whose starting state and action match x and a, say at episode t. Then a biased coin is flipped, with probability a, of coming out heads, and 1 - α, of tails. If the coin turns up heads, the episode recorded on this card is replayed, a process described below; if the coin turns up tails, this card too is thrown away and the search continues for another card matching x and a. If the bottom card is reached, the game stops in a special, absorbing, state, and just provides the reward written on this card for x, a, namely $Q_0\langle x, a\rangle$.

Replaying the episode on card t consists of emitting the reward, r_t, written on the card, and then moving to the next state $\langle y_t, t - 1\rangle$ in the ARP, where y_t is the state to which the real process went on that episode. Card t itself is thrown away. The next state transition of the ARP will be taken based on just the remaining deck.

The above completely specifies how state transitions and rewards are determined in the ARP. Define $P^{ARP}_{\langle x,n\rangle\langle y,m\rangle}[a]$ and $\Re^{(n)}_x(a)$ as the transition-probability matrices and expected rewards of the ARP. Also define:

$$P^{(n)}_{xy}[a] = \sum_{m-1}^{n-1} P^{ARP}_{\langle x,n\rangle\langle y,m\rangle}[a]$$

as the probabilities that, for each x, n and a, executing action a at state $\langle x,n\rangle$ in the ARP leads to state y of the real process at some lower level in the deck.

As defined above, the ARP is as much a controlled Markov process as is the real process. One can therefore consider sequences of states and controls, and also optimal discounted Q^* values for the ARP. During such a sequence, episode cards are only removed from the deck, and are never replaced. Therefore, after a finite number of actions, the bottom card will always be reached.

Lemmas

Two lemmas form the heart of the proof. One shows that, effectively by construction, the optimal Q, value for ARP state $\langle x,n\rangle$ and action a is just $Q_n(x, a)$. The next shows that for almost all possible decks, $P^{(n)}_{xy}[a]$ converge to $P_{xy}[a]$ and $\Re^{(n)}_x(a)$ converge to $\Re_x(a)$ as $n \to \infty$. Informal statements of the lemmas and outlines of their proofs are given below; consult the appendix for the formal statements.

Lemma A

$Q_n(x, a)$ are the optimal action values for ARP states $\langle x,n \rangle$ and ARP actions a.

The ARP was directly constructed to have this property. The proof proceeds by backwards induction, following the ARP down through the stack of past episodes.

Lemma B

Lemma B concerns the convergence of the ARP to the real process. The first two steps are preparatory; the next two specify the form of the convergence and provide foundations for proving that it occurs.

B.1

Consider a discounted, bounded-reward, finite Markov process. From any starting state x, the difference between the value of that state under the finite sequence of s actions and its value under that same sequence followed by any other actions tends to 0 *as* $s \to \infty$.

This follows from the presence of the discount factor, which weighs the $(s+1)^{th}$ state by $\gamma^s \to 0$ as $s \to \infty$.

B.2

Given any level l, there exists another yet higher level, h, such that the probability can be made arbitrarily small of straying below l after taking 5 actions in the ARP, starting from above h.

The probability, starting at level h of the ARP of straying below any fixed level l tends to 0 as $h \to \infty$. Therefore there is some sufficiently high level for which s actions can be safely accommodated, with an arbitrarily high probability of leaving the ARP above l.

B.3

With probability 1, the probabilities $P_{xy}^{(n)}[a]$ and expected rewards $\mathfrak{R}_x^{(n)}(a)$ in the ARP converge and tend to the transition matrices and expected rewards in the real process as the level n increases to infinity. This, together with B.2, makes it appropriate to consider $P_{xy}^{(n)}[a]$ rather than the ARP transition matrices $P_{\langle x,n \rangle \langle y,m \rangle}^{ARP}[a]$ i.e., essentially ignoring the level at which the ARP enters state y.

The ARP effectively estimates the mean rewards and transitions of the real process over all the episodes. Since its raw data are unbiased, the conditions on the sums and sums of squares of the learning rates $\alpha_{n(X,a)}^i$ ensure the convergence with probability one.

B.4

Consider executing a series of s actions in the ARP and in the real process. If the probabilities $P_{xy}^{(n)}[a]$ and expected rewards $\mathfrak{R}_x^{(n)}(a)$ at appropriate levels of the ARP for each of the actions, are close to $P_{xy}[a]$ and $\mathfrak{R}_x(a) \ \forall a, x, y$, respectively, then the value of the series of actions in the ARP will be close to its value in the real process.

The discrepancy in the action values over a finite number s of actions between the values of two approximately equal Markov processes grows at most quadratically with s. So, if the transition probabilities and rewards are close, then the values of the actions must be close too.

The Theorem

Putting these together, the ARP tends towards the real process, and so its optimal Q, values do too. But $Q_n(x, a)$ are the optimal Q values for the nth level of the ARP (by Lemma A), and so tend to $Q^*(x, a)$.

Assume, without loss of generality, that $Q_0(x,a) < \mathfrak{R}/(1-\gamma)$ and that $\mathfrak{R} \geq 1$

Given $\epsilon \to 0$, choose s such that

$$\gamma^s \frac{\mathfrak{R}}{1-\gamma} < \frac{\epsilon}{6}.$$

By B.3, with probability 1, it is possible to choose l sufficiently large such that for $n > l$, and $\forall a, x, y$,

$$\left| P_{xy}^{(n)}[a] - P_{xy} \right| < \frac{\epsilon}{3s(s+1)}, \text{and} \left| \mathfrak{R}_x^{(n)} - \mathfrak{R}_x(a) \right| < \frac{\epsilon}{3s(s+1)},$$

By B.2, choose h sufficiently large such that for $n > h$, the probability, after taking s actions, of ending up at a level lower than l is less than $\min \left\{ \left(\epsilon(1-\gamma)/6s\mathfrak{R} \right), \left(\epsilon/3(s+1)\mathfrak{R} \right) \right\}$. This means that

$$\left| P_{xy}'^{(n)}[a] - P_{xy} \right| < \frac{2\epsilon}{3s(s+1)\mathfrak{R}}, \text{and} \left| \mathfrak{R}_x'^{(n)} - \mathfrak{R}_x(a) \right| < \frac{2\epsilon}{3s(s+1)},$$

where, the primes on $P'^{(n)}$ and $\mathfrak{R}'^{(n)}$ indicate that these are conditional on the level in the ARP after the sth step being greater than l.

Then, for $n > h$, by B.4, compare the value $\bar{Q}_{ARP}(\langle x, n \rangle, a_1, \ldots, a_s)$ of taking actions $a_1, \ldots, a_s$ at state x in the ARP, with $\bar{Q}(x, a_1, \ldots, a_s)$ of taking them in the real process:

$$\left| \bar{Q}_{ARP}\left(\langle x, n \rangle, a_1, \dots, a_s \right) - \bar{Q}\left(x, a_1, \dots, a_s \right) \right| <$$

$$\frac{(1-\gamma)}{6s\Re} \frac{2s\Re}{1-\gamma} + \frac{2\in}{3s(s+1)} \frac{s(s+1)}{2} = \frac{2\in}{3}.$$

Where, in equation 4, the first term counts the cost of conditions for B.2 not holding, as the cost of straying below l is bounded by $2s\Re/(1-\gamma)$ The second term is the cost, from B.4, of the incorrect rewards and transition probabilities.

However, by B.1, the effect of taking only s actions makes a difference of less than $\in/6$ for both the ARP and the real process. Also since equation 4 applies to any set of actions, it applies perforce to a set of actions optimal for either the ARP or the real process. Therefore;

$$\left| Q^*_{ARP}\left(\langle x, n \rangle, a \right) - Q^*\left(x, a \right) \right| < \in.$$

So, with probability 1, $Q_n\left(x, a \right) \to Q^*\left(x, a \right)$ as $n \to \infty$ as required.

Influence of Variables

Explore vs. Exploit

The learning rate or *step size* determines to what extent newly acquired information overrides old information. A factor of 0 makes the agent learn nothing (exclusively exploiting prior knowledge), while a factor of 1 makes the agent consider only the most recent information (ignoring prior knowledge to explore possibilities). In fully deterministic environments, a learning rate of $\alpha_t = 1$ is optimal. When the problem is stochastic, the algorithm converges under some technical conditions on the learning rate that require it to decrease to zero. In practice, often a constant learning rate is used, such as $\alpha_t = 0.1$ for all t.

Discount Factor

The discount factor γ determines the importance of future rewards. A factor of 0 will make the agent "myopic" (or short-sighted) by only considering current rewards, while a factor approaching 1 will make it strive for a long-term high reward. If the discount factor meets or exceeds 1, the action values may diverge. For $\gamma = 1$, without a terminal state, or if the agent never reaches one, all environment histories become infinitely long, and utilities with additive, undiscounted rewards generally become infinite. Even with a discount factor only slightly lower than 1, Q-function learning leads to propagation of errors and instabilities when the value function is approximated with an artificial neural network. In that case, starting with a lower discount factor and increasing it towards its final value accelerates learning.

Initial Conditions (Qo)

Since Q-learning is an iterative algorithm, it implicitly assumes an initial condition before the first update occurs. High initial values, also known as "optimistic initial conditions", can encourage exploration: no matter what action is selected, the update rule will cause it to have lower values than the other alternative, thus increasing their choice probability. The first reward r can be used to reset the initial conditions. According to this idea, the first time an action is taken the reward is used to set the value of Q. This allows immediate learning in case of fixed deterministic rewards. a model that incorporates *reset of initial conditions* (RIC) is expected to predict participants' behavior better than a model that assumes any *arbitrary initial condition* (AIC). RIC seems to be consistent with human behavior in repeated binary choice experiments.

Implementation

Q-learning at its simplest stores data in tables. This approach falters with increasing numbers of states/actions.

Function Approximation

Q-learning can be combined with function approximation. This makes it possible to apply the algorithm to larger problems, even when the state space is continuous.

One solution is to use an (adapted) artificial neural network as a function approximator. Function approximation may speed up learning in finite problems, due to the fact that the algorithm can generalize earlier experiences to previously unseen states.

Quantization

Another technique to decrease the state/action space quantizes possible values. Consider the example of learning to balance a stick on a finger. To describe a state at a certain point in time involves the position of the finger in space, its velocity, the angle of the stick and the angular velocity of the stick. This yields a four-element vector that describes one state, i.e. a snapshot of one state encoded into four values. The problem is that infinitely many possible states are present. To shrink the possible space of valid actions multiple values can be assigned to a bucket. The exact distance of the finger from its starting position (-Infinity to Infinity) is not known, but rather whether it is far away or not (Near, Far).

State–Action–Reward–State–Action

SARSA stands for State-Action-Reward-State-Action. It is a technique for learning a Markov decision process (MDP) strategy, used in for reinforcement learning into the field of artificial intelligence (AI) and machine learning (ML).

SARSA very much resembles Q-learning. The key difference between SARSA and Q-learning is that SARSA is an on-policy algorithm. It implies that SARSA learns the Q-value based on the action performed by the current policy instead of the greedy policy.

$$Q(s_t,a_t) \leftarrow Q(s_t,a_t) + a[r_{t+1} + \gamma Q(s_{t+1},a_{t+1}) - Q(s_t,a_t)]$$

The action $a_{(t+1)}$ is the action performed in the next state $s_{(t+1)}$ under current policy.

SARSA Pseudo Code

SARSA (λ): Learn function $Q : \mathcal{X} \times \mathcal{A} \rightarrow \mathbb{R}$

Require

Sates $\mathcal{X} = \{1, \cdots, n_x\}$

Actions $\mathcal{A} = \{1, \cdots, n_a\}$, $A : \mathcal{X} \Rightarrow \mathcal{A}$

Reward function $R : \mathcal{X} \times \mathcal{A} \rightarrow \mathbb{R}$

Black-box (probabilistic) transition functions $T : \mathcal{X} \times \mathcal{A} \rightarrow \mathcal{X}$

Learning rate $\alpha \in [0,1]$, typically $\alpha = 0.1$

Discounting factor $\mathcal{Y} \in [0,1]$

$\lambda \in [0,1]$: Trade – off between TD and MC

procedure QLEARNING $(\mathcal{X}, A, R, T, \alpha, \gamma, \lambda)$

    Initialize $Q : \mathcal{X} \times \mathcal{A} \rightarrow \mathbb{R}$ arbitrarily

    Initialize $e : \mathcal{X} \times \mathcal{A} \rightarrow \mathbb{R}$ with o

    while Q is not converged do

        Select $(s,a) \in \mathcal{X} \times \mathcal{A}$ arbitrarily

        while s is not terminal do

            $r \leftarrow R(s,a)$

            $s' \leftarrow T(s,a)$

            Calculate π based on Q (e.g. epsilon-greedy)

            $a' \leftarrow \pi(s')$

$$e(s,a) \leftarrow e(s,a) + 1$$

$$\delta \leftarrow r + \gamma.Q(s',a') - Q(s,a)$$

for $(\tilde{s}, \tilde{a}) \in \mathcal{X} \times \mathcal{A}$ do

$$Q(s',a') \leftarrow Q(s',a') + \alpha.\delta.e(s',a')$$

$$e(s',a') \leftarrow \gamma.\lambda.e(s',a')$$

$$s \leftarrow s'$$

$$a \leftarrow a'$$

return Q

From the pseudo code above you may notice two action selection is performed, which always follows the current policy. By contrast, Q-learning has no constraint over the next action, as long as it maximizes the Q-value for the next state. Therefore, SARSA is an on-policy algorithm.

Expected Sarsa

Since Sarsa's convergence guarantee requires that every state be visited infinitely often, the behavior and therefore also the estimation policy is typically stochastic so as to ensure sufficient exploration. As a result, there can be substantial variance in Sarsa updates, since a_{t+1} is not selected deterministically.

Of course, variance can occur in updates for any TD method because the environment can introduce stochasticity through T and R. Since TD methods are typically used when a model of the environment is not available, there is little the agent can do about this stochasticity except employ a suitably low α. However, the additional variance introduced by Sarsa stems from the policy stochasticity, which is known to the agent.

Expected Sarsa is a variation of Sarsa, which exploits this knowledge to prevent stochasticity in the policy from further increasing variance. It does so by basing the update, not on $Q(s_{t+1}, a_{t+1})$, but on its expected value $E\{Q(s_{t+1}, a_{t+1})\}$. The resulting update rule is:

$$Q(s_t, a_t) \leftarrow Q(s_t, a_t) + \alpha \Big[r_{t+1} +$$
$$\gamma \sum_a \pi(s_{t+1}, a) Q(s_{t+1}, a) - Q(s_t, a_t) \Big]$$

Using this expectation reduces the variance in the update as we show formally in variance analysis. Lower variance means that in practice α can often be increased in order to speed learning. In fact, when the environment is deterministic, Expected Sarsa can employ $\alpha = 1$, while Sarsa still requires $\alpha < 1$ to cope with policy stochasticity.

Algorithm 1 shows the complete Expected Sarsa algorithm. Because the update rule of Expected Sarsa, unlike Sarsa, does not make use of the action taken in s_{t+1}, action selection can occur after the update. Doing so can be advantageous in problems containing states with returning actions, i.e. $P(s_{t+1} = s_t) > 0$. When $s_{t+1} = s_t$, performing an update of $Q(s_t, a_t)$, will also update $Q(s_{t+1}, a_t)$, yielding a better estimate before action selection occurs.

Algorithm 1 Expected Sarsa

1. Initialize $Q(s, a)$ arbitrarily for all s, a.

2. loop {over episodes}.

3. Initialize s.

4. repeat {for each step in the episode}.

5. choose a from s using policy π derived from Q.

6. take action a, observe r and s'.

7. $Vs' = \sum_a \pi(s',a) \cdot Q(s',a)$.

8. $Q(s,a) \leftarrow Q(s,a) + \alpha[r + \gamma V_{s'} - Q(s,a)]$.

9. $s \leftarrow s'$.

10. until s is terminal.

11. end loop.

Expected Sarsa can also be viewed, not as a lower variance version of Sarsa, but as an on-policy version of Q-learning. Note the similarity between the expectation value $E\{Q(s_{t+1},a_{t+1})\}$ used by Expected Sarsa and (2) relating $V^\pi(s)$ to $Q^\pi(s,a)$ Since $Q(s,a)$ is an estimate of $Q^\pi(s,a)$ its expectation value can be seen as the estimate $V(s)$ for $V^\pi(s)$ using the relation:

$$V(s) = \sum_a \pi(s,a) Q(s,a)$$.

If the policy π is greedy, $\pi(s, a) = 0$ for all a except for the action for which Q has its maximal value. Therefore, in the case of a greedy policy, $V(s) = \sum_a \pi(s,a) Q(s,a)$ simplifies to

$$V(s) = \max_a Q(s,a)$$

Thus, Q-learning's update rule is just a special case of Expected Sarsa's update rule for the case when the estimation policy is greedy. Nonetheless, the complete Expected Sarsa algorithm is different from that of Q-learning because the former is on-policy and the latter is off-policy.

Convergence

In this topic, we prove that Expected Sarsa converges to the optimal policy under some straightforward conditions given below. We make use of the following Lemma, which was also used to prove convergence of Sarsa:

Lemma 1: Consider a stochastic process (ζ_t, Δ_t, F_t), where $\zeta_t, \Delta_t, F_t : X \rightarrow \mathbb{R}$ satisfy the equations

$$\Delta_{t+1}(x_t) = (1 - \zeta_t(x_t))\Delta_t(x_t) + \zeta_t(x_t)F_t(x_t),$$

Where $x_t \in X$ and t = 0, 1, 2, ... Let P_t be a sequence of increasing σ-fields such that ζ_0 and Δ_0 are P_0-measurable and ζ_t, Δ_t and F_t-1 are Pt-measurable, t ≥ 1. Assume that the following hold:

1) the set X is finite,

2) $\zeta_t(x_t) \in [0,1], \sum_t \zeta_t(x_t) = \infty, \sum_t (\zeta(x_t))^2 < \infty$
   w.p.l and $\forall x \neq x_t : \zeta_t(x) = 0$

3) $\|E\{F_t | P_t\}\| \leq k\|\Delta_t\| + c_t$, where $k \in (0,1]$ and c_t converges to zero w.p.1,

4) $\text{Var}\{F_t(x_t) | P_t\} \leq K(1 + k\|\Delta_t\|)^2$ where K is some constant,

where $\|.\|$ denotes a maximum norm. Then Δ_t converges to zero with probability one.

The idea is to apply Lemma 1 with $X = S \times A$, $P_t = \{Q_0, s_0, a_0, r_0, \alpha_0, s_1, a_1, \ldots, s_t, a_t\}$, $x_t = (s_t, a_t)$, $\zeta_t(x_t) = \alpha_t(s_t, a_t)$ and $\Delta_t(x_t) = Q_t(s_t, a_t) - Q^*(s_t, a_t)$. If we can then prove that Δ_t converges to zero with probability one, we have convergence of the Q values to the optimal values. The maximum norm specified in the lemma can then be understood as satisfying the following equation:

$$\|\Delta_t\| = \max_s \max_a |Q_t(s_t, a_t) - Q^*(s_t, a_t)|$$

Theorem: Expected Sarsa as defined by update converges to the optimal value function whenever the following assumptions hold:

1) S and A are finite,

2) $\alpha_t(s_t, a_t) \in [0, 1]$, $\sum_t \alpha t(s_t, a_t) = \infty$ $\sum_t (\alpha t(s_t, a_t))^2 < \infty$ w.p.1 and
   $\forall(s, a) \neq (s_t, a_t) : \alpha_t(s, a) = 0$,

3) The policy is greedy in the limit with infinite exploration,

4) The reward function is bounded

Proof: To prove this theorem, we simply check that all the conditions of Lemma 1 are fulfilled. The first, second and fourth conditions of this lemma correspond to the first, second and fourth assumptions of the theorem. Below, we will show the third condition of the lemma holds.

We can derive the value of F_t as follows:

$$F_t = \frac{1}{\alpha_t}\left(\Delta_{t+1} - (1 - \alpha_t)\Delta\right)_t,$$

$$= r_t + \gamma \sum_a \pi_t(s_{t+1}, a)Q_t(s_{t+1}, a) - Q^*(s_t, a_t),$$

where all the values are taken over the state action pair (s_t, a_t), except when specified differently.

If we can show that $\|E\{F_t\}\| \le k\|\Delta_t\| + c_t$, where $k \in (0,1]$ and c_t converges to zero, all the conditions of the lemma can be fulfilled and we have convergence of Δt to zero and therefore convergence of Q_t to Q^*. We derive this as follows:

$$\|E\{F_t\}\|$$

$$= \left\|E\left\{= r_t + \gamma \sum_a \pi_t(s_{t+1}, a)Q_t(s_{t+1}, a) - Q^*(s_t, a_t),\right\}\right\|$$

$$\le \left\|E\left\{r_t + \gamma \max_a Q_t(s_{t+1}, a) - Q^*(s_t, a_t)\right\}\right\| +$$

$$\gamma\left\|E\left\{\sum_a \pi_t(s_{t+1}, a)Q_t(s_{t+1}, a) - \max_a Q_t(s_{t+1}, a)\right\}\right\|$$

$$\le \gamma \max_s\left|\max_a Q_t(s, a) - \max_a Q^*(s, a)\right| +$$

$$\gamma \max_s\left|\sum_a \pi_t(s, a)Q_t(s, a) - \max_a Q_t(s, a)\right|$$

$$\le \gamma\|\Delta_t\| +$$

$$\gamma \max_s\left|\sum_a \pi_t(s, a)Q_t(s, a) - \max_a Q_t(s, a)\right|$$

where the second inequality results from the definition of Q^* and the fact that the maximal difference in value over all states is always at least as large as a difference between values corresponding to a state s_{t+1}. The third inequality follows directly. The other inequalities are based on algebraic rewriting or definitions.

We identify $c_t = \gamma \max_s \left| \sum_a \pi_t(s, a) Q_t(s, a) - \max_a Q_t(s, a) \right|$ and $\kappa = \gamma$. Clearly, c_t converges to zero for policies that are greedy in the limit. Therefore, if $\gamma < 1$, all of the conditions of Lemma 1 follow from the assumptions in the present theorem and we can apply the lemma to prove convergence of Qt to Q*.

Variance Analysis

Expected-Sarsa converges to the optimal policy under the same conditions as Sarsa. In this topic, we further analyze the behavior of the two methods to show theoretically under what conditions Expected-Sarsa will in some sense perform better. Specifically, we show that both algorithms have the same bias and that the variance of Expected-Sarsa is lower. Finally, we describe which factors affect this difference in variance. In this topic, we use $v_t = r_t + \gamma \sum_a \pi_t(s_{t+1}, a) Q_t(s_{t+1}, a)$ and $\hat{v}_t = r_t + \gamma Q_t(s_{t+1}, a_{t+1})$ to denote the target of Expected-Sarsa and Sarsa, respectively.

The bias of the updates of both algorithms under a certain policy π is given by the following equation:

$$Bias(s, a) = Q^{\pi}(s, a) - E\{X_t\}$$

Where X_t is either v_t and $\hat{v}_t$. Both algorithms have the same bias, since $E\{v_t\} = E\{\hat{v}_t\}$. The variance is then given by:

$$Var(s, a) = E\left\{(X_t)^2\right\} - \left(E\{X_t\}\right)^2$$

We first calculate this variance for Sarsa:

$$Var(s, a) = \sum_{s'} T_{sa}^{s'}\left(\gamma^2 \sum_{a'} \pi_{s'a'} \left(Q_t(s', a')\right)^2 + \left(R_{sa}^{s'}\right)^2 \right.$$
$$\left. + 2\gamma R_{sa}^{s'} \sum_{a'} \pi_{s'a'} Q_t(s',a') - \left(E\{\hat{v}_t\}\right)^2 \right.$$

Similarly, for Expected-Sarsa we get:

$$Var(s, a) = \sum_{s'} T_{sa}^{s'} \gamma^2 \sum_{a'} \pi_{s'a'} \left(Q_t(s', a')\right)^2 + \left(R_{sa}^{s'}\right)^2$$
$$+ 2\gamma R_{sa}^{s'} \sum_{a'} \pi_{s'a'} Q_t(s',a') - \left(E\{\hat{v}_t\}\right)^2$$

Since $E\{v_t\} = E\{\hat{v}_t\}$, the difference between the two variances simplifies to the following:

$$\gamma^2 \sum_{s'} T_{sa}^{s'}\left(\sum_{a'} \pi_{s'a'} \left(Q_t(s', a')\right)^2 - \left(\sum_{a'} \pi_{s'a'} Q_t(s', a')\right)^2 \right).$$

The inner term is of the form:

$$\sum_i w_i x_i^2 - \left(\sum_i w_i x_i\right)^2,$$

where the w and x correspond to the π and Q values. When $w_i \geq 0$ for all i and $\sum_i \omega_i = 1$, we can give an unbiased estimate of the variance of the weighed values $\omega_i x_i$ as follows:

$$\frac{\sum_i w_i (x_i - \bar{x})^2}{1 - \sum_i w_i^2},$$

where $\bar{x}$ is the weighted mean $\sum_i w_i x_i$. Taking the numerator of this fraction and re-writing this gives us:

$$
\begin{aligned}
\sum_i w_i (x_i - \bar{x})^2 &= \sum_i w_i x_i^2 - 2\sum_i w_i x_i \bar{x} + \sum_i w_i \bar{x}^2 \\
&= \sum_i w_i x_i^2 - 2\bar{x}^2 + \bar{x}^2 \\
&= \sum_i w_i x_i^2 - \bar{x}^2,
\end{aligned}
$$

which is exactly the same quantity as given in $\sum_i w_i x_i^2 - \left(\sum_i w_i x_i\right)^2$. This shows that this quantity is closely related to the weighted variance of the $w_i x_i$. Therefore, the more the x_i deviate from the weighted mean $\sum_i w_i x_i$, the larger this quantity will be. In our context this occurs in settings where there is a large difference between the Q values of different actions and there is much exploration. In case of a greedy policy or when all Q values have the same value, this quantity is 0.

Temporal Difference Learning

Temporal difference learning is declared to be a reinforcement learning method. This area of machine learning covers the problem of finding a perfect solution in an un-known environment. To be able to do so, a representation is needed to define which action yields the highest rewards.

Temporal Difference methods find application in reinforcement learning tasks. Three classes are listed to solve these tasks: Dynamic Programming, Monte Carlo methods and Temporal Difference Learning, of which the latter is called the most central and novel idea in reinforcement learning.

Dynamic Programming is based on the Bellman Equation and breaks down a problem into subproblems. Dividing a big task into smaller steps, this approach is depending on a perfect model of the environment.

Monte Carlo methods do not need a model of the learning environment. From experience in form of sequences of state-action-reward-samples they can approximate future rewards. However the methods only update after a complete sequence, when the final state is reached. The Markov Return is defined as:

$$R_t = \sum_{i=t}^{T-1} \gamma^{i-t} R_{i+1} = r_{t+1} + \gamma r_{t+2} + \gamma^2 r_{t+3} + ... + \gamma^{T-t-1} r_T.$$

Temporal difference methods combine both procedures - there is no need for a model of the learning environment and updates are available at each state of the incremental procedure. The method learns directly from the raw experience in a partially unknown system with each recorded sample.

An often used example is the weather forecast for a future day, lets say Saturday. It is pointed out that learning to predict Saturday's weather from a earlier day by evaluating the prediction using the actual outcome is a supervised learning approach. In this scenario the change of weather over the course of time leading up to Saturday is ignored, only the forecast from the time the prediction was made is compared to the weather at Saturday. Taking the approach of Temporal Difference methods all days from the time of prediction up to Saturday are taken into account. In the process of learning, this means that the prediction of Saturday's weather at one day is compared to the succeeding prediction and an increment is calculated to adjust the prediction. TD methods are called bootstrapping methods, as they do not learn by the difference to the final outcome but the difference between each update step. Instead of a single update, TD methods calculate T − 1 updates for a episode of T time steps.

The TD method aims to achieve a approximation V_θ^π as close to the value function V^π as possible. The error of the approximation can be measured by the mean squared error function

$$\text{MSE}(\theta) = \frac{1}{n} \sum_{i=1}^{n} \left(V_\theta^\pi(s_i) - V^\pi(s_i) \right)^2.$$

By minimizing the mean squared error the approximation of the value function can be optimized. As $V^\pi(s)$ is unknown, it is estimated by applying equation

$$V^\pi(s) = E_\pi \{ r_t + \gamma V^\pi(s_t + 1) | s_t = s \}$$

$$= \sum_a \pi(s,a) \sum_{s'} \rho_{ss'}^a \left[\sum_{s'} R_{ss'}^a + \gamma V^\pi(s') \right] \text{ on the current approximation } V_\theta^\pi$$

$$V^\pi(s_t) \approx E \{ r_t + \gamma V_\theta^\pi(S_{t+1}) \}.$$

The application of the Bellman Equation is the core idea of Temporal Difference Learning and allows to calculate the error denoted by Equation above. However analytic computation of the minimum of the error is not possible for systems with huge state spaces. Instead, a local minimum is searched numerically by Stochastic Gradient Descent. The method calculates new search positions θ by following a approximation of the gradient of the error function. A learning rate factor α is used to adjust the step size of the SGD method and prevent overshooting.

$$\theta' = \theta - \alpha \nabla \text{MSE}(\theta)$$
$$= \theta - \alpha \left[V_\theta^\pi(s_i) - V^\pi(s_i) \right] \nabla_{\theta t} V_{\theta t}(s_t).$$

The value function approximation applied on Equation
$$\theta' = \theta - \alpha \nabla \text{MSE}(\theta)$$
$$= \theta - \alpha \left[V_\theta^\pi(s_i) - V^\pi(s_i) \right] \nabla_{\theta t} V_{\theta t}(s_t).$$

results in a sum, calculating the gradient. To reduce the number of computations needed, the gradient is approximated by $\varphi(st)$. The update function of the TD learning method can be displayed as:

$$\theta_{t+1} = \theta_t + \alpha \delta_t e_t$$
$$\delta_t = r_{t+1} + \gamma V_{\theta t}(s_{t+1}) - V_{\theta t}(s_t)$$
$$e_t = \phi(s_t)$$

The vector δ_t denotes the temporal difference. By comparing the prediction at the current state $V_{\theta t}(s_t)$ to the prediction of the next state $V_{\theta t}(s_{t+1})$ the temporal difference δ_t is used for adapting the prediction itself. This behavior is called bootstrapping. The variance of the approximation is limited at each update by this correction.

The vector e_t denotes the approximation of the gradient $\nabla_{\theta t} V_{\theta t}$. It can be pictured as the algebraic link along which the update is propagated. For this formulation the update resulting from the TD error only effects the current state s_t. Learning by this equation takes long, as the rewards only propagate one state with each update.

To speed up the process of reward propagation, eligibility traces are introduced. This vector allows the method to carry rewards backward over the sampled trajectory without the need to store the trajectory itself. The reach of this effect is depending on the factor $\lambda \in [0, 1]$. The eligibility traces replace the approximation of the gradient in Equation
$$\theta_{t+1} = \theta_t + \alpha \delta_t e_t$$
$$\delta_t = r_{t+1} + \gamma V_{\theta t}(s_{t+1}) - V_{\theta t}(s_t) \text{ with}$$
$$e_t = \phi(s_t)$$

$$e_t = \sum_{k=t_0}^{t} \lambda^{t-k} V_{\theta \theta t}(s_k).$$

The back propagation of rewards using eligibility traces is a basic mechanism of TD methods. The factor λ determines the degree to which extend the changes are propagated. For application on real tasks the value of λ is of such importance that the algorithm is named TD(λ). The algorithm is displayed as pseudo code in Algorithm 1 for the example of linear approximation of the undiscounted value function of a fixed proper policy.

The TD method is modified by λ so much that for $\lambda=1$ the method yields the same results as supervised linear regression learning on Monte Carlo returns, while a $\lambda=0$ results in a one-step look ahead. The behavior for $\lambda=1$ is problematic for value function approximation. Monte Carlo returns represent all states traversed by looking at the complete trajectory from t to T, as shown in Equation $R_t = \sum_{i=t}^{T-1} \gamma^{i-t} R_{i+1} = r_{t+1} + \gamma r_{t+2} + \gamma^2 r_{t+3} + \ldots + \gamma^{T-t-1} r_T$.
A large variance results from observing the long stochastic sequence of all future states. On the opposite the TD(0) algorithm has low variance, but uses samples inefficiently, as with each update the reward only propagates to the next state.

The TD(λ) algorithm has to be adapted for each task by tuning the step size parameter α to achieve a low error. Furthermore the choice of the λ value has influence on the error, as well as the efficiency of the use of samples. The step size factor is also a source of error. In a worst case scenario a poorly chosen α factor corrupts the minimum search by SGD.

Algorithm 1: TD(λ) for approximate policy approximation

Data:

- A simulation model for a proper policy π in MDP M.
- A feature function $\phi: S \rightarrow \mathbb{R}^K$, mapping states to feature vectors, $\phi(T) \overset{def}{=} 0$;
- A parameter $\lambda \in [0, 1]$; and
- A sequence of step sizes $\alpha_1, \alpha_2, \ldots$ for incremental coefficient updating.

Output: a coefficient vector θ for which $V^\pi(s) \approx \theta^T \phi(s)$.

Set $\theta := 0$ (or an arbitrary initial state), t := 0.

for n := 1,2,... do

Set $\delta := 0$.

Choose a start state $s_t \in$ S.

Set $e_t := \phi(s_t)$.

while $s_t \neq T$ do

Simulate one step of the process, producing a reward r_t and next state s_{t+1}.

Set $\delta := \delta + e_t \left(r_t + \left(\phi(s_{t+1}) - \phi(s_t) \right)^T \theta \right)$.

Set $e_{t+1} := \lambda e_t + \phi(s_t)$.

Set t := t + 1.

end

Set $\theta := \theta + \alpha_n \delta$

end

Least-Squares Temporal Difference Learning

The LSTD algorithm eliminates the need of adapting a step size factor α. Furthermore, it improves the learning speed compared to TD by utilizing samples more efficiently. The function approximation introduced in equation $V^\pi(s) = \sum_a \pi(s,a)Q^\pi(s,a)$. limits the value function representation to linear functions, satisfying the limitation for the application of LSTD.

Applying the limitation to linear functions $\phi(s)$ the TD learning rule in Equation $\begin{aligned}\theta_{t+1} &= \theta_t + \alpha\delta_t e_t \\ \delta_t &= r_{t+1} + \gamma V_{\theta t}(s_{t+1}) - V_{\theta t}(s_t), \\ e_t &= \phi(s_t)\end{aligned}$ for convergence analysis can be rewritten in the form

$\theta := \theta + \alpha_n (d + C\theta + \omega)$, resulting in:

$$d = E\left\{\sum_{i=0}^{T} e_i r_i\right\}; \quad C = E\left\{\sum_{i=0}^{T} e_i \left(\phi(s_{i+1}) - \phi(s_i)\right)^T\right\},$$

Where $d \in \mathbb{R}^K$ and $\dim(C) = K \times K$. The vector ω denotes a zero-mean noise vector of dimension K. In the course, it is shown that C is negative definite and that ω has only small variance from its zero-mean, which combined with the requirement for a decreasing step size α_n results in the above stated. The TD algorithm does not store sampled trajectories, and hence, wastes data which results in a low learning speed.

The LSTD(λ) algorithm does not perform gradient descent, but builds explicit estimates of C and b and stores them between trajectories. The algorithm directly solves the equation $d + C\theta_\lambda = 0$. The estimates calculated are denoted as:

$$b = \sum_{i=0}^{t} e_i r_i; \quad A = \sum_{i=0}^{t} e_i \left(\phi(s_i) - \phi(s_{i+1})\right)^T$$

The algorithm converges after n independent sample trajectories to unbiased explicit estimates

$$b = nd; \quad A = -nC.$$

Using Singular Value Decomposition the inverse of A can be computed in order to solve the equation

$$\theta_\lambda = A^{-1} b.$$

The LSTD(λ) algorithm is shown in pseudo code in Algorithm 2, to illustrate the update steps.

Algorithm 2: LSTD(λ) for approximate policy approximation:

Data:

- A simulation model for a proper policy π in MDP M;
- A feature function $\phi: S \rightarrow \mathbb{R}^K$, mapping states to feature vectors, $\phi(T) \overset{def}{=} 0$;
- A parameter $\lambda \in [0, 1]$; and
- A sequence of step sizes $\alpha_1, \alpha_2, \ldots$ for incremental coefficient updating.

Output: a coefficient vector θ for which $V^\pi(s) \approx \theta^T \phi(s)$.

Set A := 0, b := 0, t := 0.

for n := 1,2,. . . do

Choose a start state $s_t \in S$.

Set $e_t := \phi(s_t)$.

While

while $s_t \neq T$ do

Simulate one step of the process, producing a reward r_t and next state s_{t+1}.

Set $\delta := \delta + e_t \left(r_t + \left(\phi(s_{t+1}) - \phi(s_t) \right)^T \theta \right)$.

Set $b := b + e_t r_t$.

Set $e_{t+1} := \lambda e_t + \phi(s_t)$.

Set t := t + 1.

end

Whenever update coefficients are desired: Set $\theta := A -1 b$

end

The LSTD(λ) algorithm calculates a matrix inversion at the cost of $O(K^3)$ for every update of $\theta\lambda$. The update is most likely needed for every sampled trajectory. Furthermore the computation costs per time step are of $O(K^2)$. Compared to the TD(λ) algorithm the amount of computation is much higher, as the TD(λ) algorithm updates its coefficients at a linear cost of $O(K)$. For larger numbers of features K the LSTD(λ) algorithm causes significantly more computational load. The TD(λ) algorithm can reuse trajectories for learning to compensate for the inefficient use of the samples. LSTD(λ) is data efficient, hence there is no need for reusing samples. Using less samples the LSTD(λ) algorithm converges faster than TD(λ). Another advantage is the omission of the step size parameter. On the one hand an advantage in usability is achieved by eliminating the need for tuning the parameter. On the other hand the LSTD(λ) algorithm can not be slowed down by a bad choice of parameter.

TD with Function Approximation

Beyond lookup tables, TD learning can update prediction functions represented in a variety of ways. Consider, for example, the case in which each prediction is a linear function of the input signals, where each input signal xt is now a vector of real numbers

$$x_t = (x_t^1, x_t^2, \ldots, x_t^n).$$

Then the prediction function of step t applied to the signal at step t', where t' can be different from t, is defined by

$$P_t(x_{t'}) = \sum_{i=1}^{n} v_t^i x_{t'}^i,$$

where the v_t^i $i=1,\ldots,n$, are the coefficients, or weights, of the linear prediction function of step t, and the $x_{t'}^i$ are components of the vector xt'. Then TD learning adjusts the weights according to the following rule: for each $t=0,1,2,\ldots$, upon observing (x_{t+1}, y_{t+1}):

$$v_{t+1}^i = v_t^i + \alpha[y_{t+1} + \gamma P_t(x_{t+1}) - P_t(x_t)]x_t^i :$$
$$= v_t^i + \alpha\delta_{t+1}x_t^i.$$

for $i=1,\ldots,n$, where $\alpha>0$ is a step-size parameter.

This learning rule adjusts each weight in a direction that tends to reduce the TD error. It is similar to the conventional Least Mean Square (LMS) or delta rule for supervised learning with the difference being the presence of $\gamma Pt(xt+1)$ in the error term. TD learning with linear function approximation is the best understood extension of the lookup-table version. It is widely used with input vectors consisting of the outputs of a possibly large number of sophisticated feature detectors, which is equivalent to employing representations involving sophisticated basis vectors. Lookup-tables correspond to linear function approximation using standard unit basis vectors (in which case equation $v_{t+1}^i = v_t^i + \alpha[y_{t+1} + \gamma P_t(x_{t+1}) - P_t(x_t)]x_t^i :$ reduces to equation $P_{t+1}(x) = \begin{cases} P_t(x) + \alpha\delta_{t+1} & \text{if } x = x_t \\ P_t(x) & \text{otherwise,} \end{cases}$. TD $= v_t^i + \alpha\delta_{t+1}x_t^i.$ learning with nonlinear function approximation is also possible. In general, any incremental function approximation, or regression, method can be adapted for use with TD learning. In all of these cases, it is important to recognize that TD learning does not entail specific assumptions about how stimuli are represented over time. There is a wide latitude in the alternatives that can be employed, and each has implications for the behavior of the algorithm.

Eligibility Traces

TD learning can often be accelerated by the addition of eligibility traces. When the lookup-table TD algorithm described above receives input ($yt+1,xt+1$), it updates the table entry only for the immediately preceding signal xt. That is, it modifies only the immediately preceding prediction. But since $yt+1$ provides useful information for learning earlier predictions as well, one can extend TD learning so it updates a collection of many earlier predictions at each step. Eligibility traces do this by providing a short-term memory of many previous input signals so that each new observation can update the parameters related to these signals. Eligibility traces are usually implemented by an exponentially decaying memory trace, with decay parameter λ. This generates a family of TD algorithms TD(λ), $0 \le \lambda \le 1$, with TD(0) corresponding to updating only the immediately preceding prediction as described above, and TD(1) corresponding to equally updating all the preceding predictions. This also applies to non lookup-table versions of TD learning, where traces of the components of the input vectors are maintained. Eligibility traces do not have to be exponentially-decaying traces, but these are usually used since they are relatively easy to implement and to understand theoretically.

Action-Conditional Prediction

Consider a setting in which the future values of inputs (xt,yt) are influenced by an agent's actions. The prediction at step t is often denoted Q (xt,at), where xt is the input signal and at is the agent action at step t. The objective is to find a function that accurately predicts Yt, the discounted sum of future values of y, on the basis of xt and at. In the usual reinforcement learning setting of a Markov decision process, Yt also depends on all the agent's actions taken after step t. Two different cases are considered for the actions taken after step t: (1) assume that after step t, the agent selects actions that generate the largest possible value of Yt, or (2) assume that the agent follows a fixed rule, or policy, for selecting actions as a function of future inputs. In either case, the desired predictions are well-defined.

A TD learning process for case (1), known as Q-Learning, works as follows for a look-up-table representation. For each $t=0,1,2,...$, upon generating action at and observing ($xt+1,yt+1$), the prediction function Qt is updated to $Qt+1$ defined as follows:

$$Q_{t+1}(x,a) = \begin{cases} Q_t(x,a) & + \alpha \left[y_{t+1} + \gamma \max_a Q_t(x_{t+1},a) - Q_t(x_t,a_t) \right] \text{ if } x = x_t \text{ and } a = a_t \\ Q_t(x,a) & \text{otherwise,} \end{cases}$$

where x denotes any possible input signal and a denotes any of a finite number of possible actions. For case (2), the update is the same except that $\max_a Qt$ ($xt+1,a$) is replaced by Qt ($xt+1,at+1$), producing a TD learning rule called Sarsa (for state-action-reward-state-action). These learning rules can also be extended to allow function approximation.

Q-Learnng and Sarsa are useful in reinforcement learning where yt is a reward signal. An agent selecting actions that maximize $Q(x,a)$ for each current x is fully exploiting the knowledge contained in Q in its attempt to maximize the measure of long-term reward, Yt. Under appropriate conditions, both Q-Learning and Sarsa converge to prediction functions that allow an agent to make optimal action choices.

References

- Stuart J. Russell; Peter Norvig (2010). Artificial Intelligence: A Modern Approach (Third ed.). Prentice Hall. p. 649. ISBN 978-0136042594

- Shteingart, H; Neiman, T; Loewenstein, Y (May 2013). "The Role of First Impression in Operant Learning". J Exp Psychol Gen. 142 (2): 476–88. doi:10.1037/a0029550. PMID 22924882

- What-is-reinforcement-learning: geeksforgeeks.org, Retrieved 14 July 2018

- "Methods and Apparatus for Reinforcement Learning, US Patent #20150100530A1"(PDF). US Patent Office. 9 April 2015. Retrieved 28 July 2018

- Hasselt, Hado van (5 March 2012). "Reinforcement Learning in Continuous State and Action Spaces". In Wiering, Marco; Otterlo, Martijn van. Reinforcement Learning: State-of-the-Art. Springer Science & Business Media. pp. 207–251. ISBN 978-3-642-27645-3

- Reinforcement-learning: digitalvidya.com, Retrieved 31 March 2018

- Tesauro, Gerald (March 1995). "Temporal Difference Learning and TD-Gammon". Communications of the ACM. 38 (3): 58. doi:10.1145/203330.203343. Retrieved 2010-02-08

- Matiisen, Tambet (December 19, 2015). "Demystifying Deep Reinforcement Learning | Computational Neuroscience Lab". neuro.cs.ut.ee. Retrieved 2018-04-06

- Temporal-difference-learning, TD-with-Function-Approximation: scholarpedia.org, Retrieved 19 May 2018

Ensemble Learning

Ensemble learning is the process that employs learning algorithms for obtaining improved predictive performance. This chapter discusses in detail the theories and methodologies related to ensemble learning, and includes vital topics such as bootstrap aggregating, boosting, AdaBoost, gradient boosting, etc.

Ensemble learning is the process by which multiple models, such as classifiers or experts, are strategically generated and combined to solve a particular computational intelligence problem. Ensemble learning is primarily used to improve the (classification, prediction, function approximation, etc.) performance of a model, or reduce the likelihood of an unfortunate selection of a poor one. Other applications of ensemble learning include assigning a confidence to the decision made by the model, selecting optimal (or near optimal) features, data fusion, incremental learning, nonstationary learning and error-correcting.

An ensemble-based system is obtained by combining diverse models (hence forth classifiers). Therefore, such systems are also known as multiple classifier systems, or just ensemble systems. There are several scenarios where using an ensemble based system makes statistical sense, which are discussed below in detail. However, in order to fully and practically appreciate the importance of using multiple classifier systems, it is perhaps instructive to look at a psychological backdrop to this otherwise statistically sound argument: we use such an approach routinely in our daily lives by asking the opinions of several experts before making a decision. For example, we typically ask the opinions of several doctors before agreeing to a medical procedure, we read user reviews before purchasing an item, we evaluate future employees by checking their references, etc. In fact, even this article is reviewed by several experts before being accepted for publication. In each case, a final decision is made by combining the individual decisions of several experts. In doing so, the primary goal is to minimize the unfortunate selection of an unnecessary medical procedure, a poor product, an unqualified employee or even a poorly written.

Model Selection

This is perhaps the primary reason why ensemble based systems are used in practice: what is the most appropriate classifier for a given classification problem? This question can be interpreted in two different ways:

1. What type of classifier should be chosen among many competing models, such

as multilayer perceptron (MLP), support vector machines (SVM), decision trees, naive Bayes classifier, etc;

2. Given a particular classification algorithm, which realization of this algorithm should be chosen - for example, different initializations of MLPs can give rise to different decision boundaries, even if all other parameters are kept constant.

The most commonly used procedure - choosing the classifiers with the smallest error on training data - is unfortunately a flawed one. Performance on a training dataset - even when computed using a cross-validation approach - can be misleading in terms of the classification performance on the previously unseen data. Then, of all (possibly infinite) classifiers that may all have the same training - or even the same (pseudo) generalization performance as computed on the validation data (part of the training data left unused for evaluating the classifier performance) - which one should be chosen? Everything else being equal, one may be tempted to choose at random, but with that decision comes the risk of choosing a particularly poor model. Using an ensemble of such models - instead of choosing just one - and combining their outputs by - for example, simply averaging them - can reduce the risk of an unfortunate selection of a particularly poorly performing classifier. It is important to emphasize that there is no guarantee that the combination of multiple classifiers will always perform better than the best individual classifier in the ensemble. Nor an improvement on the ensemble's average performance can be guaranteed except for certain special cases. Hence combining classifiers may not necessarily beat the performance of the best classifier in the ensemble, but it certainly reduces the overall risk of making a particularly poor selection.

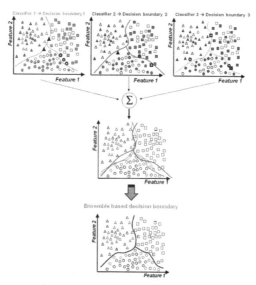

Figure: Combining an ensemble of classifiers for reducing classification error and/or model selection.

In order for this process to be effective, the individual experts must exhibit some level of *diversity* among themselves. Within the classification context, then, the diversity in the classifiers – typically achieved by using different training parameters for each classifier – allows individual classifiers to generate different decision boundaries. If proper diversity is achieved, a different error is made by each classifier, strategic combination of which can then reduce the total error. Figure graphically illustrates this concept, where each classifier - trained on a different subset of the available training data - makes different errors (shown as instances with dark borders), but the combination of the (three) classifiers provides the best decision boundary.

Too Much or Too Little Data

Ensemble based systems can be - perhaps surprisingly - useful when dealing with large volumes of data or lack of adequate data. When the amount of training data is too large to make a single classifier training difficult, the data can be strategically partitioned into smaller subsets. Each partition can then be used to train a separate classifier, which can then be combined using an appropriate combination rule. If, on the other hand, there is too little data, then bootstrapping can be used to train different classifiers using different bootstrap samples of the data, where each bootstrap sample is a random sample of the data drawn with replacement and treated as if it was independently drawn from the underlying distribution.

Divide and Conquer

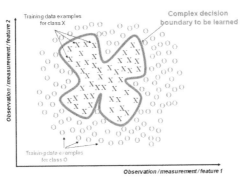

Figure: A complex decision boundary that cannot be realized by circular boundaries.

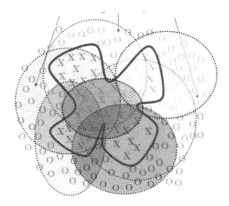

Figure: A combination of several circular boundaries can realize this complex boundary.

Certain problems are just too difficult for a given classifier to solve. In fact, the decision boundary that separates data from different classes may be too complex, or lie outside the space of functions that can be implemented by the chosen classifier model. Consider the two dimensional, two-class problem with a complex decision boundary depicted in figure. A linear classifier, one that is capable of learning linear boundaries, cannot learn this complex non-linear boundary. However, appropriate combination of an ensemble of such linear classifiers can learn any non-linear boundary. As an example, assume that we have access to a classifier model that can generate circular boundaries. Such a classifier cannot learn the boundary shown in figure. Now consider a collection of circular decision boundaries generated by an ensemble of such classifiers as shown in figure, where each classifier labels the data as class O or class X, based on whether the instances fall within or outside of its boundary. A decision based on the majority voting of a sufficient number of such classifiers can easily learn this complex non-circular boundary subject to:

i)   Classifier outputs be independent, and

ii) At least half of the classifiers classify an instance correctly.

In a sense, the classification system follows a divide-and-conquer approach by dividing the data space into smaller and easier-to-learn partitions, where each classifier learns only one of the simpler partitions. The underlying complex decision boundary can then be approximated by an appropriate combination of different classifiers.

Data Fusion

In many applications that call for automated decision making, it is not unusual to receive data obtained from different sources that may provide complementary information. A suitable combination of such information is known as data or information fusion, and can lead to improved accuracy of the classification decision compared to a decision based on any of the individual data sources alone. For example, for diagnosis of a neurological disorder, a neurologist may use the electroencephalogram (one-dimensional time series data), magnetic resonance imaging MRI, functional MRI, or positron emission tomography PET scan images (two-dimensional spatial data), the amount of certain chemicals in the cerebrospinal fluid along with the subjects demographics such as age, gender, education level of the subject, etc. (scalar and or categorical values). These heterogeneous features cannot be used all together to train a single classifier (and even if they could - by converting all features into a vector of scalar values - such a training is unlikely to be successful). In such cases, an ensemble of classifiers can be used, where a separate classifier is trained on each of the feature sets independently. The decisions made by each classifier can then be combined by any of the combination rules.

Confidence Estimation

The very structure of an ensemble based system naturally allows assigning a confidence to the decision made by such a system. Consider having an ensemble of classifiers trained on a classification problem. If a vast majority of the classifiers agree with their decisions, such an outcome can be interpreted as the ensemble having high confidence in its decision. If, however, half the classifiers make one decision and the other half make a different decision, this can be interpreted as the ensemble having low confidence in its decision. It should be noted that an ensemble having high confidence in its decision does not mean that decision is correct, and conversely, a decision made with low confidence need not be incorrect. However, it has been shown that a properly trained ensemble decision is usually correct if its confidence is high, and usually incorrect if its confidence is low. Using such an approach then, the ensemble decisions can be used to estimate the posterior probabilities of the classification decisions.

Other Reasons for using Ensemble System

The three primary reasons for using an ensemble based system:

1. Statistical;

2. Computational; and

3. Representational.

These reasons are similar to those listed above. The statistical reason is related to lack of adequate data to properly represent the data distribution; the computational reason is the model selection problem, where among many models that can solve a given problem, which one we should choose. Finally, the representational reason is to address to cases when the chosen model cannot properly represent the sought decision boundary.

Diversity

The success of an ensemble system - that is, its ability to correct the errors of some of its members - rests squarely on the diversity of the classifiers that make up the ensemble. After all, if all classifiers provided the same output, correcting a possible mistake would not be possible. Therefore, individual classifiers in an ensemble system need to make different errors on different instances. The intuition, then, is that if each classifier makes different errors, then a strategic combination of these classifiers can reduce the total error, a concept not too dissimilar to low pass filtering of the noise. Specifically, an ensemble system needs classifiers whose decision boundaries are adequately different from those of others. Such a set of classifiers is said to be diverse. Classifier diversity can be achieved in several ways. Preferably, the classifier outputs should be class-conditionally independent, or better yet negatively correlated. The most popular method is to use different training datasets to train individual classifiers. Such datasets are often obtained through re-sampling techniques, such as bootstrapping or bagging, where training data subsets are drawn randomly, usually with replacement, from the entire training data. To ensure that individual boundaries are adequately different, despite using substantially similar training data, weaker or more unstable classifiers are used as base models, since they can generate suffi-ciently different decision boundaries even for small perturbations in their training parameters.

Another approach to achieve diversity is to use different training parameters for different classifiers. For example, a series of multilayer perceptron (MLP) neural networks can be trained by using different weight initializations, number of layers / nodes, error goals, etc. Adjusting such parameters allows one to control the instability of the individual classifiers, and hence contribute to their diversity. Alternatively, entirely different type of classifiers, such MLPs, decision trees, nearest neighbor classifiers, and support vector machines can also be combined for added diversity. Finally, diversity can also be achieved by using different features, or different subsets of existing features.

Ensemble Combination Rules

The algorithms described have their built in combination rules, such as simple majority voting for bagging, weighted majority voting for AdaBoost, a separate classifier for stacking, etc. However, an ensemble of classifiers can be trained simply on different subsets of the training data, different parameters of the classifiers, or even with different subsets of features as in random subspace models. The classifiers can then be combined using one of several different combination rules. Some of these combination rules operate on class labels only, whereas others need continuous outputs that can be interpreted as support given by the classifier to each of the classes. Xu et al. defines three types of base model outputs to be used for classifier combination.

1. Abstract-level output, where each classifier outputs a unique class label for each input pattern;

2. Rank-level output, where each classifier outputs a list of ranked class labels for each input pattern; and

3. Measurement-level output, where each classifier outputs a vector of continuous-valued measures that can represent estimates of class posterior probabilities or class-related confidence values that represent the support for the possible classification hypotheses.

For the former case of abstract level outputs, the decision of the tth classifier is defined as $dt,j \in \{0,1\}$, $t=1,\cdots,T$; $j=1,\cdots,C$ where T is the number of classifiers and C is the number of classes. If tth classifier chooses class ωj, then $dt,j=1$, and 0, otherwise. For those combination rules that need continuous outputs, the classifier outputs are defined as $dt,j \in [0,1]$. Such outputs are usually normalized so that they add up to 1, which can the be interpreted as the normalized support given to clas j by classifier t, or even as the estimate of the posterior probability $Pt(\omega j|x)$.

Algebraic Combiners

Algebraic combiners are *non-trainable combiners*, where continuous valued outputs of classifiers are combined through an algebraic expression, such as minimum, maximum, sum, mean, product, median, etc. In each case, the final ensemble decision is the class j that receives the largest support $\mu j(x)$ after the algebraic expression is applied to individual supports obtained by each class. Specifically

$h_{final}(x) = \arg \max_j \mu_j(x)$, where the final class supports are computed as follows:

- Mean rule: $\mu_j(x) = \dfrac{1}{T}\sum_{t=1}^{T} d_{t,j}(x)$

- Sum rule: $\mu_j(x) = \sum_{t=1}^{T} d_{t,j}(x)$ (provides identical final decision as the mean rule)

- Weighted sum rule: $\mu_j(x) = \sum_{t=1}^{T} w_t d_{t,j}(x)$ (where w_t is the weight assigned to the tth classifier h_t according to some measure of performance)

- Product rule: $\mu_j(x) = \prod_{t=1}^{T} d_{t,j}(x)$

- Maximum rule $\mu_j(x) = max_{t=1,\cdots,T}\{d_{t,j}(x)\}$

- Minimum rule $\mu_j(x) = max_{t=1,\cdots,T}\{d_{t,j}(x)\}$ check equation from link 42

- Median rule $\mu_j(x) = \underset{t=1,\cdots,T}{med}\{d_{t,j}(x)\}$

- Generalized mean rule $\mu_{j,\alpha}(x) = \left(\dfrac{1}{T}\sum_{t=1}^{T} d_{t,j}(x)^{\alpha}\right)^{1/\alpha}$

- $\alpha \to -\infty \Rightarrow$ Minimum rule

- $\alpha \to -\infty \Rightarrow$ maximum rule

- $\alpha = 0 \Rightarrow$ Geometric mean rule

- $\alpha = 1 \Rightarrow$ Mean rule

Voting based Methods

Voting based methods operate on labels only, where dt,j is 1 or 0 depending on whether classifier t chooses j, or not, respectively. The ensemble then chooses class J that receives the largest total vote:

- Majority (plurality) voting

$$\sum_{t=1}^{T} d_{t,J}(x) = max_{j=1,\cdots,C}\sum_{t=1}^{T} d_{t,j}$$

Under the condition that the classifier outputs are independent, it can be shown the majority voting combination will always lead to a performance improvement for sufficiently large number of classifiers. If there are a total of T classifiers for a two-class problem, the ensemble decision will be correct if at least $\lfloor T/2+1 \rfloor$ classifiers choose the correct class. Now, assume that each classifier has a probability p of making a correct decision. Then, the ensemble's probability of making a correct decision has a binomial distribution, specifically, the probability of choosing $k > \lfloor T/2+1 \rfloor$ correct classifiers out of

$$T \text{ is} P_{ens} = \Sigma^T_{k=(T/2)+1} \binom{T}{k} p^k (1-p)^{T-k}$$

Then,

$$P_{ens} \to 1 ,$$

as $T \to \infty$ if $p > 0.5$

$$P_{ens} \to 0 ,$$

as $T \to \infty$ if $p < 0.5$

The requirement of $p > 0.5$ is necessary and sufficient for a two class problem, whereas it is sufficient, but not necessary for multi class problems.

- Weighted majority voting

$$\Sigma^T_{t=1} w_t d_{t,J}(x) = max_{j=1,\cdots,C} \Sigma^T_{t=1} w_t d_{t,j}$$

The optimal weights for the weighted majority voting rule can be shown to be $wt \propto P_t/1-P_t$ if the T classifiers are class-conditionally independent with accuracies $p1, \cdots, p_T$.

Other Combination Rules

There are several other combination rules, which are arguably more sophisticated than the ones listed above. These include *Borda count* which takes the rankings of the class supports into consideration; *behavior knowledge space*, which uses a lookup table that lists the most common correct classes for every possible class combinations given by the classifiers; "decision templates" which compute a similarity measure between the current decision profile of the unknown instance and the average decision profiles of instances from each class; and *Dempster-Schafer rule* which computes the plausibility based belief measures for each class. However, many empirical studies have shown that simpler rules such as the sum rule or the (weighted) majority voting often work remarkably well.

Other Applications of Ensemble Systems

Ensemble based systems can be used in problem domains other than improving the generalization performance of a classifier.

Incremental Learning

Incremental learning refers to the ability of an algorithm to learn from new data that may become available after a classifier (or a model) has already been generated from a previously available dataset. An algorithm is said to be an incremental learning algorithm if, for a sequence of training datasets (or instances), it produces a sequence of hypotheses, where the current hypothesis describes all data that have been seen thus far, but depends only on previous hypotheses and the current training data. Hence, an incremental learning algorithm must learn the new information, and retain previously acquired knowledge, without having access to previously seen data. A commonly used approach to learn from additional data - discarding the existing classifier, and retraining a new one with the old and new data combined together does not meet the definition of incremental learning, since it causes catastrophic forgetting of all previously learned information and uses previous data. Ensemble based systems can be used for such problems by training an additional classifier (or an additional ensemble of classifiers) on each dataset that becomes available. Learn^{++} primarily for incremental learning problems that do not introduce new classes, and Learn^{++}. NC for those that introduce new classes with additional datasets are two examples of ensemble based incremental learning algorithms.

Error Correcting Output Codes

Error correcting output codes (ECOC) are commonly used in information theory for correcting bit reversals caused by noisy communication channels, or in machine learning for converting binary classifiers, such as support vector machines, to multi-class classifiers by decomposing a multi-class problem into several two-class problems. Dietterich and Bakiri introduced ECOC to be used within the ensemble setting. The idea is to use a different class encoding for each member of the ensemble. The encodings constitute a binary C by T code matrix, where C and T are the number of classes and ensemble size, respectively, combined by the minimum Hamming distance rule.

Class	CLASSIFIERS														
	C_1	C_2	C_3	C_4	C_5	C_6	C_7	C_8	C_9	C_{10}	C_{11}	C_{12}	C_{13}	C_{14}	C_{15}
ω_1	1	1	1	1	1	1	1	1	1	1	1	1	1	1	1
ω_2	0	0	0	0	0	0	0	0	1	1	1	1	1	1	1
ω_3	0	0	0	0	1	1	1	1	0	0	0	0	1	1	1
ω_4	0	0	1	1	0	0	1	1	0	0	1	1	0	0	1
ω_5	0	1	0	1	0	1	0	1	0	1	0	1	0	1	0

Figure: Error correcting output codes exhaustive code matrix for five classes.

Figure shows a particular code matrix for a 5-class problem that uses 15 encodings. This encoding, suggested in (Dietterich 1995), is a (pseudo) exhaustive coding because it includes all possible non-trivial and non-repeating codes. In this formulation, the individual classifiers are trained on several meta two-class problems: for example, C_3 recognizes two meta-classes: original classes $\omega 1$ and $\omega 4$ constitute one class, and the others constitute the second class. During testing, each classifier outputs a "0" or "1" creating a $2^{C-1}-1$ long output code vector. This vector is compared to each code word in the code matrix, and the class whose code word has the shortest Hamming distance to the output vector is chosen as the ensemble decision. More specifically, the support for class ωj is given as $\mu j(x) = -\sum T t = 1 |ot - Mj,t|$ where $o_t \in \{0, 1\}$ is the output of the tth binary classifier, and M is the code matrix. The negative sign converts the distance metric into a support value, whose largest value can be zero in case of a perfect match. For example, the output [0 1 1 1 0 1 0 1 0 1 0 1 0] is closest to $\omega 5$ code word with a Hamming distance of 1 (support of -1), and hence ω_5 would be chosen for this output. Note that this output does not match any of the code words exactly, and this is where the error correcting ability of the ECOC lies. In fact, the larger the minimum Hamming distance between code words, the more resistant the ECOC ensemble becomes to misclassifications of individual classifiers.

Feature Selection

One way to improve diversity in the ensemble is to train individual classifiers different subsets of the available features. Selecting the feature subsets at random is known as the random subspace method, a term coined by, who used it on constructing decision tree ensembles. Subset selection need not be random, however: Oza and Tumer propose input decimation, where the features are selected based on their correlation with the class labels.

Bootstrap Aggregating

Bootstrap Aggregation (or Bagging for short), is a simple and very powerful ensemble method. An ensemble method is a technique that combines the predictions from multiple machine learning algorithms together to make more accurate predictions than any individual model.

Bootstrap Aggregation is a general procedure that can be used to reduce the variance for those algorithm that have high variance. An algorithm that has high variance are decision trees, like classification and regression trees (CART).

Decision trees are sensitive to the specific data on which they are trained. If the training data is changed (e.g. a tree is trained on a subset of the training data) the resulting decision tree can be quite different and in turn the predictions can be quite different.

Bagging is the application of the Bootstrap procedure to a high-variance machine learning algorithm, typically decision trees.

Let's assume we have a sample dataset of 1000 instances (x) and we are using the CART algorithm. Bagging of the CART algorithm would work as follows:

1. Create many (e.g. 100) random sub-samples of our dataset with replacement.

2. Train a CART model on each sample.

3. Given a new dataset, calculate the average prediction from each model.

For example, if we had 5 bagged decision trees that made the following class predictions for a in input sample: blue, blue, red, blue and red, we would take the most frequent class and predict blue.

When bagging with decision trees, we are less concerned about individual trees overfitting the training data. For this reason and for efficiency, the individual decision trees are grown deep (e.g. few training samples at each leaf-node of the tree) and the trees are not pruned. These trees will have both high variance and low bias. These are important characterize of sub-models when combining predictions using bagging.

The only parameters when bagging decision trees is the number of samples and hence the number of trees to include. This can be chosen by increasing the number of trees on run after run until the accuracy begins to stop showing improvement (e.g. on a cross validation test harness). Very large numbers of models may take a long time to prepare, but will not overfit the training data.

Just like the decision trees themselves, Bagging can be used for classification and regression problems.

Advantages

Bagging takes the advantage of ensemble learning wherein multiple weak learner outperform a single strong learner. It helps reduce variance and thus helps us avoid overfitting.

Disadvantages

There is loss of interpretability of the model. There can possibly be a problem of high bias if not modeled properly. Another important disadvantage is that while bagging gives us more accuracy, it is computationally expensive and may not be desirable depending on the use case.

Boosting

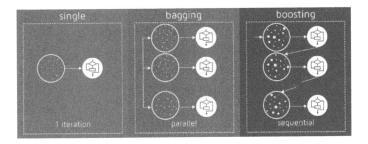

The term 'Boosting' refers to a family of algorithms, which converts weak learner to strong learners. Boosting is an ensemble method for improving the model predictions of any given learning algorithm. The idea of boosting is to train weak learners sequentially, each trying to correct its predecessor.

Boosting also creates an ensemble of classifiers by resampling the data, which are then combined by majority voting. However, in boosting, resampling is strategically geared to provide the most informative training data for each consecutive classifier. In essence, each iteration of boosting creates three weak classifiers: the first classifier $C1$ is trained with a random subset of the available training data. The training data subset for the second classifier $C2$ is chosen as the most informative subset, given $C1$. Specifically, $C2$ is trained on a training data only half of which is correctly classified by $C1$, and the other half is misclassified. The third classifier $C3$ is trained with instances on which $C1$ and $C2$ disagree. The three classifiers are combined through a three-way majority vote. The pseudocode and implementation detail of boosting is shown in figure.

Algorithm: Boosting

Input:
- Training data S of size N with correct labels ω_i, $\Omega = \{\omega_1, \omega_2\}$;
- Weak learning algorithm **WeakLearn**.

Training
1. Select $N_1 < N$ patterns without replacement from S to create data subset S_1.
2. Call **WeakLearn** and train with S_1 to create classifier C_1.
3. Create dataset S_2 as the most informative dataset, given C_1, such that half of S_2 is correctly classified by C_1, and the other half is misclassified.:
    a. Flip a fair coin. If Head, select samples from S, and present them to C_1 until the first instance is misclassified. Add this instance to S_2.
    b. If Tail, select samples from S, and present them to C_1 until the first one is correctly classified. Add this instance to S_2.
    c. Continue flipping coins until no more patterns can be added to S_2.
4. Train the second classifier C_2 with S_2.
5. Create S_3 by selecting those instances for which C_1 and C_2 disagree. Train the third classifier C_3 with S_3.

Test – Given a test instance **x**
1. Classify **x** by C_1 and C_2. If they agree on the class, this class is the final classification.
2. If they disagree, choose the class predicted by C_3 as the final classification.

Figure: Algorihm Boosting

Schapire showed that the error of this algorithm has an upper bound: if the algorithm A used to create the classifiers $C1$, $C2$, $C3$ has an error of ϵ (as computed on S), then the error of the ensemble is bounded above by $f(\epsilon)=3\epsilon^2-2\epsilon^3$ Note that $f(\epsilon)\le\epsilon$ for $\epsilon<1/2$. That is, as long as the original algorithm A can do at least better than random guessing, then the boosting ensemble that combines three classifiers generated by A on the above described three distributions of S, will always outperform A. Also, the ensemble error is a training error bound. Hence, a stronger classifier is generated from three weaker classifiers. A strong classifier in the strict PAC learning sense can then be created by recursive applications of boosting. A particular limitation of boosting is that it applies only to binary classification problems.

Boosting Pseudocode

Initialize all weights to $w = \dfrac{1}{n}$ where n is the number of instances in the dataset

- While $t < T$ (T = number of models to be grown) do.

- Create a model and get the hypothesis $h_{t(xn)}$ for all datapoints x_n in the dataset.

- Calculate the error ϵ of the training set summing over all datapoints x_n in the training set with

$$\epsilon_t = \frac{\sum_{n=1}^{N} \omega_n^{(t)} * I\left(y_n \neq h_t\left(x_n\right)\right)}{\sum_{n=1}^{N} \omega_n^{(t)}}$$

where $I(cond)$ returns 1 if $I(cond)$ = True and 0 otherwise

- Compute α with:

$$\alpha_t = \log(\frac{1-\epsilon_t}{\epsilon_t})$$

- Update the weights for the N training instances in the next $(t+1)$ model with:

$$\omega_n^{(t+1)} = \omega_n^{(t)} * \exp\left(\alpha_t * I\left(y_n \neq h_t\left(x_n\right)\right)\right)$$

- After the T iterations, calculate the final output with:

$$f\left(x\right) = sign\left(\sum_t^T \alpha_t * h_t\left(x\right)\right)$$

AdaBoost

AdaBoost is short for Adaptive Boosting. It is basically a machine learning algorithm that is used as a classifier. Whenever you have a large amount of data and you want divide it into different categories, we need a good classification algorithm to do it. We usually use AdaBoost in conjunction with other learning algorithms to improve their performance. Hence the word 'boosting', as in it boosts other algorithms! Boosting is a general method for improving the accuracy of any given learning algorithm. So obviously, adaptive boosting refers to a boosting algorithm that can adjust itself to changing scenarios.

The final equation for classification can be represented as:

$$F\left(x\right) = sign\left(\sum_{m=1}^{M} \theta_m f_m\left(x\right)\right),$$

where f_m stands for the mth weak classifier and θ_m is the corresponding weight. It is exactly the weighted combination of M weak classifiers. The whole procedure of the AdaBoost algorithm can be summarized as follow.

AdaBoost Algorithm

Given a data set containing n points, where

$$x_i \in \mathbb{R}^d, y_i \in \{-1,1\}.$$

Here -1 denotes the negative class while 1 represents the positive one.

Initialize the weight for each data point as:

$$w(x_i y_i) = \frac{1}{n}, i = 1,...,n.$$

For iteration m = 1,...,M:

(1) Fit weak classifiers to the data set and select the one with the lowest weighted classification error:

$$\in_m = E_{w_m} \left[1_{y \neq f(x)} \right]$$

(2) Calculate the weight for the mth weak classifier:

$$\theta_m = \frac{1}{2} ln \left(\frac{1 - \in_m}{\in_m} \right).$$

For any classifier with accuracy higher than 50%, the weight is positive. The more accurate the classifier, the larger the weight. While for the classifer with less than 50% accuracy, the weight is negative. It means that we combine its prediction by flipping the sign. For example, we can turn a classifier with 40% accuracy into 60% accuracy by flipping the sign of the prediction. Thus even the classifier performs worse than random guessing, it still contributes to the final prediction. We only don't want any classifier with exact 50% accuracy, which doesn't add any information and thus contributes nothing to the final prediction.

(3) Update the weight for each data point as:

$$w_{m+1}(x_i y_i) = \frac{w_m(x_i y_i) \exp\left[-\theta_m y_i f_m(x_i)\right]}{Z_m},$$

where Z_m is a normalization factor that ensures the sum of all instance weights is equal to 1.

If a misclassified case is from a positive weighted classifier, the "exp" term in the numerator would be always larger than 1. Thus misclassified cases would be updated with larger weights after an iteration. The same logic applies to the negative weighted classifiers. The only difference is that the original correct classifications would become misclassifications after flipping the sign.

After M iteration we can get the final prediction by summing up the weighted prediction of each classifier.

AdaBoost as a Forward Stagewise Additive Model

They interpreted AdaBoost as stagewise estimation procedures for fitting an additive logistic regression model. They showed that AdaBoost was actually minimizing the exponential loss function:

$$L\left(y, F\left(x\right)\right) = E\left(e^{-yF(x)}\right).$$

It is minimized at

$$\frac{\partial E\left[e^{-yF(x)}\right]}{\partial F\left(x\right)} = 0.$$

Since for AdaBoost, y can only be -1 or 1, the loss function can be rewritten as

$$E\left[e^{-yF(x)}\right] = e^{F(x)}P\left(y = -1|x\right) + e^{-F(x)}P\left(y = 1|x\right).$$

Continue to solve for F(x), we get

$$\frac{\partial E\left[e^{-yF(x)}\right]}{\partial F\left(x\right)} = e^{F(x)}P\left(y = -1|x\right) + e^{-F(x)}P\left(y = 1|x\right) = 0,$$

$$F\left(x\right) = \frac{1}{2}\log\frac{P\left(y = 1|x\right)}{P\left(y = -1|x\right)}.$$

We can further derive the normal logistic model from the optimal solution of F(x):

$$P\left(y = 1|x\right) = \frac{e^{2F(x)}}{1 + e^{2F(x)}}.$$

It is almost identical to the logistic regression model despite of a factor 2.

Suppose we have a current estimate of F(x) and try to seek an improved estimate F(x)+cf(x). For fixed c and x, we can expand L(y, F(x)+cf(x)) to second order about f(x)=0,

$$L(y, F(x) + cf(x)) = E\left[e^{-y(F(x)+cf(x))}\right]$$
$$\approx E\left[e^{-yF(x)}\left(1 - ycf(x) + c^2 y^2 f(x)^2/2\right)\right]$$
$$= E\left[e^{-yF(x)}\left(1 - ycf(x) + c^2/2\right)\right].$$

Thus,

$$f(x) = \arg\min_f E_w\left(1 - ycf(x) + c^2/2 \big| x\right),$$

where $E_w(.|x)$ indicates a weighted conditional expectation and the weight for each data point is calculated as

$$w(x_i, y_i) = e^{-y_i F(x)}, i = 1,...,n.$$

If $c > 0$, minimizing the weighted conditional expectation is equal to maximizing

$$E_w\left[yf(x)\right].$$

Since y can only be 1 or -1, the weighted expectation can be rewritten as

$$E_w\left[y\, f(x)\right] = f(x) P_w\left(y = 1|x\right) - f(x) P_w\left(y = -1|x\right).$$

The optimal solution comes as

$$f(x) = \begin{cases} 1 & \text{if } P_w\left(y = 1|x\right) > P_w\left(y = -1|x\right), \\ -1, & otherwise. \end{cases}$$

After determining f(x), the weight c can be calculated by directly minimizing L(y, F(x)+cf(x)):

$$c = \arg\min_c E_w\left[e^{-cyf(x)}\right].$$

Solving for c, we get

$$\frac{\partial E_w\left[e^{-cyf(x)}\right]}{\partial c} = E_w\left[-y\, f(x) e^{-cyf(x)}\right] = 0,$$

$$E_w\left[1_{y \neq f(x)}\right] e^c - E_w\left[1_{y = f(x)}\right] e^{-c} = 0.$$

Let epsilon equals to the weighted sum of misclassified cases, then

$$\in e^c - (1 - \in) e^{-c} = 0,$$

$$c = \frac{1}{2} \log \frac{1 - \in}{\in}.$$

C can be negative if the weak learner does worse than random guess (50%), in which case it automatically reverses the polarity.

In terms of instance weights, after the improved addition, the weight for a single instance becomes,

$$w(x_i, y_i) = e^{-y_i F(x_i) - c y_i f(x)}, i = 1, ..., n.$$

Thus the instance weight is updated as

$$w(x_i, y_i) \leftarrow w(x_i, y_i) e^{-cf(x_i) y_i}.$$

Compared with those used in AdaBoost algorithm,

$$w_{m+1}(x_i, y_i) = \frac{w_m(x_i, y_i) \exp\left[-\theta_m y_i f_m(x_i)\right]}{Z_m}$$

$$\theta_m = \frac{1}{2} \ln\left(\frac{1 - \epsilon_m}{\epsilon_m}\right)$$

we can see they are in identical form. Therefore, it is reasonable to interpret AdaBoost as a forward stagewise additive model with exponential loss function, which iteratively fits a weak classifier to improve the current estimate at each iteration m:

$$\{\theta_m, f_m(x)\} = \arg \min_{\{\theta_m, f_m\}} \sum_{i=l}^{n} L\left(y_i f^{(m-1)}(x_i) + \theta_m f_m(x_i)\right).$$

Gradient Boosting

Gradient boosting (GB) is a machine learning algorithm developed in the late '90s that is still very popular. It produces state-of-the-art results for many commercial (and academic) applications.

Working of Gradient Boosting

Gradient boosting involves three elements:

1. A loss function to be optimized.

2. A weak learner to make predictions.

3. An additive model to add weak learners to minimize the loss function.

Loss Function

The loss function used depends on the type of problem being solved. It must be differentiable, but many standard loss functions are supported and you can define your own. For example, regression may use a squared error and classification may use logarithmic loss.

A benefit of the gradient boosting framework is that a new boosting algorithm does not have to be derived for each loss function that may want to be used, instead, it is a generic enough framework that any differentiable loss function can be used.

Weak Learner

Decision trees are used as the weak learner in gradient boosting. Specifically regression trees are used that output real values for splits and whose output can be added together, allowing subsequent models outputs to be added and "correct" the residuals in the predictions.

Trees are constructed in a greedy manner, choosing the best split points based on purity scores like Gini or to minimize the loss. Initially, such as in the case of AdaBoost, very short decision trees were used that only had a single split, called a decision stump. Larger trees can be used generally with 4-to-8 levels.

It is common to constrain the weak learners in specific ways, such as a maximum number of layers, nodes, splits or leaf nodes. This is to ensure that the learners remain weak, but can still be constructed in a greedy manner.

Additive Model

Trees are added one at a time, and existing trees in the model are not changed. A gradient descent procedure is used to minimize the loss when adding trees.

Traditionally, gradient descent is used to minimize a set of parameters, such as the coefficients in a regression equation or weights in a neural network. After calculating error or loss, the weights are updated to minimize that error.

Instead of parameters, we have weak learner sub-models or more specifically decision trees. After calculating the loss, to perform the gradient descent procedure, we must add a tree to the model that reduces the loss (i.e. follow the gradient). We do this by parameterizing the tree, then modify the parameters of the tree and move in the right direction by (reducing the residual loss. Generally this approach is called functional gradient descent or gradient descent with functions.

Improvements to Basic Gradient Boosting

Gradient boosting is a greedy algorithm and can overfit a training dataset quickly. It can benefit from regularization methods that penalize various parts of the algorithm and generally improve the performance of the algorithm by reducing overfitting.

4 enhancements to basic gradient boosting:

1. Tree Constraints

2. Shrinkage

3. Random sampling

4. Penalized Learning

1. Tree Constraints

It is important that the weak learners have skill but remain weak. There are a number of ways that the trees can be constrained. A good general heuristic is that the more constrained tree creation is, the more trees you will need in the model, and the reverse, where less constrained individual trees, the fewer trees that will be required.

Below are some constraints that can be imposed on the construction of decision trees:

- Number of trees, generally adding more trees to the model can be very slow to overfit. The advice is to keep adding trees until no further improvement is observed.

- Tree depth, deeper trees are more complex trees and shorter trees are preferred. Generally, better results are seen with 4-8 levels.

- Number of nodes or number of leaves, like depth, this can constrain the size of the tree, but is not constrained to a symmetrical structure if other constraints are used.

- Number of observations per split imposes a minimum constraint on the amount of training data at a training node before a split can be considered

- Minimim improvement to loss is a constraint on the improvement of any split added to a tree.

2. Weighted Updates

The predictions of each tree are added together sequentially. The contribution of each tree to this sum can be weighted to slow down the learning by the algorithm. This weighting is called a shrinkage or a learning rate.

The effect is that learning is slowed down, in turn require more trees to be added to the model, in turn taking longer to train, providing a configuration trade-off between the number of trees and learning rate. It is common to have small values in the range of 0.1 to 0.3, as well as values less than 0.1.

3. Stochastic Gradient Boosting

A big insight into bagging ensembles and random forest was allowing trees to be greedily created from subsamples of the training dataset. This same benefit can be used to reduce the correlation between the trees in the sequence in gradient boosting models.

This variation of boosting is called stochastic gradient boosting.

A few variants of stochastic boosting that can be used:

- Subsample rows before creating each tree.
- Subsample columns before creating each tree.
- Subsample columns before considering each split.

Generally, aggressive sub-sampling such as selecting only 50% of the data has shown to be beneficial.

4. Penalized Gradient Boosting

Additional constraints can be imposed on the parameterized trees in addition to their structure.

Classical decision trees like CART are not used as weak learners, instead a modified form called a regression tree is used that has numeric values in the leaf nodes (also called terminal nodes). The values in the leaves of the trees can be called weights in some literature.

As such, the leaf weight values of the trees can be regularized using popular regularization functions, such as:

- L1 regularization of weights.
- L2 regularization of weights.

Gradient Boosting Resources

Gradient boosting is a fascinating algorithm and I am sure you want to go deeper.

Gradient Boosting algorithm

The objective of any supervised learning algorithm is to define a loss function and minimize it. Let's see how maths work out for Gradient Boosting algorithm. Say we have mean squared error (MSE) as loss defined as:

$$LOSS = MSE = \sum \left(y_i - y_i^p \right)^2$$

where, y_i = ith target value, y_i^p = ith prediction, $L\left(y_i, y_i^p \right)$ is Loss function

We want our predictions, such that our loss function (MSE) is minimum. By using gradient descent and updating our predictions based on a learning rate, we can find the values where MSE is minimum.

$$y_i^p = y_i^p + a * \delta \sum \left(y_i - y_i^p\right)^2 / \delta y_i^p$$

which becomes, $y_i^p = y_i^p - a * 2 * \sum \left(y_i - y_i^p\right)$

where, a is learning rate and $\sum \left(y_i - y_i^p\right)$ is sum of residuals

So, we are basically updating the predictions such that the sum of our residuals is close to 0 (or minimum) and predicted values are sufficiently close to actual values.

Steps to Fit a Gradient Boosting Model

Let's consider simulated data as shown in scatter plot below with 1 input (x) and 1 output (y) variables.

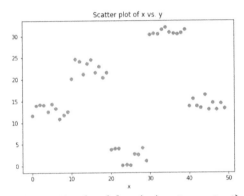

Figure: Simulated data (x: input, y: output)

Data for above shown plot is generated using below python code:

```
x = np.arange(0,50)
x = pd.DataFrame({'x':x})

# just random uniform distributions in differnt range

y1 = np.random.uniform(10,15,10)
y2 = np.random.uniform(20,25,10)
y3 = np.random.uniform(0,5,10)
y4 = np.random.uniform(30,32,10)
y5 = np.random.uniform(13,17,10)

y = np.concatenate((y1,y2,y3,y4,y5))
y = y[:,None]
```

Code Chunk 1: Data simulation

1. Fit a simple linear regressor or decision tree on data [call x as input and y as output].

```
xi = x # initialization of input
yi = y # initialization of target
# x,y --> use where no need to change original y
ei = 0 # initialization of error
n = len(yi)  # number of rows
predf = 0 # initial prediction 0

for i in range(30): # loop will make 30 trees (n_estimators).
    tree = DecisionTree(xi,yi) # DecisionTree scratch code can be found in shared github/kaggle li
                       # It just create a single decision tree with provided min. sample l
    tree.find_better_split(0)  # For selected input variable, this splits (<n and >n) data so that
                       # target variable in both splits is minimum as compared to all othe

    r = np.where(xi == tree.split)[0][0]   #  finds index where this best split occurs

    left_idx = np.where(xi <= tree.split)[0] # index lhs of split
    right_idx = np.where(xi > tree.split)[0] # index rhs of split
```

Code Chunk: (Step 1) Using decision tree to find best split (here depth of our tree is 1)

2. Calculate error residuals. Actual target value, minus predicted target value [e1= y - y_predicted1]

3. Fit a new model on error residuals as target variable with same input variables [call it e1_predicted]

4. Add the predicted residuals to the previous predictions [y_predicted2 = y_predicted1 + e1_predicted]

5. Fit another model on residuals that is still left. i.e. [e2 = y - y_predicted2]and repeat steps 2 to 5 until it starts overfitting or the sum of residuals become constant. Overfitting can be controlled by consistently checking accuracy on validation data.

```
# predictions by ith decisision tree

predi = np.zeros(n)
np.put(predi, left_idx, np.repeat(np.mean(yi[left_idx]), r))  # replace left side mean y
np.put(predi, right_idx, np.repeat(np.mean(yi[right_idx]), n-r))  # right side mean y

predi = predi[:,None]  # make long vector (nx1) in compatible with y
predf = predf + predi  # final prediction will be previous prediction value + new prediction o

ei = y - predf  # needed originl y here as residual always from original y
yi = ei # update yi as residual to reloop
```

Code Chunk: (Steps 2 to 5) Calculate residuals and update new target variable and new predictions.

References

- Ensemble-learning: scholarpedia.org, Retrieved 14 May 2018

- Bagging-and-random-forest-ensemble-algorithms-for-machine-learning: machinelearningmastery.com, Retrieved 28 June 2018

- Bagging-the-skill-of-bagging-bootstrap-aggregating-83: medium.com, Retrieved 31 March 2018

- Ensemble-learning, Boosting: scholarpedia.org, Retrieved 11 May 2018

- Boosting: python-course.eu, Retrieved 19 May 2018

- What-is-adaboost: prateekvjoshi.com, Retrieved 18 July 2018

- Gentle-introduction-gradient-boosting-algorithm-machine-learning: machinelearningmastery.com, Retrieved 24 April 2018

Permissions

We would like to thank the editorial team for lending their expertise to make the book truly unique. They have played a crucial role in the development of this book. Without their invaluable contributions this book wouldn't have been possible. They have made vital efforts to compile up to date information on the varied aspects of this subject to make this book a valuable addition to the collection of many professionals and students.

This book was conceptualized with the vision of imparting up-to-date and integrated information in this field. To ensure the same, a matchless editorial board was set up. Every individual on the board went through rigorous rounds of assessment to prove their worth. After which they invested a large part of their time researching and compiling the most relevant data for our readers.

The editorial board has been involved in producing this book since its inception. They have spent rigorous hours researching and exploring the diverse topics which have resulted in the successful publishing of this book. They have passed on their knowledge of decades through this book. To expedite this challenging task, the publisher supported the team at every step. A small team of assistant editors was also appointed to further simplify the editing procedure and attain best results for the readers.

Apart from the editorial board, the designing team has also invested a significant amount of their time in understanding the subject and creating the most relevant covers. They scrutinized every image to scout for the most suitable representation of the subject and create an appropriate cover for the book.

The publishing team has been an ardent support to the editorial, designing and production team. Their endless efforts to recruit the best for this project, has resulted in the accomplishment of this book. They are a veteran in the field of academics and their pool of knowledge is as vast as their experience in printing. Their expertise and guidance has proved useful at every step. Their uncompromising quality standards have made this book an exceptional effort. Their encouragement from time to time has been an inspiration for everyone.

The publisher and the editorial board hope that this book will prove to be a valuable piece of knowledge for students, practitioners and scholars across the globe.

Index

A
Adaboost, 22, 237, 242, 249-251, 253-254, 259
Additive Model, 251, 253-254
Artificial Intelligence, 3, 6, 8, 48, 50, 54, 69, 221, 236
Artificial Neural Networks, 16, 22, 48, 107

B
Bayes' Theorem, 32-34
Best Matching Unit, 80-84
Binary Classification, 20-21, 25, 29, 39, 42, 70, 121, 137, 248
Binary Classifier, 40, 246
Blind Source Separation, 194, 196, 198, 210

C
Competitive Learning, 50, 54-58, 82
Convergence, 175, 186, 216, 218, 223, 226
Coordinate Descent, 48, 133
Covariance Matrix, 122, 143, 161, 167, 169-170, 172, 174-175, 177, 182, 200
Covariance Method, 171, 173-174

D
Data Compression, 53-54, 143
Data Fusion, 120, 237, 240
Decision Tree, 22, 97, 154, 246, 258
Deep Learning, 1-4, 24, 54, 213
Discriminator, 69-72, 75

E
Eigenvalue, 158-161, 172-175, 179
Eigenvector, 152, 158-162, 172-173, 185, 210

F
Factor Analysis, 89, 91, 178, 181, 194
Feature Extraction, 22, 93, 141-142, 144, 147, 184
Feature Selection, 107, 141-142, 148-153, 210, 246
Fisher's Linear Discriminant, 23, 47, 165
Function Approximation, 221, 230-231, 234, 236-237

G
Gan, 69-73, 76-79, 93

Gaussian Distribution, 36, 92, 200
Gaussian Kernel, 136, 152, 184-185
Gaussian Naive Bayes, 22, 28, 30, 36, 38
Generative Model, 78, 194-195, 198
Gradient Boosting, 237, 253-255, 257
Gtm, 86-87, 89-91

H
Hebb's Rule, 16-19

I
Image Processing, 48, 58, 69, 144
Incremental Learning, 237, 244-245
Independent Component Analysis, 141, 181, 194-195, 197, 208
Information Theory, 53, 170, 245
Initialization, 84-85, 92

K
K-means Clustering, 3, 5, 178, 189, 191
Kernel Trick, 47, 130, 132
Kullback-leibler Divergence, 171, 187-188, 191

L
Learning Algorithm, 3, 5, 9-11, 47-48, 57-58, 81, 119, 127-128, 245-246, 248-249, 253
Likelihood Estimation, 47, 191, 202-203
Linear Classifier, 20, 39, 42, 46-47, 130, 240
Linear Discriminant Analysis, 24, 47, 141-142, 154, 164
Logistic Regression, 22, 24, 26-27, 29, 47-48, 94, 97, 112, 135, 165-166, 251

M
Machine Learning Algorithm, 3, 5, 127, 246, 249, 253
Markov Model, 25
Maximum Likelihood Estimation, 47, 191, 202-203
Methods for Blind Source Separation, 198
Model Selection, 237-238, 241
Multiclass Classification, 20-21, 38, 41-42, 49, 137
Multilayer Perceptron, 97, 238, 242

N

Naive Bayes Classifier, 24, 28, 32, 36, 47, 238

Neural Network, 17, 41, 48, 69, 213, 220-221, 254

Non-negative Matrix Factorization, 170, 178, 186-188, 190

Numpy, 66, 72-73, 95, 159

O

One-versus-all, 39-40, 137

P

Perceptron, 17, 24, 47-48, 87, 97, 123-125, 127, 136, 238, 242

Principal Component Analysis, 53, 141-142, 148, 154, 165-166, 176, 178, 181-182, 190, 194

Probabilistic Classification, 20, 24-26, 107

Projection Pursuit, 198, 200, 202

Q

Q-learning, 211, 214-216, 221-224, 235-236

Quantization, 50, 55, 58-59, 61, 63, 65-66, 190, 221

R

Random Forest Classifier, 27, 31, 98-99

Regression Model, 89, 91, 97, 104, 251

Reinforcement Learning, 1, 3, 6, 211-214, 221, 228, 235-236

Risk Minimization, 134-135

S

Sarsa, 221-224, 236

Self-organizing Map, 79, 81-83, 86, 93

Sobel, 144-146

Som, 79-80, 82, 84-86

Stochastic Gradient Descent, 22, 230

Supervised Machine Learning, 5, 94, 127

Support Vector Machine, 47, 94, 112, 118, 127, 134, 138-139, 191

T

Temporal Difference Learning, 211, 228-229, 236

U

Unsupervised Learning, 1, 5, 12, 47, 50, 53-54, 117, 122, 137

V

Variance Analysis, 223

Vector Quantization, 50, 55, 58-59, 65-66, 190

CPSIA information can be obtained
at www.ICGtesting.com
Printed in the USA
BVHW011732220519
549014BV00003B/312/P